COMPUTER
CONCEPTS

Denise Seguin

Paradigm
PUBLISHING

St. Paul

Managing Editor:	Daryl Bruflodt
Production Editor:	Lori Michelle Ryan
Cover Designer:	Leslie Anderson
Senior Design and Production Specialist:	Jaana Bykonich
Copy Editor:	Susan Capecchi
Indexer:	Schroeder Indexing Services

Care has been taken to verify the accuracy of information presented in this book. However, the authors, editors, and publisher cannot accept responsibility for Web, e-mail, newsgroup, or chat room subject matter or content, or for consequences from application of the information in this book, and make no warranty, expressed or implied, with respect to its content.

Trademarks: Some of the product names and company names included in this book have been used for identification purposes only and may be trademarks or registered trade names of their respective manufacturers and sellers. The authors, editors, and publisher disclaim any affiliation, association, or connection with, or sponsorship or endorsement by, such owners.

We have made every effort to trace the ownership of all copyrighted material and to secure permission from copyright holders. In the event of any question arising as to the use of any material, we will be pleased to make the necessary corrections in future printings. Thanks are due to the aforementioned authors, publishers, and agents for permission to use the materials indicated.

ISBN 978-0-76385-181-1

Preface

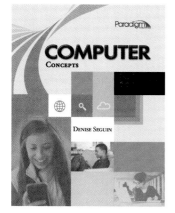

Overview of Course and Textbook

Today's students have grown up with technology all around them and are more connected than any generation before them. They have always had the Internet as a source of information, entertainment, and communication. Students in the classroom today likely started using the Internet and a word processor in grade school. Some students never turn off their cell phones, even when they go to bed at night. For more than one generation, the cell phone has become integral to daily life. Some of you are probably breaking in a second or third smartphone. Having the latest gadget with the coolest apps and being in constant touch with friends and family is a normal way of life for many.

So what can a textbook on introductory computer concepts provide as value to this technology-driven audience? The answer lies within the pages you are about to read. Knowing how to type an essay in a word processor and look up information for a history course on the Internet is not all there is to this digital world in which we live. To be successful in any career, one needs an understanding of how technology is put together and how the tools at one's disposal can be used effectively. In the pages that follow you will learn about all of the equipment and programs that are combined to provide you with technology applications for communicating and performing tasks in one's personal and professional life.

All of this information is presented in short topics with many visual aids so that reading time is minimized; you will learn just what you need to know to succeed. You want to spend your time doing something—not just reading. With that in mind, at the end of each topic is a hands-on activity. Your instructor will assign these for you to do if he or she wants you to dig deeper into the topic that you've just read. Some activities involve getting out and asking classmates, friends, or family what they do with technology; other activities have you try out the technology yourself; and some activities require investigative research on your own. Learning by discovery can be the most rewarding learning of all.

At the end of each chapter you will have a chance to review a summary of the topics, do some objective summary tasks, and then dig into projects that will reinforce and expand the knowledge you've gained. Each chapter concludes with seven to nine projects, some of which are to be done individually, in pairs, or within a team. Your instructor will assign projects based on his or her goals for your level of learning. Each chapter includes a project on green computing and a project on computer-related ethics so you can engage in meaningful discussions with your classmates about issues that face everyone in this digital world.

What Topics Are Included?

Computer Concepts provides instruction in achieving a basic understanding of the components that comprise computer hardware, system software, application software, Internet connectivity and resources, and the security and privacy issues related to technology. No prior experience with computer concepts is required. Even those with some technological savvy can benefit from completing the course by digging deeper into topics of interest with the instructor's guidance. After completing a course that uses this textbook, students will be able to:

- Identify various types of computers; explain how data is converted into information; and understand technological convergence, cloud computing, green computing, and ergonomics.
- Identify hardware and software needed to connect to the Internet; explain broadband connectivity options; recognize popular web browsers, plug-ins, and players; search the web effectively; and distinguish various online services.

- Recognize and explain the components in a system unit, input devices, output devices, and network adapters; understand how data is represented on a computer; and distinguish various options for storage and storage capacity.
- List the major functions of operating system software and recognize popular operating systems used for computing devices; explain the purpose of embedded and cloud operating systems; describe commonly used utility programs for maintaining a computer; and use troubleshooting tools in system software for solving computer issues.
- Identify productivity and multimedia applications used in workplaces and by individuals; differentiate web-based and open source applications; explain the process to acquire, install, uninstall, and upgrade software; and provide examples of mobile apps.
- Describe popular social networking, social bookmarking, media sharing, blogging, and wiki websites; and provide examples of how businesses are using social media strategies to connect and communicate with consumers.
- Explain various risks to security and privacy encountered by connected individuals, and describe strategies for protecting against security and privacy intrusions from unwanted sources.

Chapter Features

This textbook is divided into seven chapters, which can be done in any order. Some instructors will follow the chapter sequence as written; however, others may assign the chapters in a different order. For example, your instructor may prefer that you study the social media content before you learn about hardware. Regardless of the order of the chapters, each chapter begins with a brief introduction to the chapter content along with a list of chapter objectives. Following each chapter opener, key features to help you learn and master the content are described next.

- Content is presented in topics that fit within two or four pages of reading with visual aids that could be pictures, illustrations, diagrams, or screen captures from software programs.

Check This Out
Related websites at which you can explore more information

Did You Know?
Related interesting or fun facts or trivia about the topic

Blog Topic
A chance for you to write about your experience or opinions on the topic

Explore Further
An activity where you do something to learn more or achieve a greater understanding of the topic or a related topic

- Job information is provided to spark interest and invite exploration of computer-related careers by students.

- Tips for security and privacy are inserted where appropriate to help students learn safe computing practices.

Be Aware of Shoulder Surfers!

If you are viewing sensitive information on a mobile device, protect your screen from shoulder surfers. Privacy screens for notebooks, tablets, and smartphones prevent shoulder surfers from seeing personal or confidential information.

- Multiple-choice, crossword puzzle, and matching exercises give you an opportunity to practice and review your understanding of the concepts.

- Seven to nine projects of various complexity at the end of each chapter provide opportunities to work individually, in pairs, or in a team to produce documents, presentations, tables, spreadsheets, blogs, and in some cases a video or podcast that demonstrate your understanding of topics and how the topics apply to the workplace or an individual application.

- Information that can be presented in a table format is included whenever possible to minimize reading load.

Table 3.2	Storage Units and Capacities in Bytes		
Storage Unit	Abbreviation	Popular Reference	Approximate capacity in bytes
Kilobyte	KB	K	1,000 (one thousand)
Megabyte	MB	meg	1,000,000 (one million)
Gigabyte	GB	gig	1,000,000,000 (one billion)
Terabyte	TB	TByte	1,000,000,000,000 (one trillion)

- A chapter summary provides a review of the main chapter content and key words learned.

SNAP Web-Based Training and Assessment

This textbook may or may not be packaged with Paradigm Publishing's SNAP product. SNAP provides additional resources that supplement the learning in the textbook. Your instructor will provide you with information on the resources that have been scheduled for you in SNAP such as tutorials on computer concepts, key term definitions, blogs, surveys, wikis, games, podcasts, or other summary activities. Tutorials use animation, audio, and video that will appeal to visual and auditory learners.

Instructor Resources

Instructor support is available on CD and at the password-protected instructor area of the Internet Resource Center at www.paradigmcollege.net/computerconcepts. These materials include the following:

- syllabus and course-planning suggestions
- sample lesson plans and teaching hints by chapter
- PowerPoint® presentation for student study or classroom instruction for each chapter
- EXAMVIEW® software and test banks

Acknowledgments

The author and editors would like to thank the following for their involvement in this project: Denise Gauthier, Lakehead University, Thunder Bay, Ontario; Lenny E. Andrews, CIT/NT Program Head, Montgomery Community College; Prof. Lorraine Mastracchio, Senior Chairperson, Faculty/Curricula, Chair Office Technologies, The College of Westchester; Scott Cline, Southwestern Community College; Karen J Allen, Assistant Professor, Community College of RI; Janet Blum, Professor, Fanshawe College.

About the Author

Denise Seguin has served in the Faculty of Business at Fanshawe College of Applied Arts and Technology in London, Ontario, since 1986. She has developed curriculum and taught a variety of office technology, software applications, and accounting courses to students in postsecondary Information Technology diploma programs and Continuing Education courses. Seguin has served as Program Coordinator for Computer Systems Technician, Computer Systems Technology, Office Administration, and Law Clerk programs and was acting Chair of the School of Information Technology in 2001. Along with authoring *Computer Concepts* she has also authored Paradigm Publishing's *Microsoft® Outlook* 2000 to 2010 editions and co-authored *Our Digital World* first and second editions, *Benchmark Series Microsoft® Office* 2007 and 2010 series, *Marquee Series Microsoft® Office* 2000 to 2010 series, and *Using Computers in the Medical Office* 2003 to 2010 editions.

Table of Contents

COMPUTER
CONCEPTS

Chapter 1

Living in a Digital World

After successfully completing this chapter, you will be able to:

Define *Computer* and identify the various types of computers

Give an example of technological convergence and ubiquitous computing

Define *Information Technology* and describe the four processes of a computer: input, output, processing, and storage

Explain cloud computing and list advantages to individuals and businesses

Describe the goals of green computing and identify green computing practices

Recognize ways to use computing devices that conform to good ergonomic design

Individuals and businesses interact with computers in numerous ways every day. Some of these interactions occur while you are at home, at work, or at school using a laptop, smartphone, or tablet. Many times you are interacting with a computing device while shopping, dining, or traveling. Consider the number of times you withdraw money from an ATM, gas up your car, swipe a debit or credit card to complete a purchase, use a self-checkout at the grocery store, or program your alarm clock or coffee maker. Many times throughout the day you are interacting with a computer without thinking about it.

To be successful in today's world requires some understanding of computers and how they work. In this chapter, you will begin your introduction to the digital world by learning to distinguish the various types of computers, recognize the impact of computer innovation and convergence in our lives, explain how data is transformed into useful information, and identify trends and issues such as cloud computing, green computing, and ergonomics.

This chapter is an introduction to the terminology and concepts you will explore in more detail in the chapters that follow.

Personal Computers

A **computer** is an electronic device that has been programmed to process, store, and output data that has been accepted as input. Computers come in many sizes and shapes to meet a variety of computing needs. Most people are familiar with a desktop, laptop, or tablet and recognize it as a computer. Other electronic devices that contain a programmed chip such as a digital camera, game console, GPS, or even some children's toys also have computer capabilities designed to perform limited functions.

A computer needs both **hardware** (all of the physical components and devices) and **software** (instructions that tell the computer what to do) in order to be useful. You will learn about hardware in Chapter 3, operating system programs in Chapter 4, and productivity software applications in Chapter 5.

Personal Computers

A **personal computer (PC)** is a computer in which the input, processing, storage, and output are self-contained. A PC is generally used by one person at a time, although PCs can be connected to a network where other people can access a PC's resources such as a file on a storage medium. A PC is sometimes referred to as a microcomputer.

Figure 1.1 A desktop computer with a vertical system unit (called a tower)

Figure 1.2 Apple's iMac sports an all-in-one case where the monitor, processor, memory, and storage mediums are housed in one unit.

A **desktop computer** is a PC in which the computer's processing, memory, and main storage device are housed within a horizontal or vertical case called the **system unit**. A vertical case is sometimes referred to as a tower. A separate monitor, keyboard, and mouse sit alongside or near the system unit as shown in Figure 1.1. An all-in-one case integrates the system unit and monitor into one device as shown in Figure 1.2.

Mobile Computers

A **mobile computer** is a PC that can be moved from place to place. Mobile computers are also referred to as portable computers and come in a number of configurations that vary in size, shape, and weight. A **laptop computer** fits comfortably on a person's lap and is also referred to as a **notebook**. These PCs often replaced desktops as monitor sizes grew and processors, memory, and storage equaled what previously had been available only in desktops. A typical notebook has a clamshell-style design that when opened has the monitor swivel up to reveal a keyboard with the processor, memory, storage media, and battery housed below the keyboard as shown in Figure 1.3.

Figure 1.3 Laptops, also referred to as notebooks, have a clamshell design where the monitor opens up to reveal the system unit.

A **netbook** (Figure 1.4) is a smaller version of a notebook designed for people who primarily only need access to web-based applications such as email and the Internet. These notebooks contain some productivity software applications but do not have DVD drives. Netbooks offer a lower cost alternative to a traditional notebook.

A type of notebook that is thinner, lighter in weight, but just as powerful as a traditional notebook is called an **ultrabook**. Ultrabooks were originally named by Intel (a company that manufactures computer chips) to differentiate the newer notebook design that aims to achieve faster processing and storage while extending battery life in a slim (most are 0.6 to 0.7 inches thick), lightweight (average 2.5 pounds) notebook. Apple's MacBook Air shown in Figure 1.5 is a popular ultrabook; however, all of

Figure 1.4 Netbooks are popular with people who primarily only use email and the Internet.

the other major hardware manufacturers such as Lenovo, Acer, Toshiba, HP, Dell, and Samsung have also released ultrabooks.

Tablet PCs are lightweight notebooks with smaller screens that you interact with using a touch screen or special pen called a stylus. Slate tablets have an onscreen keyboard only while other tablets come with a keyboard that pivots or plugs into the tablet so that the tablet acts more like a traditional notebook. The popularity of Apple's iPad tablet has led other manufacturers to produce tablets, giving consumers a variety of models to choose from. Figure 1.6 shows Apple's iPad.

Figure 1.5 Ultrabooks such as Apple's MacBook Air are slim, lightweight, yet as powerful as a notebook.

Protect Your Mobile Device

Notebook theft is on the rise. In some areas, organized criminals use people to distract you while another steals your device. Use anti-theft software or devices to track your notebook and protect your data in case of theft. Always have backups just in case!

Figure 1.6 Apple's iPad is a popular tablet.

Blog Topic

Is the personal computer dead?

Smartphones and tablets are increasingly powerful with all of the tools offered on a notebook. Desktop sales have been steadily decreasing. Some people argue that mobile devices are simply supplementing the traditional desktop and notebook and that sales data are misleading since desktops and notebooks are lasting longer.

1. Write and post a blog entry with a paragraph that describes the number of computing devices you own and how you use them. State your opinion to the blog topic *Is the personal computer dead?* and provide your rationale.

2. Read at least two of your classmates' blog entries and post one comment to each.

3. Submit your blog URL and the URLs of the two classmates' blogs to your instructor in the manner she or he has requested.

EXPLORE FURTHER

Compare Ultrabooks with Tablet PCs

Assume the manager at the office where you intern is interested in buying a new mobile computer. The manager is not sure whether an ultrabook or a tablet PC is the better choice.

1. Research the similarities and differences between ultrabooks and tablet PCs. Choose one model of each for your comparison. Specifically, find out the physical characteristics of each (weight and screen size), connectivity options (ports, wireless, Bluetooth options), input options (keyboard, touchscreen), storage options, and processor speeds.

2. Create a table in a document or spreadsheet to present the comparison of an ultrabook to a tablet PC by each criterion. Clearly identify the model of each device you are presenting and include the URLs of the websites from which you obtained the specifications.

3. Save the document or spreadsheet as **C1-Intro-UltrabookvsTablet-Your Name**.

4. Submit the document or spreadsheet to your instructor in the manner she or he has requested.

Mobile Devices, Wearable Computers, and Embedded Computers

TOPIC 1.2   Handheld computing devices smaller than notebooks are referred to as **mobile devices**. These devices have smaller screens and store programs and data within the unit or on a memory card. Some devices rely entirely on touch-based input while others have a built-in or slide-out keyboard. Wearable computers are devices that can be worn on the body by attaching to an arm, belt, helmet, eyeglasses, or clothing. These computers are used to perform special functions such as health monitoring or assist with other hands-free work. Embedded computers reside within an electronic device that is designed to perform a specific task such as the programs found in many household appliances and electronic gadgets.

Mobile Devices

Increasingly, mobile devices are expanding computer use outside our homes and offices. Examples of mobile devices shown in Figure 1.7 include:

- **Smartphones** are cell phones with built-in cameras that offer software applications (called apps), Web-browsing, and messaging capabilities.
- **Ultra-Mobile PC (UMPC)** is a small handheld computer that supports touch, digital pen input, or includes a compact keyboard depending on the design.
- **Portable Media Players** are devices used to play music, watch videos, view photos, play games, and/or read electronic books.

Figure 1.7 A smartphone, handheld computer, and portable media player are popular mobile devices.

Wearable Computers

A computing device that can be worn on the body and functions while the individual is walking or otherwise moving around is called a **wearable computer**. These devices are usually always-on, include sensors for various purposes, and provide for hands-free use with communications capability. Devices may provide for input with voice commands, hand movements, joysticks, buttons, or touch. Wearable computers are used to assist or monitor individuals with health conditions, track items, provide real-time information, access documentation, or engage in virtual reality simulations. For example, the Department of Defense helped develop wearable computers for soldiers that monitor the battlefield environment.

Google's Project Glass eyeglasses (Figure 1.8) use a heads-up virtual display that interacts with the wearer to provide information and communication technologies without the wearer having to use his or her smartphone. Google's eyeglasses could bring wearable computers to the mainstream consumer electronics market.

Figure 1.8 Google's Project Glass eyeglasses use voice commands to display in front of your eyes up-to-date information, take photos, and communicate.

Embedded Computers

Numerous household appliances and consumer electronics incorporate **embedded computers** that have processors programmed to perform a particular task (Figure 1.9). Examples include: a microwave oven calculates defrost time depending on weight, a refrigerator sounds an alarm when the inside temperature becomes problematic, and a car's navigation console displays a map of your current location.

Digital cameras, game consoles, electronic thermostats, electronic vending machines, ATMs, digital alarms, and digital thermometers are just a few other examples of devices with an embedded system. Digital devices are everywhere and so prevalent that many times you may not be aware you are using a computer!

Figure 1.9 Electronic devices with embedded systems are designed to perform a specific task such as this navigation system, digital camera, and handheld game console.

EXPLORE FURTHER

Favorite Computing Devices

1. Conduct a survey with at least 10 relatives, friends, neighbors, or classmates to find out each person's favorite computing device.
2. Compile the results and create a table or chart in a document, spreadsheet, or presentation that presents the results of your informal survey.
3. Save the document, spreadsheet, or presentation as **C1-PCs-DeviceSurvey-Your Name**.
4. Submit the table or chart to your instructor in the manner she or he has requested.

Computers for Connecting Multiple Users and Specialized Processing

Larger, more powerful computers are used by organizations that need to connect many people to resources and store and process large amounts of data. Individuals use PCs to connect via a network to these larger computers for access to programs, processing, and storage resources. A high-end computer with multiple processors, large amounts of memory and storage capacity can function as a server in a small network; however, larger organizations purchase midrange servers and mainframes when hundreds or thousands of users need to process transactions simultaneously. Supercomputers are used when massive computing power is needed to perform advanced calculations.

Servers

A **server** is a computer with hardware and software that allows it to link together other computers in order to provide services such as Internet access and share resources such as programs, data, printers, and storage. The computers that connect to a server are called **clients**. Servers are high-performance computers often stacked in racks (Figure 1.10) and stored in a room called a **server room** that is maintained to avoid heat, humidity, and dust.

A **midrange server** is used in small and medium-sized organizations that need to connect hundreds of client computers at the same time. Midrange servers are more powerful than a PC but not as powerful as a mainframe.

A computer connected to a network that does not store any data or software on the local PC is called a **thin client**. Some companies use thin clients to reduce costs and/or maintain tighter security on software licensing and data.

Figure 1.10 Servers mounted in racks are stored in a separate room protected from excessive heat, humidity, and dust.

Mainframes

A large, powerful, and expensive computer used by government and large organizations such as banks, insurance companies, and other corporations to connect hundreds or thousands of users simultaneously is known as a **mainframe** (Figure 1.11). These computers have specialized hardware and software capable of processing millions of transactions and retaining massive volumes of data.

Figure 1.11 Mainframe computers connect thousands of computers simultaneously and process and store millions of transactions.

Supercomputers

The most powerful of all computers is a **supercomputer**. A supercomputer is the fastest, most expensive, and most powerful computer, capable of performing trillions of calculations per second. These massive computers are usually designed for a specific task such as the complex mathematical calculations needed for weather forecasting, nuclear research, oil exploration, or to conduct scientific research analysis.

Supercomputing speed is expressed in **petaflops**. A petaflop (a measurement used in scientific calculations) represents a quadrillion floating point operations per second. In June 2012, a supercomputer named Sequoia (Figure 1.12), installed at the Department of Energy's Lawrence Livermore National Laboratory, achieved 16.32 petaflops per second and was named the top supercomputer in the Top 500 list of most powerful computers.

Check This Out

www.top500.org

Go here to read about the location of supercomputers around the world. A list of the top 500 sites for the most powerful computers is released twice per year.

Figure 1.12 In June 2012, Sequoia, installed at the Department of Energy's Lawrence Livermore National Laboratory, was named the top supercomputer in the Top 500 list of most powerful computers in the world.

EXPLORE FURTHER

History of Computing Time Line

The Computer History Museum located in Mountain View, California, offers information about the most influential people, technology, and events in computing history. An online exhibit *Timeline of Computer History* offers an interactive exploration into the origins of computers.

1. Go to www.computerhistory.org/timeline to view the online Timeline exhibit.
2. Pick five consecutive years in the time line that are of interest to you, click the year, and read the information presented in the online exhibit. *Note: Your instructor may instead choose to assign you a time period for this activity in order to have a complete time line presented to the class.*
3. Create a presentation with one slide per year and provide a brief summary in your own words that describes the significant people, technology, or event that was shown in the time line.
4. Save the presentation as **C1-PCs-ComputerTimeline-Your Name**.
5. Submit the presentation to your instructor in the manner she or he has requested.

Computer Innovations and Converging Technologies

TOPIC 1.4

At home you use a computer to communicate with others via email or social media websites; track and pay bills; play games; watch videos, television shows, and movies; listen to music or radio stations; do homework; and more. Computers are put to work in every type of business in a variety of ways. Technology is constantly evolving, meaning there will always be change in the devices and methods that we use for completing tasks at home, at work, and at school. Technologies are also converging, meaning that a device that originally was designed for one purpose, such as a cell phone designed only to make voice calls, is now capable of performing multiple functions such as browsing the Web, taking photos, sending and receiving email, and creating documents.

Ubiquitous Computing

Dictonary.com defines *ubiquitous* as an adjective that means "*existing or being everywhere, especially at the same time; omnipresent.*" **Ubiquitous computing** means that computing technology is everywhere within our environment and used all of the time. Effectively, the technology mostly fades into the background and the user becomes unaware of the technology as the person focuses on the task at hand. With the rapid pace of technology innovation, ubiquitous computing will become even more prevalent to all of us. Consider these five examples of recent computer innovations in various industries:

Retail Macy's is using a new handheld computer at some of its stores that will inform the retail clerk if the store has stock in the customer's shoe size and send a message to a stock person indicating which two doors of the stockroom are closest to the customer. The clerk uses the device, which is about the size of a remote control, to scan the bar code on a shoe, enter the customer's shoe size, and receive instant notification of stock status.

At Macy's, store clerks can get instant stock status by scanning a bar code and entering a customer's shoe size.

Restaurant A digital noise-cancelling technology designed by Meyer Sound and the owner of a restaurant in California uses speakers, microphones, iPads, and sound-dampening materials disguised as art hanging on the walls to make the restaurant as loud or as quiet as the owner sees fit. The system monitors sound levels picked up by microphones that are processed by the computer and used to control sound reverberation levels. If the owner thinks the restaurant is too loud, the system dampens the noise so that diners can easily converse with their guests.

New technology for restaurants lets the owner dampen sound when the noise level becomes too loud for comfortable conversation among guests.

Did You Know?

Intel cofounder Gordon E. Moore described a trend in 1965 in which the number of transistors that could be placed on a circuit doubled every two years. He predicted the trend would continue and this became known as Moore's Law, which became a guiding principle for the computer industry.

Manufacturing High-end 3-D printers use materials such as hard and flexible plastics, glass, metal powders, and even chocolate to make objects layer by layer, using an array of heat- or light-activated materials sold in cartridges. These printers have led to the emergence of on-demand manufacturing, meaning companies will no longer have to maintain inventories of spare parts. Items can be saved in a database and printed on demand when needed.

3-D printing is leading to manufacturing on demand.

Police officers can use their iPhone or iPod touch to take fingerprints.

Law Enforcement A low-cost sleeve that snaps onto an iPhone or iPod touch is being used by law enforcement agencies in the field to collect fingerprints of suspects, detainees, or even deceased individuals for rapid identification. The device for the mobile phone avoids the costs associated with providing laptops and fingerprint scanners to all officers in a police force.

Sony's Playstation 4 concept image (new console under development at time of writing)

Medicine A new knee brace allows doctors to monitor remotely a patient's healing progress after discharge from the hospital for knee surgery. The brace is embedded with motion sensors. When the patient is moving, the motion is simulated by a 3-D avatar on a remote computer and transmitted to the patient's doctor for viewing on a PC or smartphone.

Convergence

Technological convergence, where innovation merges several technologies into a single device, is not just about cell phones becoming multipurpose smartphones. Game consoles used to just play video games, but today's multipurpose consoles are also used to play movies from Blu-ray, DVD, or the Web. You can also surf the Web, browse through photos, and play music on newer systems.

Doctors can remotely monitor a patient's healing progress.

EXPLORE FURTHER

What new technology innovation is occurring in your field of study?

Technological innovation occurs every day, and a computer innovation will likely occur in your field of study while you are still in school.

1. Either by searching the Web or by interviewing someone who works in your field of study, investigate a technology innovation that is occurring in your field or is to occur by the time you graduate.
2. Create a document with a brief description of the innovation you learned about and the impact the innovation is expected to have within the industry. At the end of the document, include the URLs of websites you used or a reference for the person you interviewed.
3. Save the document as **C1-Intro-ComputerInnovation-Your Name**.
4. Submit the document to your instructor in the manner she or he has requested.

Information Technology and the Information Processing Cycle

TOPIC 1.5

Information technology (IT) refers to the use of computers, software, networks, and other communication systems and processes to store, retrieve, send, process, and protect information. The IT department in an organization is tasked with managing the hardware, software, networks, and other systems that form the information infrastructure. IT specialists are involved with designing, developing, implementing, and maintaining information systems.

Characters that are typed or otherwise entered into a computer are called **raw data**. At the entry stage the data is not meaningful as it is just a string of characters. Software programs provide the instructions for the computer to process and organize the data into meaningful and useful **information**. The **Information Processing Cycle** includes the operations involved in transforming *data* into *information* and includes: input, processing, output, and storage as shown in Figure 1.13.

Computer calculates
total with tax and
shipping charges

INPUT
Raw data is entered

PROCESSING
Data is processed

OUTPUT
Information is presented

Customer clicks items
he wants to purchase
at online shopping
website and enters
quantities

Online checkout
form displays total
due to the customer

After checkout, order is
sent to company staff for
fulfillment and shipping

STORAGE
Data and Information
are stored

Order is stored temporarily
while processing and
permanently when completed
for later retrieval

Figure 1.13 The Information Processing Cycle includes four operations to transform raw data into useful information.

Input

Any device used to enter raw data or communicate instructions to the computer is an **input device**. Commonly used devices include a keyboard, mouse, and microphone similar to the ones shown in Figure 1.14. A scanner, bar code reader, digital camera, digital pen, webcam, or touch-screen device can also be used to enter input.

Figure 1.14 A keyboard, mouse, microphone, and touch screen are common devices used to enter input.

Processing

A computer chip called the **central processing unit (CPU)** carries out the instructions given by the software to perform the **processing** cycle. Think of the CPU as the brain of the computer. A CPU is a silicon chip referred to as the **microprocessor** and is housed on the computer's motherboard (printed circuit board that contains the main computer components). Microprocessors today are typically manufactured with multiple cores, which are independent units on the same chip that can process data simultaneously. These **multi-core processors** significantly increase speed and performance. Intel is a leading designer and manufacturer of microprocessors (Figure 1.15).

Figure 1.15 Intel's popular Core series of microprocessors is available in several variations to suit individual and business users.

Output

Anything used to view the information processed and organized by the computer is an **output device**. Typically, you view information on a monitor and/or print it on a printer similar to the ones shown in Figure 1.16. Other output devices include speakers and screens such as those on mobile devices and televisions.

Figure 1.16 A monitor and printer are commonly used to view information processed by the computer; however, mobile devices such as a tablet or smartphone can also be considered output devices.

Storage

While processing, instructions and data are temporarily stored in a holding area called **random access memory (RAM)**. RAM is also housed on the computer's motherboard. RAM is temporary storage that is emptied when power to the computer is lost.

Cache memory is located either on the CPU chip or on a separate chip between the CPU and RAM and is used to store frequently used data. Speed and performance are increased with cache memory since the CPU checks cache memory first before checking RAM. The faster retrieval of frequently used data saves the processor time.

Permanent storage (Figure 1.17) is any device where data and information are saved for later use; these devices are referred to as **storage media**. Several storage media, some portable and some housed inside the system unit, are available in various capacities. An internal hard disk drive is housed inside the system unit while portable storage media such as USB flash drives (also called memory sticks), external hard drives, and optical discs such as CDs, DVDs, and Blu-ray are also available. An increasingly popular trend is to store information using **cloud storage** where you log in to a website and copy documents, photos, or other information to a web service. Cloud storage such as Flickr (a website used to store photos) or Dropbox (a website where you can store any type of file) have become popular since they offer free online storage that can be shared easily or accessed anywhere you have access to the Internet.

Figure 1.17 Permanent storage is available in media with various capacities such as the internal hard disk drive shown with the top metal cover removed, a USB flash drive, an external hard disk drive, and optical discs.

In today's highly connected world, a fifth operation called communications is often added to the information processing cycle. Computers accept input and send output to/from other computers via various wired and wireless communication channels such as cables, telephone lines, satellite, cellular, microwave, and Bluetooth transmission media. A **communications device** is any component used to facilitate the transmission of data such as a cable modem, DSL modem, or router (Figure 1.18).

In this topic, you have been introduced to terminology and hardware in the information processing cycle that will be explored in more detail in Chapter 3.

Integrated modem and wireless router used to connect the computer devices on the home network to the Internet

Figure 1.18 Computers connect to other computers to receive input and send output using communications devices such as the integrated modem and wireless router shown.

Career Connection

IT Jobs in Demand

If you enjoy working with computers you may want to consider an IT career. *Computerworld* magazine surveyed more than 300 IT executives for its 2012 forecast and included the following in its top IT jobs in demand: programming and application development with emphasis on mobile application developers, project management, help desk and technical support, networking, business intelligence, data center operations and systems integration, security, and telecommunications. If any of these careers are of interest to you, look at courses offered in postsecondary programs in computer engineering, computer science, information systems, information technology, and software engineering.

EXPLORE FURTHER

IT Job Profile

You have read in Career Connection that IT jobs are in demand. You are interested in working with computers but want to learn more about specific job openings to find out what employers are looking for in new employees.

1. Using a job search website such as Monster.com, locate a current job ad for an IT job that interests you within your area. *Hint: Use titles from the Career Connection section.*

2. Create a document that describes in your own words the job opportunity including the job title, the company offering the job, the duties involved in the job, and the qualifications required. Include information on compensation if the ad lists a salary range. At the end of the document include the URL for the job ad.

3. Save the document as **C1-Intro-ITJobAd-Your Name**.

4. Submit the document to your instructor in the manner she or he has requested.

TOPIC 1.6

Cloud Computing

Individuals and businesses are increasingly turning to providers of software and computing services that are accessed entirely on the Internet. This delivery model of software and services is called **cloud computing**. With cloud computing, all you need is a computer with a web browser in order to get your work done since all of the software and the documents you need to access are stored online.

Cloud computing got its name because the Internet has always been identified with a cloud in technology documentation. Cloud computing places the processing and storage operations of the Information Processing cycle at an online service provider's server and/or data center rather than using the hardware and software on your own PC or mobile device (Figure 1.19). In some cases you can use cloud computing services for free. For example, at Google Drive you can use up to 5 GB of cloud storage for free (with an option to pay a fee for more storage space).

The delivery of software applications using the Internet is referred to as **software-as-a-service (SaaS)**. Advantages and disadvantages of cloud computing are listed in Table 1.1.

Figure 1.19 Using cloud computing services means that your software applications and/or data are accessed from your web browser and stored on the service provider's equipment.

Table 1.1	Advantages and Disadvantages of Cloud Computing
Advantages	**Disadvantages**
Applications and data are available at any time from any place since all you need is an Internet connection	You are totally dependent on your Internet connection; if the service goes down, you cannot access your programs or files
Updates to software are automatic and immediately available	You do not have control over changes made to software—upgrading is not at your discretion
The service provider makes continual investment in hardware and software. Pay only the subscription fees after you have purchased your computer and Internet connectivity	Over a long period of time, monthly subscription fees could end up costing more than the initial outlay of cash for hardware and software and ongoing Internet connectivity
Web applications are generally easy to use and navigate	Web applications may be too limiting to meet your needs
Web-based applications are generally compatible with PCs, Macs, and mobile devices—you can use any device	Some businesses may have compatibility issues with exchanging data with legacy systems or infrastructure
Documents, photos, music, videos, and other files are stored offsite. If you experience equipment malfunction, theft, or some other disaster, all that is lost is the physical equipment, which is easily replaced	Large cloud computing vendors have reliable and secure storage; however, there is a risk that personal and/or sensitive data could be accessed by unauthorized users. Also be mindful of who actually owns the data you are storing online—is it you or the provider?

If you open your web browser to check email, create documents, or upload photos, music, videos, or other files to store and share with others, then you are already using SaaS services. A few popular cloud computing services include Google Drive (formerly Google Docs), Dropbox, iCloud, and SkyDrive. Many more cloud computing service providers exist to meet the growing demands and needs of many individuals and businesses.

Figure 1.20 illustrates Google Presentations. If you are familiar with presentation software, creating a presentation in Google Presentations web-based application will be easy for you since the program contains tools similar to what you would find in other presentation programs. As more people become aware of and convert to using web-based applications, traditional office productivity suites may no longer be the mainstream choice.

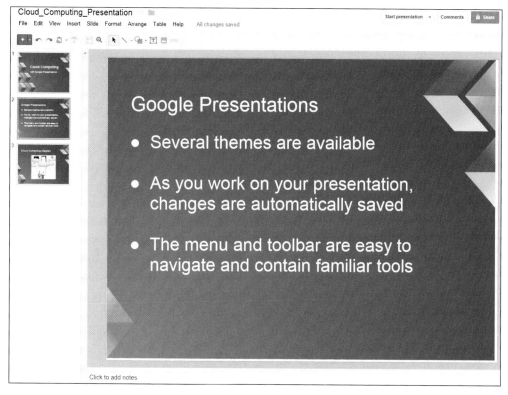

Figure 1.20 Sign in to Google Drive using a Gmail account to access Google Presentations and create a presentation similar to the one shown.

EXPLORE FURTHER

What are IaaS and PaaS?

In this topic you learned about one type of cloud computing known as software-as-a-service (SaaS). Two other types of cloud computing are infrastructure-as-a-service (IaaS) and platform-as-a-service (PaaS).

1. Look up the definitions of IaaS and PaaS.
2. Create a document that explains in your own words what these two types of cloud computing services are and the advantages offered to businesses for these services.
3. Save the document as **C1-Intro-CloudComputing-Your Name**.
4. Submit the document to your instructor in the manner she or he has requested.

Green Computing

TOPIC 1.7

Green computing refers to the use of computers and other electronic devices in an environmentally responsible manner. Green computing can encompass new or modified computing practices, policies, and procedures. This trend is growing with more individuals and businesses adopting green computing strategies every year. Strategies include the reduction of energy consumption of computers and other devices; reduction in use of paper, ink, and toner; and reuse, recycling, or proper disposal of electronic waste (referred to as **e-waste** or **e-trash**).

In addition to changes in computing practices, manufacturers are working to produce electronics that are more energy efficient, reduce the amount of toxic chemicals used in computers, and incorporate more recyclable components and packaging. Finally, governments and industry are making available more recycling programs to reuse or properly dispose of electronics.

Five Ways to Go Green

1. Make sure you use Energy Star certified devices.

   The Energy Star label on a device means the manufacturer has reached or exceeded the minimum federal standards for reduced energy consumption.

This label identifies a device as being Energy Star compliant.

2. Turn off devices when you are not using them and unplug them if you will not be using them for an extended period of time. Even better—use smart power strips that automatically reduce the power to devices when not in use.

   In 2012, the Department of Energy proposed new standards for microwave ovens that would limit standby energy use to 1 watt. Estimates are that the savings over 30 years of this one new standard will equal the energy used by approximately 2 million U.S. homes in one year. Imagine the savings if this standard is applied to all other electronics that use standby power.

A smart power strip reduces energy consumption by controlling the flow of power to peripheral devices when the main device is not in use or is in standby mode.

3. Reduce printing to only those documents, messages, or photos that absolutely must be in paper copy and make sure what you print uses the least amount of paper.

   Make it a policy to distribute PDF copies of documents and messages and share photos online with friends and relatives. When you must print consider using both sides of the paper and/or using narrower margins to print more on a page. The cost savings from reduced paper consumption, toner, and ink cartridges is significant. Consider also that fewer print cartridges will end up in the landfills.

Reduce printing—only print what you absolutely must have in a paper copy.

4. Modify the default power options on your computer to conserve more energy.

   Most Windows-based desktop and notebook computers default to a balanced power plan, which aims to balance performance with energy conservation. You

Check This Out

www.energy.gov/oe/green-button

Go here to read about the U.S. Green Button standard launched in 2012 to assist consumers with managing their energy consumption.

Did You Know?

Devices that consume power when turned off or in standby mode are called energy vampires. The Department of Energy estimates the average home spends $130 per year to power energy vampires.

can adjust the sleep and display settings to turn off power sooner than the default times. Choose *Power Options* in the Hardware and Sound category of the Control Panel.

 Modify power options on your PC to conserve more energy.

On Mac computers, adjust the energy features using the Energy Saver pane in System Preferences.

5. Consider reselling or donating equipment you no longer need.

Computers, cell phones, and electronics that are still in working order can be sold or donated to schools, churches, or nonprofit groups. If you must dispose of electronics, try to drop off the e-waste at an electronics recycling facility.

In the U.S. approximately 3 million tons of e-waste is thrown away each year. Most of this discarded electronic equipment ends up in landfills or is exported to countries such as China and India.

Whenever possible divert e-waste from landfills.

Did You Know?

According to estimates by the Environmental Protection Agency, only 15 to 20 percent of e-waste is recycled.

 Blog Topic

Are you green?

Do you practice green computing? If yes, are there ways you can improve your green computing practices? If no, which green computing strategies can you start to use? Have you purchased a new PC or mobile device within the last year? If yes, how did you dispose of your older equipment?

1. Write and post a blog entry that provides your answers to the questions.

2. Read at least two of your classmates' blogs and post one comment to each.

3. Submit your blog URL and the URLs of your classmates' blogs for which you provided a comment to your instructor in the manner she or he has requested.

EXPLORE FURTHER

Understanding Eco-labeling

An eco-label is awarded to a product or service that is determined to have met specified environmental standards or criteria. Eco-labeling is a voluntary program to identify electronics that meet environmental performance certification. Eco-labels and standards vary depending on the organization that has developed the program. An understanding of the meaning of various eco-labels will assist with making responsible electronic purchasing decisions.

1. Research three eco-labels that are used on electronics. Find the organization that manages the label and the standards by which the label is evaluated.

2. Create a document that summarizes the three eco-labels in your own words. Insert an image of each eco-label in the document. *Hint: One way to insert an image is to right-click the eco-label image on a website and choose* Copy *from the shortcut menu. Next, click in your document window where you want the image to appear and then click the Paste button in the ribbon.*

3. Save the document as **C1-Intro-Eco-labels-Your Name**.

4. Submit the document to your instructor in the manner she or he has requested.

TOPIC 1.8

Computers and Your Health

Frequent use of computing devices can adversely affect your health if proper care and preventive strategies are not used. Physical ailments that can occur include fatigue, eyestrain, blurred vision, backaches, wrist and forearm pain, finger numbness or pain, and neck and shoulder pain. A leading job-related illness and injury in North America is **repetitive-strain injury (RSI)**. RSI is an injury or disorder of the joints, nerves, muscles, ligaments, or tendons.

Two common computer-related RSI injuries are **tendonitis** and **carpal tunnel syndrome (CTS)**. Tendonitis occurs when a tendon in your wrist becomes inflamed. CTS occurs when the nerve that connects the forearm to the palm of the hand becomes inflamed. Both of these conditions are caused by excessive typing, mouse scrolling, mouse clicking, and thumb typing/movements on mobile devices. Symptoms of tendonitis and CTS are listed in Table 1.2.

Tendonitis and carpal tunnel syndrome are two common RSI injuries from computer use that cause pain in the wrist and hand.

Table 1.2	Symptoms Associated with RSI Injuries from Computer Use
Symptoms of Tendonitis	**Symptoms of Carpal Tunnel Syndrome (CTS)**
Tingling or numbness in the fingers	Numbness and tingling in the thumb and the first two fingers especially at night (can cause you to awaken from sleep)
Pain in the forearm and wrist	Burning sensation when the nerve is compressed
Decreased mobility of your wrist or fingers	Decreased grip strength leading you to drop objects
Loss of strength in your hand	Loss of strength in your hand

Computer vision syndrome affects 50 to 90 percent of computer users.

Computer Vision Syndrome

Computer vision syndrome (CVS) is a temporary condition caused by prolonged computer use that involves eye strain; weak, itchy, burning, or dry eyes; blurred or double vision; difficulty with focus; sensitivity to light; headaches; and neck pain. According to the American Optometric Association, 50 to 90 percent of computer workers will experience some CVS symptoms.

Posture-Related Injuries

Pain in the lower back, neck, shoulders, and arms are common complaints from computer workers. Sitting for long periods of time in the same position causes fatigue and reduces circulation to muscles and tendons, which can lead to stiffness and soreness.

Neck pain is a common complaint among computer workers.

Prevention Strategies to Reduce Risk of RSI, CVS, and Muscular Pain

Knowing the three primary risk factors for developing health issues when using a computer is key to identifying strategies to reduce risk of injury: poor posture, poor technique, and excessive use. Prevention strategies are listed in Table 1.3. Many of these strategies involve the use of **ergonomics** to improve the computer workspace design. Ergonomics involves the design of equipment and a person's workspace to promote safe and comfortable operation of the equipment by the individual. In other words, good ergonomic design fits the computer equipment to the worker by adjusting components to the optimal height, distance, and angles.

An ergonomically correct computer workspace helps prevent RSI injuries.

Table 1.3	Preventive Strategies for Avoiding Computer-Related Illness
Take frequent breaks. Get up out of the chair and walk around, stretch, and do another activity for a few moments.
Maintain good posture by sitting up straight with feet flat on the floor, shoulders relaxed, head and neck balanced and in line with torso, and your lower back supported by your chair or a rolled towel. If the desk height is not adjustable, use a foot rest.
Sit in a chair that has five legs for stability and allows adjustments to height and angle of backrest, seat, and arm rests.
When typing, the keyboard should be at elbow level with the elbows close to your body and supported by your chair. Wrists and hands should be positioned in line with forearms. If using a notebook computer, consider plugging in an external keyboard so that you can adjust the height and position.
The top of the computer screen should be at or slightly below your eye level. If using a notebook computer, consider using an external monitor that you can adjust to the correct height. Optimal viewing distance is 20 to 40 inches. Increase font size in documents and browsers if necessary to avoid eye strain.
Remember to blink—studies have shown computer users tend to blink about five times less than normal. Also minimize glare and use ambient lighting rather than overhead fluorescents if possible.
Look away from the computer screen once in a while and spend a few moments focusing on something that is off in the distance. For example, look out the window at something outside.

Check This Out
www.osha.gov/SLTC/etools/ computerworkstations
Go here for an interactive eTool to learn more about proper workstation setup or view setup checklists.

EXPLORE FURTHER

Notebook, Texting, and Smartphone Ergonomics

Good ergonomic workspace design for a notebook PC involves some factors not discussed in Table 1.3. Increased smartphone use can become a risk for some people. For example, the term **BlackBerry thumb** was devised to describe pain that developed in BlackBerry users in the thumb or wrist from excessive texting.

1. Research ergonomics for laptops and smartphones. Specifically, find at least two articles that address the unique needs of mobile computing device users.
2. Develop a checklist or table with ergonomically correct usage of mobile devices. Include the URLs of the articles you used at the end of the document.
3. Save the document as **C1-Intro-MobileErgonomics-Your Name**.
4. Submit the document to your instructor in the manner she or he has requested.

Concepts Review

Topic	Key Concepts	Key Terms
Personal Computers	A computer needs both hardware and software to work. A PC is a self-contained computer with input, processing, storage, and output. A desktop computer includes a system unit and a separate monitor, keyboard, and mouse. A mobile computer is a computer that can be moved around. A typical laptop (notebook) has a monitor that when swiveled up reveals a keyboard with the remaining components housed below. A netbook is a small notebook designed primarily for email and Internet access. Ultrabooks are thinner, lighter, and more powerful notebooks. A tablet PC is a lightweight notebook with a smaller screen that you interact with using touch or a digital pen.	Computer Hardware Software Personal computer (PC) Desktop computer System unit Mobile computer Laptop computer Notebook Netbook Ultrabook Tablet PCs
Mobile Devices, Wearable Computers, and Embedded Computers	Mobile devices are handheld computing devices with small screens and with programs and data stored within the unit. Smartphones, ultra-mobile PCs, and portable media players are popular mobile devices. A computer connected to a network that does not store any data or software on the local PC is called a thin client. Wearable computers contain sensors that are always on and provide for hands-free interaction and communications.	Mobile devices Smartphones Ultra-mobile PC (UMPC) Portable media players Wearable computer Embedded computers
Computers for Connecting Multiple Users and Specialized Processing	A server is a high-end computer that connects other computers and is stored in a specially maintained server room. Computers that connect to a server are called clients. A computer that relies on the server for all programs and data is called a thin client. Midrange servers are used to connect hundreds of clients at the same time. Mainframes are large, powerful, and expensive computers that are capable of handling hundreds or thousands of users. A supercomputer is the fastest, most expensive computer capable of processing trillions of calculations per second. Supercomputing speed is measured in petaflops where one petaflop is a quadrillion floating point operations per second.	Server Clients Server room Midrange server Thin client Mainframe Supercomputer Petaflops

continued....

Computer Innovations and Converging Technologies	Ubiquitous computing means that computing technology is everywhere within our environment and used all of the time.	Ubiquitous computing Technological convergence
	Macy's is using a handheld computer to provide instant stock status based on a customer's shoe size.	
	A restaurant owner helped design a noise-dampening technology system that reduces noise when the restaurant gets too loud.	
	3D printers have led to the emergence of on-demand manufacturing.	
	Law enforcement officers can now use a sleeve that attaches to an iPhone or iPod touch that scans fingerprints for rapid identification.	
	A knee brace embedded with motion sensors allows a surgeon to monitor remotely a patient's healing progress.	
	Technological convergence involves the blending or merging of multiple technologies into a single device such as a smartphone or game console.	
Information Technology and the Information Processing Cycle	Information technology involves the use of technology to store, retrieve, send, process, and protect information.	Information technology (IT) Raw data Information Information Processing Cycle Input device Central processing unit (CPU) Processing Microprocessor Multi-core processors Output device Random access memory (RAM) Cache memory Storage media Cloud storage Communications device
	IT specialists are involved with designing, developing, implementing, and maintaining information systems.	
	Raw data are characters entered into a computer that software transforms into meaningful information.	
	The Information Processing Cycle includes four operations: input, processing, output, and storage.	
	Devices used to enter raw data are input devices.	
	Processing is carried out by the central processing unit (CPU), also called a microprocessor.	
	Multi-core processors have independent units on the same silicon chip that allow multiple processes to run simultaneously.	
	Devices used to view information on the computer are output devices.	
	Random access memory (RAM) is temporary storage used to hold data while processing.	
	Cache memory is where frequently used data is stored.	
	Permanent storage media such as hard disk drives, USB flash drives, optical discs, and cloud storage are where data is stored for later use.	
	Communications devices such as a cable modem or router transmit data to/from computers.	

continued....

Topic	Key Concepts	Key Terms
Cloud Computing	Cloud computing is a delivery model where software and computing services are accessed entirely from the Web. Cloud computing places the processing and storage operations in the Web. Some cloud services, such as Google Drive, are free. Several advantages and disadvantages of cloud computing must be considered before signing up for a cloud service. A few popular cloud computing services are Google Drive, Dropbox, iCloud, and SkyDrive.	Cloud computing Software-as-a-Service (SaaS)
Green Computing	Using computers and other electronic devices in an environmentally responsible manner is known as green computing. Green computing practices, policies, and procedures strive to reduce energy consumption; reduce use of paper and paper supplies; and reuse, recycle, or properly dispose of electronics. Five ways to practice green computing include: use Energy Star rated devices, turn off or unplug devices when not in use, reduce printing of documents, modify power options on your computers, and resell or donate old equipment.	Green computing e-waste e-trash
Computers and Your Health	Repetitive-strain injury (RSI) is the leading cause of job-related injury in North America and involves a disorder of the joints, nerves, muscles, ligaments, or tendons. Tendonitis occurs when a tendon in your wrist becomes inflamed. Carpal tunnel syndrome (CTS) occurs when the nerve that connects the forearm to the palm becomes inflamed. Both tendonitis and CTS are caused by computer overuse. Symptoms of tendonitis and CTS include pain, numbness, tingling, decreased mobility and decreased strength in the hand. Computer vision syndrome (CVS) is temporary problems with your eyes caused by prolonged computer use. Ergonomic design involves adjusting components to optimal height, distance, and angles to prevent computer-related injury.	Repetitive-strain injury (RSI) Tendonitis Carpal tunnel syndrome (CTS) Computer vision syndrome (CVS) Ergonomics BlackBerry thumb

Multiple Choice

1. Apple's MacBook Air is an example of this type of notebook computer.
   a. Netbook
   b. Laptop
   c. Tablet PC
   d. Ultrabook

2. Which of the following computers is NOT a personal computer (PC)?
   a. Mainframe
   b. Laptop
   c. Netbook
   d. Desktop computer

3. Google's Project Glass eyeglasses fit into this category of computers.
   a. Supercomputer
   b. Wearable
   c. Server
   d. Desktop PC

4. These computers have a processor that is programmed to perform a particular task.
   a. Multi-core processors
   b. Embedded computers
   c. Servers
   d. Thin clients

5. This type of computer is used to link together other computers in order to share resources.
   a. Ultra-mobile PC (UMPC)
   b. Ultrabook
   c. Netbook
   d. Server

6. Supercomputing speed is measured in
   _____.
   a. Megabytes
   b. Gigabytes
   c. Petaflops
   d. Gigahertz

7. This term is used to describe computing that is everywhere at the same time.
   a. Technological convergence
   b. 24/7 access
   c. Supercomputing
   d. Ubiquitous computing

8. This term describes the merging of multiple technologies into a single device such as a game console being used to play movies and surf the Web.
   a. Ubiquitous computing
   b. Supercomputing
   c. Technological convergence
   d. Embedded computing

9. Which of the following operations is NOT in the Information Processing Cycle?
   a. Printing
   b. Processing
   c. Input
   d. Output

10. A scanner is an example of this type of device used in the Information Processing Cycle.
    a. Input
    b. Processing
    c. Output
    d. Storage

11. The computer chip that carries out the instructions given by software is called the
    _____.
    a. Random Access Memory (RAM)
    b. Central Processing Unit (CPU)
    c. Cache memory
    d. Storage media

12. This term describes a delivery method where software applications are accessed from the Web.
    a. Software-as-a-Service (SaaS)
    b. Infrastructure-as-a-Service (IaaS)
    c. Cloud-as-a-Service (CaaS)
    d. Subscriptions-as-a-Service (SaaS)

13. Cloud computing places the processing and _____ operations in the Information Processing Cycle at the service provider's server.
    a. Output
    b. Storage
    c. Input
    d. Communications

14. This label on a device indicates the manufacturer has met or exceeded minimum federal standards for energy consumption.
    a. Green Star
    b. Star Plus
    c. Energy Star
    d. Eco Star

15. A leading cause of job-related illness in North America is _____.
    a. Computer vision syndrome
    b. Repetitive-strain injury
    c. Computer fatigue
    d. Repetitive-work injury

16. This term describes the design of equipment and workspace for the individual's safety and comfort.
    a. Healthy computing
    b. Work smart
    c. E-computing
    d. Ergonomics

Crossword Puzzle

ACROSS

4   Computer that can be moved around

7   Small notebook for e-mail and the Web

9   Use of technology to manage information

10 Environmentally responsible

12 Fastest, most expensive computer

14 Internet

15 Characters entered into computer

16 Connects thousands, processes millions of transactions

DOWN

1   Blending multiple functions into one unit

2   Inflamed tendon in wrist

3   Eye strain

5   Everywhere, all of the time

6   Thin, light notebook

8   Discarded electronics

11 Hard disk drive

13 Self-contained computer

Matching

Match the term with the statement or definition.

_____ 1. Desktop PC

_____ 2. Multipurpose cell phone

_____ 3. Microwave oven

_____ 4. Midrange server

_____ 5. Multi-core processor

_____ 6. Web-based applications

_____ 7. E-trash

_____ 8. Carpal tunnel syndrome

a. Independent units on the same CPU

b. Connects hundreds of clients

c. Mobile device

d. Repetitive-strain injury

e. Obsolete electronics

f. Apple iMac

g. Embedded computer

h. Cloud computing

Project 1 Technology at Your School

Individual, Pairs, or Team
Deliverable: Presentation

Your school uses technology to meet a variety of needs by different users and perform many different types of tasks. Consider the different uses of technology at your school that would be needed by students, faculty, and administrators. Pick one of the three user groups and list all of the technology that the group would access and the types of tasks for which the technology would be used. You may want to interview someone from faculty or administration to help you complete this task. *Note: Your instructor may instead assign a user group to you for this project.*

1. Create a presentation with one slide for each use of technology by the user group. Describe the hardware or software that is used and how it is used to complete a task. If you have access to a digital video camera and permission to shoot video from participants, include short videos of the technology being used.
2. Save the presentation as **C1-Project1-SchoolTech-Your Name**.
3. Submit the presentation to your instructor in the manner she or he has requested.

Project 2 Mobile Device Usage

Pairs or Team
Deliverable: Table or Chart

Conduct an informal survey of 20 to 30 friends, relatives, neighbors, or students in another class asking them to estimate the time they spend using technology on a mobile device for the following activities: Talking or Video Calling, Texting, Surfing, Taking Pictures, Playing Games, Other. Ask each person to list activities rated as Other.

1. Compile your results and create a table or a chart in a word processor, spreadsheet, or presentation program to show the results. Include below the chart a list of the activities rated as Other.
2. Save the table or chart as **C1-Project2-MobileUsage-Your Name**.
3. Submit the table or chart to your instructor in the manner she or he has requested.

Project 3 Information Processing Cycle

Individual
Deliverable: Flowchart or Table in a Document or Presentation

Take a task that you completed today using technology and break the task down into each of the four operations in the Information Processing Cycle. Consider the hardware and software that would be used at each operation. Review Figure 1.13 for assistance.

1. Create a flowchart similar to Figure 1.13 or list the operation and place the description in a table in a document or presentation. Include at the beginning of the document or presentation a brief description of the task you analyzed including a list of the hardware and software you determined was used.
2. Save the document or presentation as **C1-Project3-IPCycle-Your Name**.
3. Submit the document or presentation to your instructor in the manner she or he has requested.

Project 4 Comparison of Two Cloud Computing Service Providers

Pairs or Team
Deliverable: Document

Assume you work as interns at a local business magazine. You have been asked to write an article about cloud computing. The editor has asked you to write the article geared toward a small business owner that explains cloud computing and compares two of the leading cloud computing service providers.

1. Research top cloud computing service providers and pick two providers for your article.
2. Create a document written as a magazine article for small business owners that explains cloud computing and describes the services offered by the two providers you selected.
3. Save the document as **C1-Project4-CloudComputing-Your Name**.
4. Submit the document to your instructor in the manner she or he has requested.

Project 5 RSI Costs and Benefits of Ergonomics

Individual, Pairs, or Team
Deliverable: Presentation

You intern at the membership office of the professional association for your industry. At next month's association dinner meeting the president would like to show a presentation that informs the members of current statistics and cost of RSI illness in the workplace. The president would also like to provide information about ergonomics.

1. Research current statistics and costs for RSI in the workplace and the benefits of investing in ergonomics.
2. Create a presentation that could be used by the president at the next association dinner meeting to show statistics, costs, and information about ergonomics as a benefit to reducing RSI injuries.
3. Save the presentation as **C1-Project5-RSIandErgonomics-Your Name**.
4. Submit the presentation to your instructor in the manner she or he has requested.

Project 6 Greener Computing

Individual, Pairs, or Team
Deliverable: Blog Entry

Your workplace does not have a green computing initiative in place. You decide to convince management that the company should embrace green computing practices and policies.

1. Write and post a blog entry that will convince management to adopt green computing in the workplace.
2. Submit your blog URL to your instructor in the manner she or he has requested.

Optional

Read the blog entry for this project of at least two other classmates and post a comment to each. Submit the URLs of your classmates' blogs with Step 2.

Project 7 Technology Innovation

Individual, Pairs, or Team
Deliverable: Blog Entry

How could a technology innovation improve your life? Consider the answer to this question and brainstorm a hardware or software technology that could solve the problem.

1. Write and post a blog entry that describes the problem and how a new technology could improve the situation.
2. Submit your blog URL to your instructor in the manner she or he has requested.

Optional

Read the blog entry for this project of at least two other classmates and post a comment to each. Submit the URLs of your classmates' blogs with Step 2.

Project 8 Discussion—Is Technology Good or Bad?

Team
Deliverable: Document, Blog Entry, or Presentation

Technology has allowed people to live better, more safely, and to access a wealth of resources for personal and work enjoyment and efficiency. Some would argue that technology has made us an "always-on" society where workers have no free time, people are vulnerable to abuse through cyber bullying, and people experience technology burnout from the rapid pace of change.

1. Within your team discuss whether technology innovation is good or bad for society.
2. Prepare a summary of your team's discussion in a document, blog entry, or presentation.
3. Save the document or presentation as **C1-Project8-TechDiscussion-Your Name**.
4. Submit the document, presentation, or blog entry to your instructor in the manner she or he has requested.

Project 9 Ethics Discussion on Personal Use of Technology at Work

Team
Deliverable: Document, Blog Entry, or Presentation

A friend at your workplace who sits near you uses her computer for personal reasons several times throughout the day when she should be working. You have observed her updating her Facebook page, watching YouTube videos, shopping online, and looking at online travel websites. One time at lunch you casually mentioned that you noticed she uses the Web a lot for personal reasons and she told you she prefers the high speed access at work over her home setup.

1. Within your team discuss how you should handle this situation. Should you ignore the situation since you are not her manager? If you answer yes, would your answer be different if the employee was not your friend? In what instances, if any, is it OK to use employer equipment for personal use? How could you convince your friend to stop using the employer's computer for personal use? How should management deal with employees' use of company-provided technology for personal reasons?
2. Prepare a summary of your team's discussion in a document, blog entry, or presentation.
3. Save the document or presentation as **C1-Project9-PersonalUseDiscussion-Your Name**.
4. Submit the document, presentation, or blog entry to your instructor in the manner she or he has requested.

Chapter 2

Exploring the World Using the Internet

After successfully completing this chapter, you will be able to:

Describe the Internet and the World Wide Web

Identify the hardware, software, and service you need to connect to the Internet

List and explain the various types of Internet connectivity options

Recognize four popular web browsers used to view content

Distinguish parts of a URL and search, browse, and evaluate online content

Recognize plug-ins and players used on web pages to enrich content

Explain online services such as e-commerce, email, and VoIP

Chances are you have used the Internet today at home, at school, or at work to search for information, access study notes, play games, watch videos or movies, update your status, upload photos, or post a comment on a social media site. For many people reading this book, the Internet has always been available to accomplish these tasks, and the ability to connect and share information online with anyone in the world is taken for granted. Society has been shaped in many ways by the proliferation of the Internet over the last 20 years, and the increased use of the Internet on mobile devices is promising to bring even more innovation to the future.

Today's consumers and workers need to be Internet savvy. Knowing how to find the right information quickly, connect with others, and communicate professionally are essential skills for personal and professional success. In this chapter you will learn the difference between the Internet and the World Wide Web, study the equipment options used for Internet connectivity, review the most popular web browsers, search and evaluate web content, understand how multimedia pages access plug-ins and players, and identify the various services available to you in the online world.

Following this introduction to the Internet you will learn to communicate and connect with others using social media and Web publishing options in Chapter 6.

Networks, the Internet, and the World Wide Web

A **network** is two or more computers or other devices (such as a printer) that are linked together to share resources and communicate with each other. Computers are linked by a communications medium such as a wireless signal or a cable that physically connects each device. You may have a small home network set up to share Internet access among a desktop and a laptop, tablet, or other mobile device. Often, home networks also share a printer.

Networks exist in business, government, and other organizations in a variety of sizes and types to facilitate sharing and communicating among workers. These larger networks share software, storage space, printers, copiers, and other devices in addition to Internet access.

The Internet

The **Internet (Net)** is a global network that links together other networks such as government departments, businesses, nonprofit organizations, educational and research institutions, and individuals. Think of the Internet as the physical structure that connects thousands of other networks together to make a worldwide network. In order for this network to transmit data around the world, special high-speed communications and networking equipment is needed to provide the pathway on which the data travels. For example, an email message you send to someone in another state, province, or country would travel through several networks including telephone, cable, or satellite networks to reach its destination. This collection of networks (Figure 2.1) that provides the pathway for data to travel is the Internet.

Figure 2.1 The Internet is a global network connecting thousands of other networks providing the pathway for data to travel the world.

You connect your PC or mobile device to the Internet by subscribing to Internet service through an **Internet Service Provider (ISP)**, a company that provides access to the Internet's infrastructure for a fee. You will learn about connecting to the Internet in the next topic.

The World Wide Web

The global collection of electronic documents circulated on the Internet in the form of **web pages** make up the **World Wide Web (Web** or **WWW)**. A web page is a document that contains text and multimedia content such as images, video, sound, and animation. Web pages are usually linked to other pages so that one can start at one page and click links to several other related pages. Web pages are stored in a format that is read and interpreted for display within a **web browser** (a software program used to view web pages). A **website** is a collection of related web pages for one organization or individual. For example, all of the web pages about your school that are available for viewing on the Internet make up your school's website. All of the web pages and resources such as photos, videos, sounds, and animations that make the website work are stored on a special server called a **web server**. Web servers are connected to the Internet continuously so that anyone can access them at any time from any place.

While the Internet provides the path on which a web page is transmitted, web pages are just one type of data that uses the Internet. Other services that use the same network include email messages, instant messages, voice-over-IP services (telephone service via the Internet), and file transfer services. Figure 2.2 illustrates how the Internet delivers the Web content to you at your PC or mobile device while Figure 2.3 provides an example of web pages with multimedia.

Figure 2.2 A web page travels along the Internet's collection of networking equipment and telecommunications systems to your PC or mobile device.

A website includes a navigation area with the main headings or topics for the site. In these pages, the navigation area is at the top.

The starting page for a website is called the home page.

Web pages contain text and multimedia content such as video, sound, images, and animations. Related web pages are linked together.

Figure 2.3 Web pages can contain text, images, video, sound, and animation. A website is a collection of related web pages such as these from the U.S. Navy.

Web 2.0 Initially, web pages mostly were a one-way communication medium where the organization or individual controlled the content and used the Web simply as a means to provide information. Over time, a second generation of two-way communication web pages became available that allowed people to interact with the organization or with each other by sharing ideas, feedback, content, and multimedia. These websites that encourage and facilitate collaboration and sharing and allow users to add or edit content became known as **Web 2.0**.

Web 3.0 The next generation of the Web under development is known as
Web 3.0 or the **Semantic Web**. In this generation of the Web, meaningful
connections between data and Web pages will exist, allowing you to find more
complex information more easily and quickly. For example, you might type a
question such as *Where is the nearest Blue Flag rated beach and a campground?* and the
browser will automatically check your geographic location to respond with the
closest locations. Web 3.0 will use automated agents or intelligent agents, machines
that will adapt and learn the type of content to show you based on previous searches
and browsing that you have done. Imagine in the future typing *Where is a good place
to eat out tonight?* and the browser responds with a list of restaurants for the type of
food you have searched for in the past within a few miles of your current location.

Career Connection

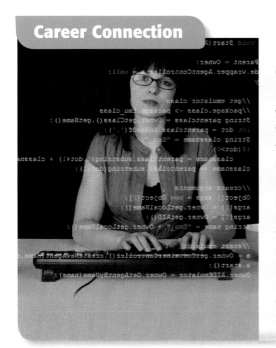

Careers for the Web

Every business needs to have a well-designed, functional
website that appeals to its target consumer. Consumers
typically turn first to the Web when looking for information
to make a purchase. The increase in the use of the Internet
on mobile devices means demand for people who can
develop websites that display well in mobile web browsers is
growing. Web designers design the look, feel, and function of
a website, while Web developers specialize in programming
the website. Both specialists work together to create a
dynamic and interactive site that enhances an organization's
brand. If either of these professions interests you, look at
online ads for Web designers and Web developers to see
what training and experience you will need.

EXPLORE FURTHER

What is Internet2?

If the Internet is the world's largest network of networks, what is Internet2? What is the purpose of
Internet2, how is it managed, and what benefits will be gained?

1. Search the Web to locate answers to the above questions.
2. Create a document with a summary of your findings in your own words. Include the URLs of the web
   pages you used to create your summary.
3. Save the document as **C2-Web-Internet2-Your Name**.
4. Submit the document to your instructor in the manner she or he requested.

Connecting to the Internet

At work or school you connect to the Internet using the high-speed service installed on the organization's network. After logging in by providing your user name and password, you can immediately launch a web browser and start searching the Web. The networks you use in these settings are designed to handle more functions beyond sharing Internet access. In this topic, you will learn about Internet connectivity options for a small home network.

Components Needed for Internet Access

Computers and mobile devices sold today are already equipped with the hardware that is needed to connect to a network. For example, a notebook may be sold equipped with a **network interface card (NIC)**, often referred to in computer ads as an **Ethernet port**. With this type of hardware you plug one end of an Ethernet cable (a twisted-pair cable similar to a telephone cable but larger) into the notebook and the other end into a device that connects to the Internet. Most PCs and all mobile devices also come equipped with a built-in **wireless interface card** that allows you to connect to a network using wireless technology. Newer notebooks and mobile devices may also integrate **Bluetooth** connectivity, which offers the ability to connect to another Bluetooth-enabled device such as your smartphone.

In addition to your network-enabled PC, notebook, or mobile device, you will also need the following account service, hardware, and software to connect to the Internet and browse the Web:

- An account with an Internet Service Provider (ISP)
- Networking equipment (usually provided by your ISP) such as a cable modem, DSL modem, wireless modem, or satellite modem
- A router may be needed if you will be connecting multiple devices (newer modems integrate a wireless router within the same equipment)
- A web browser such as Internet Explorer, Firefox, Chrome, or Safari (you will learn about these software programs in the next topic)

Internet Service Providers (ISPs)

ISPs are companies that sell Internet access by providing the equipment and servers that allow your PC or mobile device to connect to the Internet backbone. Typically, you contract with a telephone or cellular provider, cable company, satellite company, or dedicated Internet access company such as EarthLink.

Fees for Internet access vary and usually are based on the connection speed that you want. High-speed access costs more than a slower connection and is usually priced at various speed levels. Also be aware of download limits (called data caps) in your contract. Some ISPs attach a data cap to a service and if you exceed the cap additional fees may be charged.

Deciding on the connection speed you should sign up for is generally based on your anticipated usage of the Internet. If you primarily only use email and browse web pages, you can get by with a slower speed than someone who wants to participate in online games, watch movies, or stream live music or radio programs.

Conduct a search for ISPs that operate in your area at your school or library to find the best deal and compare services. Generally, along with Internet access you also receive multiple email accounts and security tools to keep your PC or mobile device virus- and spam-free.

HOW MUCH MORE CAN YOU DO WITH EARTHLINK HIGH SPEED INTERNET?

A blazing-fast Internet connection means doing more in less time with less waiting around. See how many more photos and songs you can download using 3 different speed levels of EarthLink High Speed compared to dial-up.

DOWNLOADING PHOTOS (average 1MB file)

| 6.0 MBPS HIGH SPEED | 3.0 MBPS HIGH SPEED | 1.5 MBPS HIGH SPEED | 56K DIAL UP |
| 45 PHOTOS IN 1 MIN. | 22 PHOTOS IN 1 MIN. | 11 PHOTOS IN 1 MIN. | 1/2 PHOTO IN 1 MIN. |

DOWNLOADING MUSIC (average 3MB file)

| 6.0 MBPS HIGH SPEED | 3.0 MBPS HIGH SPEED | 1.5 MBPS HIGH SPEED | 56K DIAL UP |
| 15 SONGS IN 1 MIN. | 7.5 SONGS IN 1 MIN. | 4 SONGS IN 1 MIN. | 1/6 SONG IN 1 MIN. |

Figure 2.4 ISP EarthLink provides this chart at its website that compares the number of photos and songs that can be downloaded at various connection speeds.

High-Speed Internet Connectivity

High-speed Internet access is called **broadband**, which is a term used to refer to any always-on connection capable of carrying a large amount of data at a fast speed. Speed for broadband connectivity is expressed as **megabits per second (Mbps)**, meaning data transfers at the rate of 1 million bits per second. See Table 2.1 for a list of typical connection speeds by type of connection. When you evaluate ISP contracts, a higher Mbps value means a higher subscription fee. The chart shown in Figure 2.4 puts meaningful context to connection speed by comparing the number of photos and songs that can be downloaded at four speed levels. Various options for broadband access are described below.

Table 2.1	Internet Connectivity Average Connection Speeds
Type of Internet Connectivity	**Average Speed**
Cable	5 to 20 Mbps More expensive plans offer 50 to 75 Mbps access
DSL	1 to 10 Mbps
Fiber-Optic	50 Mbps Some plans available at 75, 150, and 300 Mbps
Satellite	1Mbps

Cable Internet Access

Cable Internet access is provided by the same cable company with which you subscribe for television service. A cable modem connects to your cable network outlet using a coaxial cable. From the cable modem, you use a twisted-pair cable to plug into your computer or wireless router to enable Internet access. Cable connections are very fast; however, you share the connection with others in your neighborhood so performance can vary.

Did You Know ?

Actual connection speed will vary due to numerous factors such as distance from ISP, time of day (congestion slows down networks), and the Web activities of others sharing the connection.

Check This Out

www.speedtest.net

Go here to perform a speed test from your PC or mobile device. Compare speed results at different times of the day until you find when speed is fastest.

A cable modem is connected to the cable company network using coaxial cable.

A DSL modem is connected to the telephone company network using twisted-pair cable.

Check This Out

www.broadbandmap.gov

Go here, type in your city and state, and click Find Broadband to view statistics about broadband providers in your area.

DSL Internet Access

A **Digital Subscriber Line (DSL)** provided by your telephone company connects using telephone lines. A DSL modem uses twisted-pair cable to plug into your telephone jack and your computer or wireless router. With DSL, your telephone line is not tied up while you are using the Internet.

Fiber-to-the-Premises

Fiber-to-the-Premises (FTTP) also referred to as **Fiber-to-the-Home (FTTH)** or **Fiber-Optic-Service (FiOS)** involves the ISP running a fiber-optic cable directly to your home or business. This is the most expensive option and not yet widely available. A piece of networking equipment is installed to convert optical signals transmitted over fiber-optic cable to and from the electrical signals transmitted by your computer devices.

Fiber-optic networks transmit beams of light capable of speeds measuring in the billions of bits per second.

Satellite

Satellite Internet access is an option in rural areas where cable or DSL is not available. Satellite requires the installation of a satellite dish and satellite modem. Access is slower and more expensive.

Satellite Internet is used in rural areas where cable and DSL are not available.

Fixed Wireless Internet Access

Fixed wireless Internet access involves installing an antenna outside your home to send and receive radio signals. A wireless modem is used to connect to your computer or router.

Wi-Fi Hotspots

In a **Wireless Fidelity (Wi-Fi)** network, wireless access points and radio signals are used to transmit data. Wi-Fi is commonly used in public spaces for free Internet access. An area where a Wi-Fi network is within range is called a **hotspot**. Wi-Fi is also commonly used in homes, schools, and workplaces to provide connectivity to notebooks, tablets, and smartphones. A Wi-Fi hotspot encompasses a short distance, which makes it attractive for home users to connect a mobile device via a wireless router connected to their cable or DSL modem, or temporarily access the Internet in an airport, café, library, or other public space.

Depending on the Wi-Fi equipment being used, connection speeds fall within the range of 5 to 6 Mbps for older equipment, 25 to 30 Mbps for mid-range equipment, and 150 to 160 Mbps for newer devices.

A wireless access point is used in a Wi-Fi network to provide access to wireless users.

Mobile Broadband Sticks

Mobile broadband sticks are portable modems that plug into a USB port on your mobile device and connect via a cellular network. The advantage to a mobile broadband stick is that you can carry your Internet connection with you.

3G and 4G Cellular Communications

Most smartphones used today will be either **3G** (third generation) or **4G** (fourth generation) devices that provide Internet access through cell towers. Average speed for a 3G connection is around 1 Mbps; however, performance varies depending on location. Average speed for 4G devices is often advertised as 10 times faster than 3G and is often described as a 4G **LTE network**, which is the fastest network for mobile devices. These networks use the 4G technology standard with advanced design to improve speed. Devices have to be able to send and receive using 4G technology to take advantage of the higher speed.

A mobile broadband stick is a portable modem that you plug into a USB port.

In some communities, broadband Internet access may not be available, or the cost may be too high for some people. A low-cost way of connecting to the Internet is to use **dial-up**, in which you connect your PC to your telephone system via a modem built into your PC. The ISP provides you with a local telephone number that the computer dials to get on the Internet. The main disadvantages to dial-up are the slow speed and that you cannot use your telephone to make voice calls while the computer is online.

The ISP will provide you with instructions to install and connect to the ISP's network. Generally, the installation requires you to plug in the modem and run a software program from a CD, DVD, or USB flash drive. Appendix B provides instructions for setting up a wireless network in your home.

Once you've established a physical network connection, you are ready to explore the Web using a web browser.

At the time of writing, a 4G LTE device on an LTE network experiences the fastest speed for a mobile user.

EXPLORE FURTHER

What is tethering?

Assume you are planning a vacation in a remote cabin where there is no Internet access. You are bringing your smartphone and notebook with you to the cabin. Your smartphone plan includes Internet access. You decide to investigate tethering as a means to get Internet access on your notebook.

1. Search for information on tethering. Specifically, find out how a cell phone can be used as a modem for another device such as a notebook or tablet. How does it work? What do you need to do to connect the two devices? Are there any issues with tethering that you should be aware of before going to the cabin?

2. Create a document that summarizes your answers to the questions in your own words. At the end of the document, include the URLs of the main articles you used for this topic.

3. Save the document as **C2-Web-tethering-Your Name**.

4. Submit the document to your instructor in the manner she or he has requested.

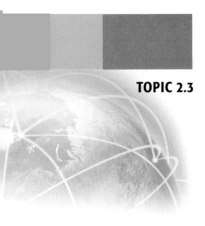

Popular Web Browsers

Once you have established an Internet connection, you are ready to start browsing, shopping, watching videos, playing games, or checking out what your friends and family are posting at social media websites. Web pages are viewed using browser software. A web browser is a program that locates a web page on the Internet and interprets the code in which the web page has been stored to compose the page as text and multimedia. Many web pages are created using a markup language called **HTML**, which stands for **Hypertext Markup Language**. A markup language uses tags to describe page content. In this topic you will review four popular web browsers for PCs: Internet Explorer, Firefox, Chrome, and Safari. You will also be introduced to the unique needs of mobile web browsers.

Internet Explorer

Internet Explorer (IE) is the web browser included with Microsoft Windows. In Figure 2.5, Internet Explorer is displayed with version 9 (included with Windows 7) on the left and version 10 (included with Windows 8) on the right. Notice the browser in Windows 8 provides more page viewing area. IE 10 is designed to provide more web page viewing with a simpler design. Tools, multiple page tabs, and customization options are only revealed when needed.

Since Windows has such a large market share, IE enjoyed the status as the most popular web browser for many years. People did not look for alternatives when IE was already on one's desktop; however, recently IE has been losing ground to Google's Chrome browser.

Tabs allow you to open multiple web pages and switch back and forth between them. In IE 10, multiple page tabs are hidden until you swipe down from the top of the page or right-click the mouse.

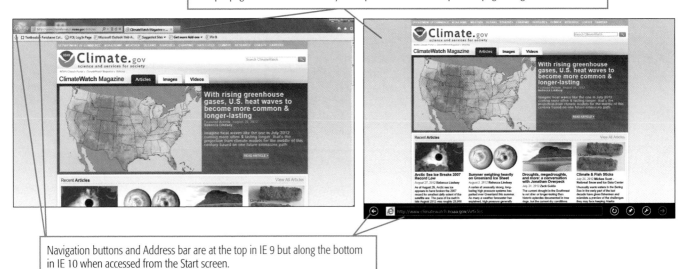

Navigation buttons and Address bar are at the top in IE 9 but along the bottom in IE 10 when accessed from the Start screen.

Figure 2.5 Internet Explorer (IE) is the web browser included with Microsoft Windows. At the left, IE version 9 in Windows 7 is shown, while the same web page in IE version 10 in shown at the right. IE 10 has a larger page viewing area and simpler design than earlier versions.

Chrome

Google's **Chrome** is a free web browser that runs on Windows-compatible PCs. The browser was initially released in 2008 with features that included fast page loading and the ability to search directly in the Address bar. In Figure 2.6, Chrome is shown with the web page for Grand Canyon National Park.

As of June 2012, Chrome and Internet Explorer were both hovering near the 30 percent market share statistic according to two popular web usage statistic counters, StatCounter and W3Counter. With future trends indicating mobile browsers will be favored over PC browsers, these market share statistics could vary widely going forward.

Figure 2.6 Google's Chrome browser delivers fast page loading and the ability to search from the address bar.

Firefox

Firefox is a free web browser available at mozilla.org by the Mozilla Foundation. The browser will run on a Windows-compatible PC, a Mac, or a Linux computer. Since the initial release of Firefox version 1 in 2004, the browser's use has been steadily rising. At the time of writing, Firefox was the third most popular browser. Figure 2.7 shows Firefox version 13 with the web page for the Library of Congress. You will notice similarities to IE version 9 with the placement of the navigation buttons, Address bar, and tabs for browsing multiple pages. Fans of Firefox indicate they favor the browser's speed in loading web pages.

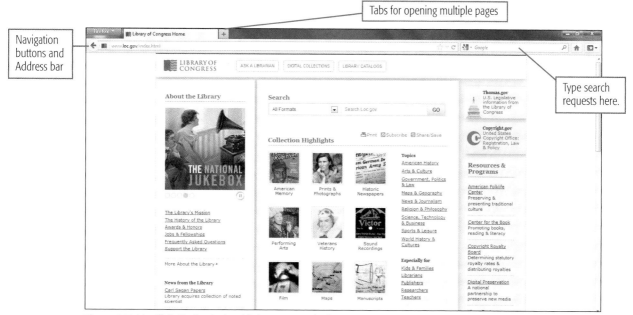

Figure 2.7 Mozilla's Firefox is the third most popular browser.

Type search
requests here.

Navigation
buttons and
Address bar

You can add
pages you want
to read later
to the Reading
List. Safari
keeps the list
up-to-date for
all devices such
as your iPhone
or iPad via
iCloud.

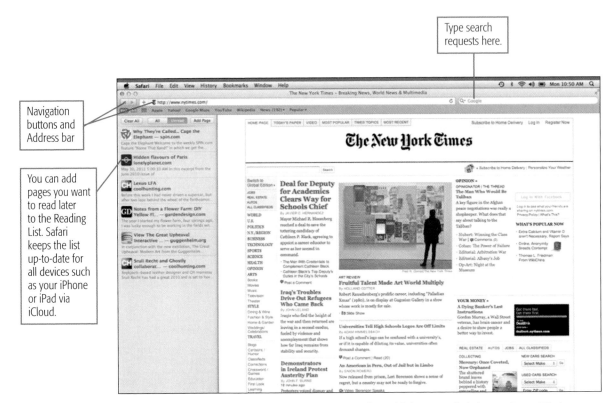

Figure 2.8 Safari is the browser supplied on Macs, iPads, and iPhones. Safari also works on Windows-compatible PCs and is available to download for free at Apple.com.

Safari

Apple's **Safari** browser is used on Mac and Apple mobile devices such as iPads and iPhones. The browser is also available as a free download for a PC. Safari 5 includes new features such as the Reading List shown in Figure 2.8 and full-screen browsing.

All of the top four web browsers share similar features and navigation options designed to assist with finding and viewing web pages. Regardless of the browser you use, web addressing and search techniques discussed in the next topic are universal.

Figure 2.9 Opera Mobile is a popular browser for mobile devices.

Mobile Browsers

Mobile web browsers are designed to quickly display web pages optimized for the smaller screens on devices such as tablets and smartphones. The challenge for mobile browsers is that web pages designed for larger screens have to be readable in a smaller viewing area. Mobile browsers incorporate text wrapping and try to avoid the user having to scroll sideways. Mobile versions of IE, Chrome, Firefox, and Safari are available in addition to numerous other browser apps for Android and Apple devices.

In Figure 2.9, Opera Mobile is shown on a smartphone. Opera also provides a browser for Windows-compatible, Mac, and Linux computers.

Blog Topic

Which browser(s) do you favor?

Which browser do you use? Have you tried one of the other browsers mentioned in this topic? Do you use multiple browsers? If yes, why? If you could develop your dream browser, what would it do differently than what you use now?

1. Write and post a blog entry that provides the answers to the above questions.
2. Read at least two of your classmates' blogs and post one comment to each.
3. Submit your blog URL and the URLs of your classmates' blogs for which you provided a comment to your instructor in the manner she or he requested.

EXPLORE FURTHER

What other web browsers are available?

Other web browsers are available for PCs and Macs in addition to the four mentioned in this topic. Each of these other web browsers is designed to be different in various ways from IE, Chrome, Firefox, and Safari.

1. Research other web browsers that are available for a PC or a Mac. Pick one alternative web browser and learn more about what it does and why people use it.
2. Create a document that describes the alternative web browser in your own words. At the end of the document include the URLs of the articles you used.
3. Save the document as **C2-Web-AlternativeBrowsers-Your Name**.
4. Submit the document to your instructor in the manner she or he has requested.

Understanding Internet and Web Addresses and Navigating Web Pages

TOPIC 2.4

If you are invited to visit a friend at his house, you need to know the address so you know where to go to find his home. Similarly, on the Internet, you locate a computer by using an address. When a computing device is connected to the Internet, it is assigned a unique address called an **Internet Protocol (IP) address** so that the device can communicate with other computers. An IP address is a series of four numbers from 0 to 255 separated by periods. For example, in Figure 2.10, the IP address is 209.46.18.200. **ICANN (Internet Corporation for Assigned Names and Numbers)** is a nonprofit organization that is in charge of keeping track of the Internet addresses and names all around the world.

The system of addressing that uses four groups of numbers is referred to as IPv4. A new system called IPv6 was launched because the number of unique IPv4 addresses was running out. IPv6 uses eight groups of characters separated by colons, where a character can be a number 0 through 9 or a letter a through f. With IPv6 there will be enough IP addresses for years to come. For now, both IPv4 and IPv6 will coexist since some equipment and software connected to the Internet cannot handle IPv6 addressing.

Did You Know?

On June 6, 2012, World IPv6 Launch Day was held during which hundreds of websites including heavyweights Google, Microsoft, and YouTube permanently enabled IPv6 addressing.

Figure 2.10 A URL contains a domain name that allows you to locate a website using a text-based name rather than the numeric IP address.

Web Addresses

If you know the numeric address for a computer on the Internet, you can navigate to the site by typing it in the browser's Address bar. For example, typing 209.46.18.200 in the Address bar of your browser will bring you to the EMC Corporation website (the publishing company for this textbook). However, most people do not know or could not remember a numeric address. Instead, we use a **web address**, which is a text-based address, to navigate to a website. A web address is also called a **uniform resource locator (URL)**. In Figure 2.10, the URL for the EMC Corporation website is *http://www.emcp.com*. The four parts of this URL are explained in Table 2.2. Each part of a URL is separated by punctuation consisting of a colon (:), one (/) or two slashes (//), and periods (.) referred to as "dots." For example, when telling someone the URL for EMC Corporation you would say "*emcp dot com*."

When you type a URL in the Address bar of a browser, a server has to locate the IP address for the domain name so that data can be transmitted to the correct computer. A server that holds this directory is known as a **Domain Name System (DNS) server** and is owned by a business or ISP.

Table 2.2	The Parts of a URL	
Part of URL	**What It Represents**	**Examples**
http	The protocol for the page. A protocol is a set of rules for transmitting data. Since http is used most of the time, you can omit it when typing the URL.	http Hypertext transfer protocol ftp File transfer protocol https Hypertext transfer protocol secure
www	World Wide Web server Since most servers are World Wide Web servers, you can omit www when typing the URL.	
emcp	The organization's **domain name**, also referred to as a second-level domain name. Domain names are the text-based version of the IP address and are usually the name or an abbreviation of a company or organization.	emcp EMC Corporation domain name nytimes New York Times domain name google Google Inc.'s domain name navy U.S. Navy's domain name loc Library of Congress domain name
com	The part of the domain name that identifies the **top-level domain (TLD)**. TLDs identify the type of organization associated with the domain name. Several TLDs with three or more characters are known as **generic top-level domains (gTLDs)**. ICANN is expanding the number of approved gTLDs. Watch for websites in the future with domain names such as myroadsideinn.*hotel* or mylawfirm.*legal*. Two-character TLDs are country codes called **ccTLDs**.	com Commercial organizations edu Educational institution gov Government website mil Military site net Network providers such as ISPs org Nonprofit organizations biz Business ca Canada

Navigating Web Pages

Most people browse the Web in one of two ways: by typing the web address of a company or organization to go directly to a website (Figure 2.11), or, by typing a search phrase into a search engine website such as Google or Bing to search for information (Figure 2.12). In the next topic you will learn more about using search engines to find information.

1. Type the web address into the Address bar of the browser you are using. For example, typing *nps.gov* in the IE10 address bar and pressing Enter caused the home page for the National Park Service to appear.

2. Click a hyperlink to a topic that interests you.

3. Continue clicking hyperlinks until you find what you need.

Figure 2.11 Navigating the Web starting from a web address

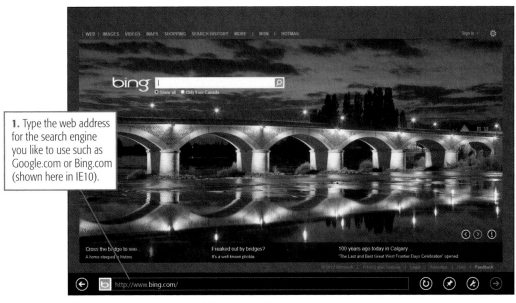

1. Type the web address for the search engine you like to use such as Google.com or Bing.com (shown here in IE10).

2. Type a search phrase and press Enter or click the Search button.

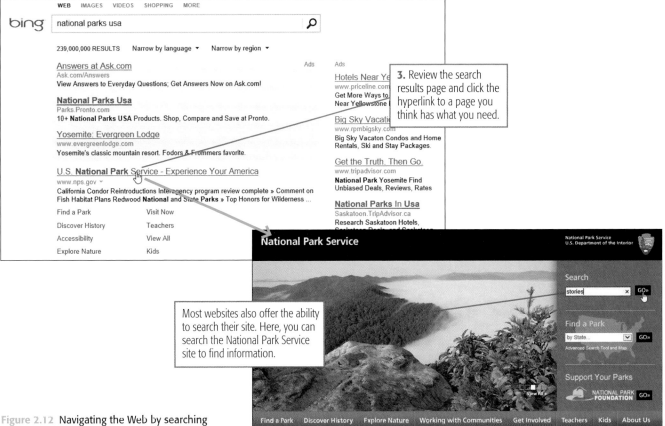

3. Review the search results page and click the hyperlink to a page you think has what you need.

Most websites also offer the ability to search their site. Here, you can search the National Park Service site to find information.

Figure 2.12 Navigating the Web by searching

The first page of a website that displays when the web address is requested is called the **home page**. Main headings appear along the top or edges and are organized by topic to guide you to subpages within the site. Web pages contain **hyperlinks** (**links** for short) that when clicked or tapped on a touchscreen take you to a related web page. Any item on a web page can be hyperlinked to another page. For example, a title, word, phrase, photo, video, graphical icon such as a button, or audio object may be a hyperlink. As you move the mouse around a page, the white arrow pointer will change to a white hand with the index finger pointing upward when you are pointing at text or an object that is a hyperlink. Hyperlinked text is usually a different color, in bold, or underlined. Click when you see the icon change or tap the text or object to move to the related web page.

You can also type the web address of a linked web page directly into the Address bar. For example, typing *nytimes.com/pages/todayspaper/index.html* takes you directly to Today's Paper at The New York Times website.

 Blog Topic

What type of Web activity do you do most often?

Most people do a variety of tasks on the Internet, but one or two types of activities generally predominate. In what activity do you spend most of your time on the Web? Is it reading news or reading or writing blogs? Is it online shopping? Is it connecting with friends and family? Is it sharing photos, videos, or music? Is it looking for information for work, school, or personal interest? How many hours per week on average do you estimate you spend on each of these activities?

1. Write and post a blog entry that provides the answers to the above questions.
2. Read at least two of your classmates' blogs and post one comment to each.
3. Submit your blog URL and the URLs of your classmates' blogs for which you provided a comment to your instructor in the manner she or he requested.

EXPLORE FURTHER

How do I register a domain name?

Assume you are planning to start a new business when you graduate. You know you will need to have a website but are not sure how to go about getting a domain name for your organization.

1. Find out how to check for an available domain name and how to register the name.
2. With millions of websites already in existence, the name you want to use may already be taken. Find out what alternatives you have if the domain name you want is already in use.
3. Create a document that summarizes in your own words what you have learned about domain names in Steps 1 and 2. At the end of the document include the URLs of the articles you used.
4. Save the document as **C2-Web-DomainNames-Your Name**.
5. Submit the document to your instructor in the manner she or he has requested.

TOPIC 2.5

Searching the Web

A **search engine** is a company that searches web pages and indexes the pages by **keywords** or by subject. When you type a search phrase at a search engine website, the results list that displays contains links to the web pages that have been associated with the keywords you used in your search phrase. To generate indexes, search engines use programs called **spiders** or **crawlers** that read web pages and other information to generate index entries. Generally, website owners submit their website information to search engines to make sure they are included in search results.

Some search engines display a subject directory that provides links to categories of information such as *Music, News, Shopping,* or *Travel.* Clicking a category brings you to another page with subtopics for that category. In most cases, you can specify if you want search results to come from the entire Web or from indexes associated with images, maps, news, shopping, or videos. Table 2.3 contains a list of five popular search engines; however, be aware that many other search engines exist.

Did You Know?

Some browsers contain an Instant Search text box usually located to the right of the Address bar. Type a search phrase in this box to search using a default search engine. If you prefer to use a different search engine, customize the browser options.

Did You Know?

According to Hitwise (a company that measures Internet traffic) Google (65%) and Bing (28%) were the two leading search engines used in June 2012. More than 50 percent of searches in the same period used only one or two words in the search phrase.

Table 2.3	Popular Search Engines
Search Engine	**URL**
Google	google.com
Bing	bing.com
Yahoo!	yahoo.com
Ask	ask.com
Dogpile	dogpile.com

You will get different results from various search engines. Figure 2.13 displays the search results from the same search phrase *xeriscape gardening* entered at two search engines, Yahoo! and Ask. Differences in results can occur for a variety of reasons. For example, spider and index program parameters differ by search engine, some search engines locate and index new or updated pages at different speeds or times, and page relevance to the search phrase may be ranked differently.

The same search phrase returns different search results at two search engines. Search engine spider and index programs vary.

Figure 2.13 Search engines provide different results for the same search phrase for many reasons, including the way in which spiders and indexers find and rank pages and keywords.

Fine-Tuning a Search

Regardless of the search engine you like to use, knowing how to fine-tune a search request will make your searching quicker and easier. With practice, you will develop a search technique that works best for you. Following are some guidelines for searching:

- A search phrase in quotations returns pages where the keywords are in the same sequence; otherwise, the search results may have the keywords in any order. For example, "endangered animals" returns pages with the word *endangered* immediately followed by the word *animals.*
- Type a minus symbol in front of a keyword to *exclude* the keyword from the search results; for example, "endangered animals" –tiger returns pages about endangered animals other than tigers.
- Rather than searching the entire Web, consider using a search engine's category such as News, Images, Videos, or Blogs to restrict the search results to a specific type of page or object (Figure 2.14).
- Check out a search engine's advanced search tools to further refine your search terms, domain, or region (Figure 2.14).
- Most search engines allow you to restrict searches to a specific time frame; for example, in Google's search tools you can filter results by *Past hour, Past 24 hours, Past week, Past month, Past year,* or *Custom date range* (Figure 2.14).
- Look for Help at the search engine's website to learn more about how the search engine indexes pages and the recommendations for searching at its site.

Figure 2.14 Using a search engine's search tools can help you narrow a search.

Some search engines are **metasearch search engines** that send your search phrase to other search engines and then compile the results in one list. Using a metasearch search engine allows you to type your search phrase once and access results from a wider group of search engines. Dogpile is an example of a metasearch search engine that provides search results in one place from Google, Bing, and Yahoo! among others.

Some metasearch search engines specialize in one type of search service such as KAYAK (kayak.com), which specializes in searching travel websites to provide you with a comparison of flights, hotels, and car rentals in one place (Figure 2.15).

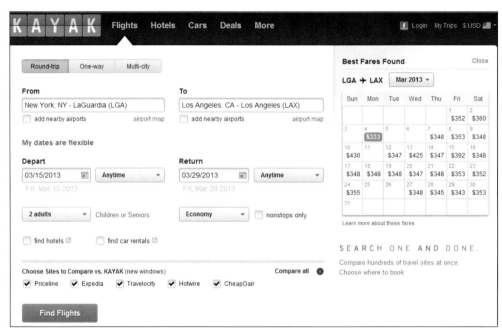

Figure 2.15 KAYAK, a metasearch search engine, specializes in searching travel websites.

Content Aggregators

A **content aggregator** is an organization that searches the Web for new content, and collects and organizes the content in one place. Some content aggregators send updates automatically to subscribers. Subscribers receive the updates, sometimes referred to as *feeds*, based on selections made for the type of information in which the subscriber is interested. For example, you can elect to receive new items related to news or music. Some content aggregators provide this service for free while others charge a fee to send out updates to subscribers. The advantage to subscribers is that the content aggregator does the work of searching the Web and organizing related information.

Click the RSS or Google Reader icon at websites to subscribe to update feeds.

Really Simple Syndication (RSS) is a specification used by content aggregators to distribute updates to subscribers. Updates are read using an RSS reader (program used to read RSS feeds) on your PC or mobile device. Another reader by Google called Google Reader can be used to subscribe to updates at websites, which are viewed by signing in with your Gmail account at reader.google.com.

Popurls.com is a content aggregator that lists on one page all of the latest headlines from the most popular sites on the Internet (Figure 2.16). Another aggregator, Techmeme (Techmeme.com), tracks changes to technology news and presents a summary each day.

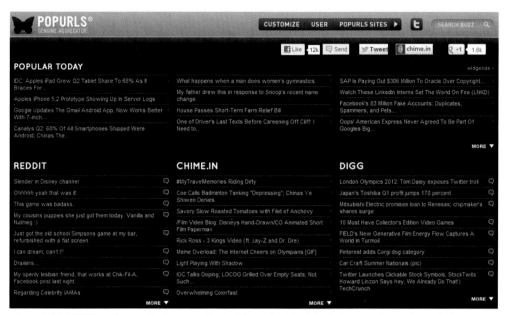

Figure 2.16 POPURLS is a content aggregator that lists all of the latest changes at popular websites.

EXPLORE FURTHER

Try out your search skills

Assume you need to find information on cybersquatting with respect to the concern that cybersquatting will increase in the future when ICANN releases new gTLDs. You need to find out what cybersquatting means and why it may become a greater concern. Only pages published within the past 12 months are desired.

1. Conduct a search using your favorite search engine using only a search phrase. What search phrase did you use and how many pages were in the search results list?
2. Next, explore the search engine's tools for conducting advanced searches and narrow your search results as specified above. How did you refine your search and how many pages were in the revised search results list?
3. Read one or two articles about the topic.
4. Create a presentation that summarizes in your own words a definition of cybersquatting and a few points about why cybersquatting is expected to rise with the release of new gTLDs. Include a slide for each of Step 1 and Step 2's answers. End your presentation with the URLs of the article(s) you read.
5. Save the presentation as **C2-Web-CybersquattingSearch-Your Name**.
6. Submit the presentation to your instructor in the manner she or he has requested.

TOPIC 2.6

Evaluating Web Content

Increasingly, the Web is becoming the only resource people turn to when looking for information, news, shopping, connecting with others, and sharing media. Anyone with an Internet connection and space allocated on a web server can publish a page on the Web. Many websites rely on users to generate the content that is posted. With thousands of new websites coming online every year, how can you be sure the information that is presented at a site is true, accurate, and timely?

Start at the Web Address

Look at the domain name in the web address. Is it an organization you recognize and trust? For example, an article published at nytimes.com would be associated with a highly recognizable media organization, The New York Times. A web address that ends with .gov, .org, or .edu would indicate the source is a government department or agency, a nonprofit organization, or an educational institution—all trusted sources.

Look at domain names for publishers of content in the print-based world with which you are familiar. For example, if you are familiar with *Psychology Today* magazine, then you will be comfortable reading content at psychologytoday.com (Figure 2.17).

Check the domain name in the web address for a recognizable name that you trust.

Figure 2.17 Begin evaluating web content by looking in the web address for a domain name that is an organization you recognize and trust.

If you do not recognize the domain name in the web address, consider doing a search for the domain name owner and searching the owner's name to find out whether the organization is reputable.

Look for an Author and the Author's Affiliation

Check for an author's name at the page. Is the author affiliated with the organization in the web address? Is the author an expert as evidenced by credentials after his or her name or evidenced in the introduction or other biographical information?

If no author name is found, try to determine if the information is credible by other means. For example, check for a link that describes the organization presenting the content. Most websites have an About Us or a Contact Us link (Figure 2.18). Check these sources to determine if a bias might exist for the information you are reading.

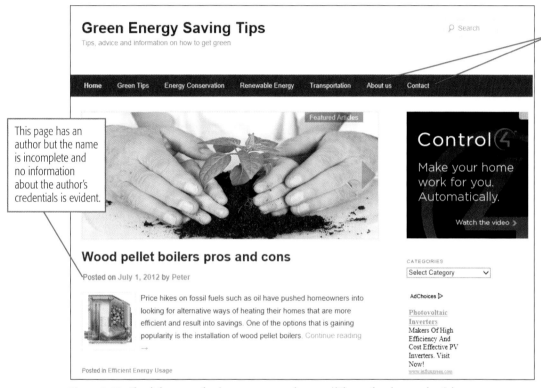

Figure 2.18 Check for an author's name on a web page; if the author has credentials or other biographical information, that helps you evaluate the validity of the content.

Check the Publication Date

In most cases you want to find the most recent information about a topic. Look for the date of publication on the page (Figure 2.19). Use the search engine's advanced search tool to filter your search results by a recent time frame and see if the page remains in the list. Sometimes, the original publication date may be older but a notation may appear (usually near the top or bottom of the page) that provides a date the content was updated. Finally, a clue to the date of publication may appear in the linked web address. For example, a linked page may have an address similar to: http://www.companyname.com/archives/2013/March/pagename.html.

If no date can be found, consider whether the content seems dated. For example, look for something in the article that may give a clue to the time frame it was published such as a reference to an event. When in doubt, corroborate the content by finding another source that is published with a recent date.

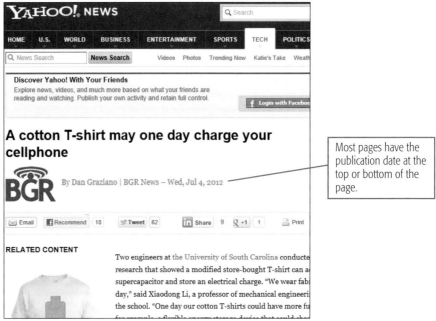

Figure 2.19 Always look for a publication date to evaluate if the content is current.

A link such as ASK AN ALIEN is probably just showing the author's sense of fun; however, the wording, page design, lack of author or date all indicate that you should verify this content with another source.

Most pages have the publication date at the top or bottom of the page.

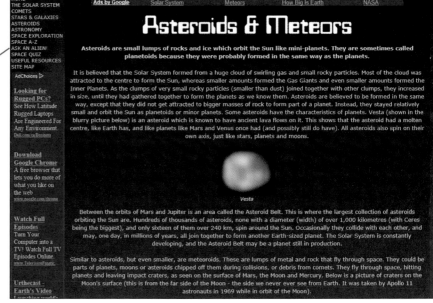

Figure 2.20 A page's design including layout, organization, and choice of colors can reveal whether the page has been published by a professional organization.

Purpose and Design of the Site

Finally, consider the purpose and design of the page you are reading. Is the organization that has published the page a company in the business of marketing a product or service? If yes, a bias may be present toward convincing you to buy the product or service.

A web page's design, spelling, and grammar will also indicate the page's credibility. A professionally designed, well written page will invite trust. The page shown in Figure 2.20 may indeed be presenting accurate information on asteroids and meteors; however, the page design uses layout, colors, and organization not used by professionals, and links such as *ASK AN ALIEN!* are cause for further inspection.

A poorly designed web page that is lacking a recognizable domain name, an author's name, and a recent publication date indicates a page that you need to be careful with. The information may indeed be accurate and credible, but you should do some additional checking to be sure.

 Blog Topic

Is Wikipedia a valid source of information for a research paper?

Wikis are websites where the page content is created by the user community. Generally, anyone can add content, and additions or changes that are wrong may be visible for a while before errors are caught. The openness of wikis has led some in the academic world to discredit sources such as Wikipedia (the most popular encyclopedia with content developed by volunteers). What do you think?

1. Go to wikipedia.org and read the information on the *About Wikipedia* page.

2. Create and post a blog entry with your opinion on whether Wikipedia content is an acceptable source for a research paper and state your rationale.

3. Read at least two of your classmates' blogs and post one comment to each.

4. Submit your blog URL and the URLs of your classmates' blogs for which you provided a comment.

EXPLORE **FURTHER**

Evaluate information on geocaching in your area

Geocaching is an outdoor activity where participants use a GPS or other mobile device to locate a container that has been hidden by other participants. The container usually contains a logbook and may also have a prize of small value. When a participant finds the geocache, he or she updates the logbook and trades or leaves the prize for the next person.

1. Find information on geocaching in your area. Pick a web page and evaluate the web page. Is it accurate? Is the page from a credible source? Is the information current?

2. Create a document with a screen capture of the web page and below the screen capture list the elements that you used to evaluate the web page in Step 1. Provide the URL at the bottom of the document. *Hint: One way to make a screen capture of a web page is to display the desired web page, press the Print Screen key on your keyboard, and then use the Paste button in Word to paste the image into a document.*

3. Save the document as **C2-Web-PageEvaluation-Your Name**.

4. Submit the document to your instructor in the manner she or he has requested.

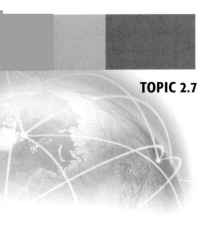

Popular Web Plug-ins and Players for Multimedia Content

TOPIC 2.7

Most web pages have some multimedia content such as images, animations, audio, and video. This type of rich content enhances the experience. In order for some multimedia content to work, a **plug-in** (also referred to as an **add-on**) or **player** may need to be installed. Plug-ins, add-ons, or players all refer to the same type of program—a software program that allows the browser to display enhanced content that it cannot display on its own.

Some plug-ins and players are included in the browser or with your operating system (Windows Media Player); however, you may display a web page with a message similar to the one shown in Figure 2.21 indicating that you need to install a plug-in or player to view the content. When you encounter a message like this, a link will be provided to the source program, which you can download for free. Click or tap the link and follow the instructions to download and install the software (Figure 2.22).

Popular plug-ins and players used on the Web are listed in Table 2.4.

Table 2.4	Common Plug-ins and Players You May Be Prompted to Download and Install	
Plug-in or Player Name	**Description**	**URL**
Adobe Reader	Used to view PDF documents. PDF documents are popular for exchanging richly formatted documents on the Web. PDFs are formatted as they would look when printed without requiring the source program in which the document was created to view or print.	adobe.com
Adobe Flash Player	Used often for animations on web pages with high-quality graphics, sound, and interactivity. Many browsers include the Flash Player since it is a popular plug-in; however, some such as Firefox will require you to download and install the application.	adobe.com
Shockwave Player	Used for Web content that includes interactive games, high-quality video or audio	adobe.com
Java	Java is a programming language used on some web pages to add interactivity to applications run from web pages or play online games.	java.com
Microsoft Silverlight	Plug-in from Microsoft used for interactive applications and high-quality video or audio	microsoft.com
Real Player	Used to play video and music files such as MP3 files	real.com
QuickTime	QuickTime is from Apple and built into Mac computers and mobile devices. PCs will also need QuickTime if the web page has video or animation provided in the QuickTime format.	apple.com

Depending on the plug-in or player you have had to install, the content may become visible immediately, or you may need to close and reopen the browser and then return to the web page you were trying to view.

A link will be provided to the plug-in or player that is needed. Click the link to download and install the latest version from the software program's website. In this case clicking the link connects you to adobe.com.

Figure 2.21 A message such as this one will appear if you display a web page that requires a plug-in or player that is not installed.

Watch for messages that will add extra software or toolbars to your browser that you may not want. If necessary, deselect these options and then click the Download button.

Figure 2.22 Install a plug-in or player by following the steps provided at the software program's website.

Plug-in and Player Updates

From time to time you will be prompted to install an update to a plug-in or player. Generally, when these messages occur, you should install the updates so that web pages work as expected.

Be Alert for Fake Plug-Ins and Players!

Some viruses appear on web pages as spoofs of popular plug-ins and players. These viruses look like the real player but clues will exist that they are not real. Look for typos in the name of the player (missing spaces between words) or linked web page. If in doubt, go directly to the source URL provided in Table 2.4 to download a plug-in or player.

EXPLORE FURTHER

Add-on toolbars for your browser

Some programs, such as many antivirus applications, install add-on toolbars to your browser automatically. As shown in Figure 2.22, you may inadvertently install an add-on when you download a plug-in or player. Some browsers refer to add-ons as *extensions*.

1. Using your favorite browser, find out how to enable and disable add-ons/extensions.
2. Create a handout specifying the browser and version that provides step-by-step instructions for the reader on how to turn on or turn off additional toolbars in the browser.
3. Save the document as **C2-Web-AddOnToolbars-Your Name**.
4. Submit the document to your instructor in the manner she or he has requested.

TOPIC 2.8

E-Commerce, Messaging, and Internet Telephone and Conferencing Options

The Internet is not used just for connecting with others at social media websites or looking up information you need for work, school, or your personal life. Many people turn to the Internet for shopping (e-commerce), communicating using messaging services such as electronic mail (email), and for telephone calls or conferencing services.

E-Commerce

E-commerce is the abbreviation for electronic commerce, which involves buying or selling over the Internet (Figure 2.23). Most software is now purchased directly via the Internet where the link to download the program becomes available once you have paid for the license fee. Shopping online for music, videos, books, clothing, and other merchandise generally requires that you have a credit card for payment although, increasingly, some merchants are making available the ability to pay directly from your bank account or use a third-party payment service such as Google Checkout. With Google Checkout, your Gmail account can be linked to a credit or debit card and referred to as Google Wallet, which you can use to pay for purchases at websites. E-commerce on mobile devices is a fast-growing market as consumers love to shop for favorite apps or music to use on a smartphone or tablet. Table 2.5 describes three categories of e-commerce.

Table 2.5	Types of E-Commerce Transactions
E-Commerce Activity	**Description**
Business-to-consumer (B2C)	This is a familiar category of e-commerce if you have ever bought music, software, or other merchandise on the Web. A business such as Amazon sets up a website that is available to any consumer for purchasing merchandise or services. Businesses that sell online to consumers are often referred to as **e-tailers** (abbreviation for electronic retailers). Figure 2.23 illustrates the typical steps in a B2C transaction.
Business-to-business (B2B)	In this category, a business sells directly to other businesses using the Web. In some cases, B2B transactions occur at websites used by consumers. For example, if you are on a website where ads are shown and you click the ad, a payment is charged to the business that posted the ad. B2B ads at websites allow the website owner to provide the website free of charge to consumers.
Consumer-to-consumer (C2C)	C2C activity occurs at websites such as Craigslist or eBay where transactions occur directly between two consumers. C2C websites generally also involve B2C or B2B transactions since the website owner that provides the service charges fees to advertisers and/or sellers to post ads.

Step 1
Customer visits an electronic storefront and views the online catalog.

Step 2
Items are selected and placed into the shopping cart.

NAME: ********
ADDRESS: *********
CREDIT CARD: ********

Step 5
Customer receives confirmation notice of the purchase.

Step 3
Customer accesses checkout and enters personal and financial data.

bank's server

Step 4
E-tailer verifies shopper's financial data at a banking website.

e-tailer's secure server

Figure 2.23 Steps in the online shopping process for B2C transactions

Keep Your Personal Data Safe

When paying online make sure you are using a secure website before entering personal data such as your credit card number. The Web address should start with https, and some browsers show an icon of a closed lock indicating your personal data is safe. You will learn about secure websites in Chapter 7.

Email

Electronic mail **(email)** is the sending and receiving of digital messages using the Internet, sometimes with documents or photos attached. Businesses were using the Internet for email long before consumers embraced the service when PCs became mainstream in the 80s and 90s. In today's workplaces, email is the standard communication medium and often is preferred over voice conversation since email provides a written record of what has been agreed upon.

When you sign up for an account with an ISP, one or more email accounts are included with your Internet service. An **email address** is used to connect to your email account at the ISP server and is generated in the format *username@mailserver. com* or *username@mailserver.net*. Your ISP will provide the means for you to create your own user name to include before the @ symbol. The text after the @ symbol is the ISP's server name. Once your email account is created you can use a program called an **email client** such as Microsoft's Outlook or Apple's Mail to send and receive messages.

Did You Know

In 1971 the first message was sent across a network with the @ symbol used to separate the user name from the computer name.

Web-based email such as Hotmail or Gmail are popular among email users since you do not need a separate email client program to send and receive messages. When you use Hotmail or Gmail, you sign in from your browser to access email. Once logged in, all messages are created, sent, stored, and otherwise managed from the browser window as shown in Figure 2.24.

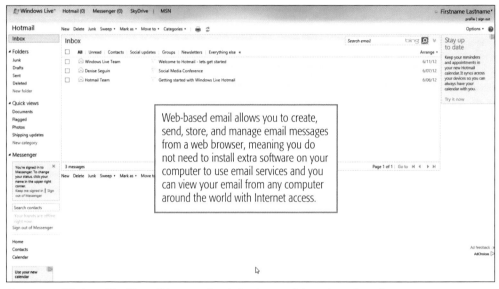

Figure 2.24 Windows Live Hotmail is a popular choice for a web-based email service.

Text and Instant Messaging Messaging between mobile devices is often preferred over email since the messages can be sent more quickly without the need to go to a special email program. **Text messages** are short text exchanges, referred to as **texting**, that you send to another mobile device using a service called **Short Message Service (SMS)**. Some mobile devices provide the ability to use **instant messaging** (exchanging text messages in real time) between other users of similar devices. Examples of instant messaging services on mobile devices are BlackBerry's BBM and Apple's iMessage.

Internet Voice and Conferencing Services

The ability to call someone using the Internet and engage in a voice conversation is called **Voice over Internet Protocol (VoIP)**. Skype is a popular service for making free calls over the Internet and includes the ability to make video calls using web cameras to allow each party to see one another while chatting. Software and hardware on your PC or mobile device convert your voice and/or picture into digital signals that travel the Internet.

www.voipreview.org
Go here to learn more about Internet telephone service and compare plans.

Text or instant messaging from a mobile device is a popular method of communicating with others.

Skype is a popular choice for people who want to make video calls using the Internet.

Web Conferencing **Web conferencing** is a program that allows a group of individuals to connect online to engage in a meeting. Web conferencing software similar to that shown in Figure 2.25 allows each participant to talk and share ideas and information using presentations or online whiteboards. A person's desktop can be shared so that others participating in the meeting can watch a demonstration. Online meetings allow businesses to save the cost of expensive travel to bring together a group of people.

Other services use the Internet such as newsgroups, chat rooms, and remote access support providers. New applications for the Internet that will make creative use of text, video, and audio are sure to be invented!

Web conferencing programs provide the ability to talk and share documents or presentations with a group of individuals. Tools are included to annotate and mark up the online whiteboard during the conference.

Participants can pose and answer questions with the group in this window.

Figure 2.25 Web conferencing software allows a group of individuals to connect and collaborate using the Internet.

EXPLORE FURTHER

Netiquette Guidelines

With so much communication taking place over the Internet, rules for acceptable social interactions have been developed called **netiquette**, which is short for *Internet etiquette*. Without the visual cues that are present in face-to-face communication, messages can often be misunderstood. What are some common netiquette guidelines?

1. Research netiquette and pick what you think are the five most important rules.
2. Create a presentation with one rule per slide and provide an example of appropriate and inappropriate netiquette to demonstrate the rule. Include a slide at the end with the URLs of the sites from which you obtained your rules.
3. Save the presentation as **C2-Web-Netiquette-Your Name**.
4. Submit the presentation to your instructor in the manner she or he has requested.

Concepts Review

Topic	Key Concepts	Key Terms
Networks, the Internet, and the World Wide Web	Networks link computers together to share resources. The Internet is the physical structure that represents a global network linking other networks from around the world. Connection to the Internet is provided by ISPs for a fee. Web pages circulated on the Internet make up the World Wide Web. Web pages stored on web servers are viewed using a web browser. Websites are a collection of related web pages. Web 2.0 refers to a second generation of two-way communication using web pages. Web 3.0 is expected to incorporate automated agents that will adapt and learn the type of content you want to see on the Web.	Network Internet (Net) Internet Service Provider (ISP) Web page World Wide Web (Web or WWW) Web browser Website Web server Web 2.0 Web 3.0 Semantic Web
Connecting to the Internet	Computers sold today come equipped with a network interface card and/or a wireless interface card to facilitate connection to the Internet. ISPs provide the equipment and servers to connect to the Internet backbone. Fees for Internet access vary and are based on connection speed. High-speed Internet access is referred to as broadband. Internet access is measured in megabits per second (Mbps). Cable Internet access requires a cable modem that connects a coaxial cable from the cable company's network to your computer. A Digital Subscriber Line is provided by a telephone company, which supplies a DSL modem that uses twisted-pair cable to connect into the telephone jack and into your computer. Fiber-optic service requires that the ISP run a fiber-optic cable to your home, where a piece of equipment converts optical signals to electrical signals. Satellite Internet access is usually found in rural areas and requires the installation of a satellite dish and satellite modem. Fixed wireless Internet access requires you to install an antenna outside your home, and a wireless modem sends/receives radio signals. A Wi-Fi network uses wireless access points and is a popular choice for public spaces and homes. Mobile broadband sticks are portable modems that connect to the Internet via a cellular network. Smartphones and tablets connect using a third-generation (3G) or fourth-generation (4G) network.	Network interface card (NIC) Ethernet port Wireless interface card Bluetooth Broadband Megabits per second (Mbps) Cable Internet access Digital Subscriber Line (DSL) Fiber-to-the-Premises (FTTP) Fiber-to-the-Home (FTTH) Fiber-Optic Service (FiOS) Satellite Internet access Fixed wireless Internet access Wireless Fidelity (Wi-Fi) Hotspot Mobile broadband sticks 3G 4G LTE network Dial-up

continued....

	A 4G LTE network is the fastest network for mobile devices. Where broadband is not available or is too expensive, you can connect to the Internet using a dial-up modem that uses your telephone line.	
Popular Web Browsers	Web pages are viewed using web browser software that interprets the code the page is stored in as text and multimedia content. HTML is a markup language used in many web pages that describes page content using tags. Internet Explorer is the browser included with Microsoft Windows. Chrome, provided free by Google, runs on Windows-compatible PCs and is becoming popular due to its fast page loading and ability to search in the Address bar. Firefox is a free browser for PCs, Macs, or Linux computers available from the Mozilla Foundation. Apple's Safari is used on Mac and Apple mobile devices such as iPads and iPhones. Mobile web browsers are designed to quickly display web pages optimized for much smaller screens.	HTML Internet Explorer (IE) Chrome Firefox Safari Mobile web browsers
Understanding Internet and Web Addresses and Navigating Web Pages	Every computing device connected to the Internet is assigned an IP address. ICANN is a nonprofit organization in charge of keeping track of IP addresses around the world. An IP address with four groups of numbers from 0 to 255 separated by periods is known as IPv4. IPv6 was developed because the number of unique IPv4 addresses was running out. A web address, also called a URL, is a text-based address used to navigate to a website. A DNS server holds the directory that associates an Internet address with a web address. The http in a URL refers to the Hypertext Transfer Protocol used for displaying pages. A domain name is the text-based name for an organization within the URL. The three- or four-character extension in a domain name is called the top-level domain and identifies the type of organization. Generic top-level domains are being expanded by ICANN. Two-character extensions in a domain name are country codes. The first page you see when you visit a web page is called the home page. Web pages contain hyperlinks that take you to a related web page when clicked or tapped.	Internet Protocol (IP) address ICANN (Internet Corporation for Assigned Names and Numbers) Web address Uniform Resource Locator (URL) Domain Name System (DNS) server Domain name Top-level domain (TLD) Generic top-level domain (gTLD) ccTLDs Home page Hyperlinks Links

continued....

Topic	Key Concepts	Key Terms
Searching the Web	Search engines read web pages and create indexes using keywords associated with the page. Spiders and crawlers are programs used by search engines to find and index web pages. Some search engines provide categories of topics and subtopics that you can use to narrow your search. You will get different results from different search engines using the same search phrase because spider and index programs vary, pages may be updated at different times, and rankings may differ. A metasearch search engine compiles results from other search engines in one place. Typing a quotation or minus symbol in the search phrase helps to narrow the results list. Use a search engine's advanced tools to fine-tune a search.	Search engine Keywords Spiders Crawlers Metasearch search engine Content aggregator Really Simple Syndication (RSS)
Evaluating Web Content	Domain names in the web address can provide clues to a web page's authenticity. Check a web page for an author's name and author's affiliation; if no name is present, try reading the About us or Contact links. Look for dates to make sure the information you are reading is the most recent; if no date exists look for clues in the content or web address. Evaluate the purpose of a website to help decide if a bias may exist in the information presented. A poorly designed website with errors in spelling and grammar should have its content corroborated by another source.	
Popular Web Plug-ins and Players for Multimedia Content	Plug-ins, players, and add-ons are all software programs needed by a browser to display multimedia content. Adobe Reader is a program used to view PDF documents. Adobe Flash Player and Shockwave Player are programs used to view animations with high-quality graphics, sound, and interactivity. Java is a programming language used to add interactivity to games and web page applications. Silverlight is a plug-in from Microsoft for interactivity applications and high-quality audio or video. Real Player is used for music files such as MP3s. QuickTime from Apple is used for videos or animations. Once installed, plug-ins and players will periodically require updating.	Plug-in Add-on Player
E-Commerce, Messaging, and Internet Telephone and Web Conferencing Options	E-commerce involves transactions online between businesses and consumers, businesses and other businesses, and consumers and other consumers. Shopping online generally requires a credit card or account with a third party payment service such as Google Checkout.	E-commerce E-tailers Email

continued....

E-Commerce, Messaging, and Internet Telephone and Web Conferencing Options	E-tailer is a term that refers to a business with an electronic storefront.	Email address
	Email is the sending and receiving of messages that can have attachments such as documents and photos.	Email client
		Text messages
	An email address connects you to your ISP's mail server to send and receive messages.	Texting
		Short Message Service (SMS)
	An email client is a program used to compose and manage email messages.	Instant messaging
		Voice over Internet Protocol (VoIP)
	Texting involves sending short messages to a mobile device.	Web conferencing
	Instant messaging allows you to send/receive text messages in real time.	Netiquette
	VoIP is a technology that allows you to make telephone calls over the Internet.	
	Web conferencing software allows a group of individuals to collaborate online.	

Multiple Choice

1. The collection of networks that provides the pathway for data to travel is the _____.
   a. Web
   b. Internet
   c. Internet4
   d. Superhighway

2. This refers to the global collection of web pages circulated on the internet.
   a. Internet
   b. Superhighway
   c. World Wide Web
   d. Web server

3. High-speed Internet access is referred to by this term.
   a. Broadband
   b. Megabits per second (Mbps)
   c. Superhighway
   d. Baseband

4. Which of the following connections is NOT high speed?
   a. Cable
   b. DSL
   c. FTTP
   d. Dial-up

5. This is the web browser included with Microsoft Windows.
   a. Internet Explorer
   b. Chrome
   c. Safari
   d. Firefox

6. This browser allows you to type search phrases directly in the Address bar.
   a. Chrome
   b. Internet Explorer
   c. Firefox
   d. Safari

7. This is the nonprofit organization that keeps track of Internet addresses for the world.
   a. IPv6
   b. IPv4
   c. ICANN
   d. IPANN

8. A Web address is called a(n) _____.
   a. IP address
   b. URL
   c. DNS
   d. Hyperlink

9. A search engine uses this type of program to search the Web for keywords to index.
   a. Hyperlinks
   b. HTTP
   c. Metaindex
   d. Spider

10. A search engine that compiles results from other search engines is called a _____ search engine.
    a. category
    b. hypertext
    c. metasearch
    d. cybersearch

11. Which of the following is NOT a strategy to help you evaluate a web page's credibility?
    a. Look at the domain name for an organization you recognize.
    b. Check for an author's name and affiliation.
    c. Evaluate the page design.
    d. Look for the same page at a different search engine.

12. If a publication date is not on the web page, a clue may appear in this linked address.
    a. IP address
    b. Web address
    c. Mailing address for the organization
    d. DNS

13. This player allows you to read PDF documents.
    a. Adobe Reader
    b. Adobe Flash Player
    c. Shockwave Player
    d. Real Player

14. This player is a programming language used on web pages.
    a. QuickTime
    b. Real Player
    c. Silverlight
    d. Java

15. E-tailers are primarily involved in this category of e-commerce.
    a. B2C
    b. B2B
    c. B2W
    d. C2C

16. This type of software allows a group of individuals to collaborate online in a meeting.
    a. VoIP
    b. Email
    c. Instant messaging
    d. Web conferencing

Crossword Puzzle

ACROSS

3 emcp.com
7 First page that displays
9 A collection of related web pages
11 Company that sells Internet access
12 Program used to view web pages
13 Search engines index pages by these
14 Web address TLD indicating a trusted source
15 May indicate a page's credibility

DOWN

1 Player from Apple
2 Your Name@mailserver.com
4 Free browser from Google
5 Free browser from Mozilla
6 Company that finds and indexes web pages
8 Plug-in from Microsoft
9 Wireless network that uses access points and radio signals
10 Buying and selling on the Internet

Matching

Match the term with the statement or definition.

_____ 1. Web 2.0
_____ 2. Wireless interface card
_____ 3. Mobile web browsers
_____ 4. IPv6
_____ 5. Minus symbol
_____ 6. Publication date
_____ 7. Adobe Flash Player
_____ 8. C2C

a. Included with many browsers
b. eBay
c. Indicates keyword to be excluded
d. Optimized for smaller screens
e. Evaluate web page's currency
f. Equipment in mobile device
g. Second generation web pages
h. System of Internet addresses

Project 1 Broadband Options and Questions for ISPs

Individual, Pairs, or Team
Deliverable: Presentation

The manager at the local senior community center where you volunteer has asked you to prepare a presentation for the seniors that compares the various high-speed Internet connection options in your area. The manager wants you to include questions that seniors should ask an ISP before signing a contract for Internet access.

1. Research the available broadband connection options in your area.
2. Prepare a list of questions someone should ask an ISP before signing a contract. Consider services, speed, support, and cost questions.
3. Create a presentation that could be shown to seniors with the information from Steps 1 and 2.
4. Save the presentation as **C2-Project1-InternetConnections-Your Name**.
5. Submit the presentation to your instructor in the manner she or he has requested.

Project 2 Which Browser Is the Favorite?

Pairs or Team
Deliverable: Table or Chart

Conduct an informal survey of at least 20 friends, relatives, neighbors, or students in another class asking them which browser they use on the Web.

1. Compile your results and create a table or chart in a word processor, spreadsheet, or presentation program to show the results.
2. Save the table or chart as **C2-Project2-BrowserChart-Your Name**.
3. Submit the table or chart to your instructor in the manner she or he has requested.

Project 3 Google versus Bing

Individual or Pairs

Deliverable: Document or Presentation

Google and Bing are the two leading search engines used on the Web. Pick a topic you are interested in and perform searches for your topic using both search engines. Make sure to use each search engine's advanced tools to narrow the search results. When finished, compare and contrast the experience you had with each search engine. What did you like or dislike about each set of advanced search tools? Which search engine do you think gave the best results?

1. Create a document or presentation that summarizes your search experience at Google and Bing. Include

descriptions or examples of the advanced search tools you used and how the results improved. Provide answers to the above questions.

2. Save the document or presentation as **C2-Project3-GooglevsBing-Your Name**.

3. Submit the document or presentation to your instructor in the manner she or he has requested.

Project 4 Evaluating the Credibility of Content on a Web Page

Pairs or Team

Deliverable: Document or Presentation

Within your pair or team pick a topic of interest and search the Web for pages related to the topic you chose. Find a web page that you believe is missing key information that would help evaluate the page's credibility. For example, find a page missing an author or a publication date, a page published by an unknown organization, or a page with poor design or poorly written content.

1. Create a document or presentation that includes a hyperlink to the web page. Include a brief description of the page and the reasons why you believe the page's credibility needs to be verified.

2. Save the document as **C2-Project4-TeamPageEvaluation-Your Name**.

3. Submit the document to your instructor in the manner she or he has requested.

Project 5 Comparing C2C Options

Pairs or Team

Deliverable: Presentation

A neighbor wants your help selling her Xbox games online. She has never sold anything using the Web before and is not sure if she should use an auction, a classified ad, or an online marketplace. Learn about the differences between an auction site such as eBay, a classified ad site such as Craigslist, and an online marketplace such as Amazon Marketplace. Compare an ad for an Xbox game at each venue and the cash the neighbor may realize from a similar sale.

1. Create a presentation with a brief summary of how each type of C2C site operates. What are the advantages and disadvantages of each site? Which venue do you think would provide the best return for your neighbor?

2. Save the presentation as **C2-Project5-C2COptions-Your Name**.

3. Submit the presentation to your instructor in the manner she or he has requested.

Project 6 Greener Computing

Individual, Pairs, or Team

Deliverable: Blog Entry

You have just purchased a new 4G smartphone and are not sure what to do with your older 3G smartphone that you no longer want. Research ways in which you can recycle or reuse the 3G smartphone in your area.

1. Write and post a blog entry that describes what you learned and which method you would probably use if you had an older smartphone to discard and give your reasons.

2. Submit your blog URL to your instructor in the manner she or he has requested.

Optional

Read the blog entry for this project of at least two other classmates and post a comment to each. Submit the URLs of your classmates' blogs with Step 2.

Project 7 Online Meeting or Face-to-Face Meeting— Which Is Better?

Individual, Pairs, or Team
Deliverable: Blog Entry

The ability to collaborate using web conferencing software means a group of individuals could meet virtually any time, anywhere. The technology could even be used when a group is housed within the same building but prefers the online collaborative environment. When, if ever, is a face-to-face meeting more desirable than a web conference? Could web conferencing be used for all types of meetings? If necessary, consult a parent or relative, or interview someone with work experience that involves meetings.

1. Write and post a blog entry that describes your opinions about the above questions.
2. Submit your blog URL to your instructor in the manner she or he has requested.

Optional

Read the blog entry for this project of at least two other classmates and post a comment to each. Submit the URLs of your classmates' blogs with Step 2.

Project 8 Ethics Discussion—Posting Negative Reviews

Team
Deliverable: Document, Blog Entry, or Presentation

You overheard one of your colleagues at work while she was talking on the telephone to a friend telling the friend she has posted negative reviews about one of your company's products at various websites. She said she was doing it to get even with her manager for treating her poorly. What should you do?

1. Within your team discuss how you should handle this situation. Should you ignore the situation since the conversation did not directly involve you? Should you confront the person? Should you tell her manager? Is there any other option you should consider?
2. Prepare a summary of your team's discussion in a document, blog entry, or presentation.
3. Save the document or presentation as **C2-Project8-EthicsDiscussion-Your Name**.
4. Submit the document, presentation, or blog entry to your instructor in the manner she or he has requested.

Chapter 3

Computer Hardware

After successfully completing this chapter, you will be able to:

- Recognize and explain the purpose of the major components in a system unit

- List and recognize various types of input devices

- List and recognize various types of output devices

- Identify network adapters for connectivity purposes

- Understand how data is represented on a computer

- State various options for storage and storage capacities

As you learned in Chapter 1, computers come in all shapes and sizes. Whether you are working with a desktop, laptop, netbook, ultrabook, tablet, or other mobile device, certain components are found in each one. All computers have a CPU, input device(s), output device(s), memory, connectivity adapters, and storage. These electronic and physical components found in a computing device are collectively known as the computer's hardware.

Some hardware is visible to you such as the screen, keyboard, and mouse, while other hardware is housed inside the system such as the CPU, memory, network adapter, and some storage. Hardware used for input, output, connectivity, or storage that you plug in or connect to your computer wirelessly such as a USB storage medium or printer is called a **peripheral** device.

If you have looked at ads for computers you know that a basic understanding of the terminology and hardware components is helpful to making a purchase decision. In Chapter 1 you were introduced to many of the hardware components found in a PC. In Chapter 2 you learned about hardware such as cable modems and DSL modems that provide connectivity to the Internet. In this chapter you will explore what's inside the system unit, input and output devices, network adapters, digital data representation, and storage options in more detail. Appendix A contains tips for buying a computer or mobile device.

The System Unit

As stated in Chapter 1, the system unit is the horizontal or vertical (tower) case in which the computer's microprocessor, memory, and storage are located. In a mobile device such as a laptop, tablet, or smartphone, these components are inside the unit below the integrated keyboard and/or screen. In an all-in-one system, these components are mounted in the same case in which the monitor is housed. Regardless of the configuration, the main components in the system unit are the power supply with cooling fan, motherboard, ports for plugging in peripherals, and storage devices. In this topic you will learn about the power supply, motherboard components, and ports. In a later topic you will learn about storage.

Figure 3.1 shows the inside view of a notebook's system unit.

Figure 3.1 Inside view of a notebook

Power Supply

All computers need power to operate. In a tower or desktop the power supply is positioned at the back of the unit where you plug in the power cord. A notebook or tablet is powered by a charged battery or the power adapter when the power adapter is plugged into a power outlet. A cooling fan is located near a power supply to draw heat away from the CPU and prevent the CPU from overheating. A heat sink is also installed near a CPU to draw heat away from the processor.

Notebooks are powered by a charged battery or by using a power adapter plugged into a wall unit.

Motherboard

The main circuit board in the computer is called the **motherboard**. All of the other devices plug directly into or communicate wirelessly with the motherboard. Figure 3.2 shows a typical motherboard you might find inside a PC.

Expansion slots

CPU

Memory modules

Figure 3.2 The motherboard is the hub that connects all of the devices together and is designed to support a certain type of CPU.

The motherboard includes the CPU, memory, expansion slots, and circuitry attached to ports that are used to plug in external devices. Many computers integrate video and sound electronics into the motherboard's main circuit board while other computers may include these components as **expansion cards** that plug into an expansion slot on the motherboard. Expansion slots are used to plug in additional circuit boards to your computer to either add or improve functionality. Another common use of an expansion card in a tower unit is to provide a network adapter into which a cable, called an Ethernet cable, is plugged for connectivity to a network. Notebook computers also have built-in card readers that allow you to insert a memory card from a digital camera or plug in a card used for wireless networking.

Data travels between the components on the motherboard to the CPU and memory over wires called **data buses**. Think of a data bus as a highway upon which data is routed. The size and speed of a data bus affects performance since a data bus that can carry more data to the CPU and memory at a faster rate of speed performs better. Similarly, traveling by car on a four-lane highway at a high speed means you arrive at a destination faster than if you traveled on a two-lane highway at a slower speed.

CPU As you learned in Chapter 1, the CPU performs the processing cycle and is often referred to as the "brain" of the computer. Today's computers can do **parallel processing**, which involves having multiple microprocessor chips (more than one CPU chip on the motherboard), or a multi-core processor (one CPU chip separated into independent processor cores). Parallel processing provides the ability to execute multiple instructions at the same time. Most notebooks today are configured with a two- or four-core microprocessor. Parallel processing has vastly improved system performance when software has been written to take advantage of its capabilities.

Apple's A6 ARM CPU at the time of writing is expected to be the processor in iPhone5 and/or the next iPad. ARM processors use less energy, making them a popular choice for mobile devices such as iPhones and iPads.

A CPU goes through an **instruction cycle** that involves the CPU retrieving, decoding, executing, and storing an instruction. The speed at which a CPU operates is measured in the number of instruction cycles the CPU can process per second, referred to as **clock speed**. Clock speed is typically measured in **gigahertz (GHz)**, which is 1 billion cycles per second. A CPU in most notebooks and tablets sold today run at speeds between 1 and 2.5 GHz.

In Chapter 1 you were introduced to cache memory, which is memory either built into the CPU or stored next to the CPU on a separate chip on the motherboard that is used for storing frequently used instructions and data. Cache memory stored closest to the CPU is called **Level 1 (L1) cache**. L1 cache is memory built on the CPU chip and operates the fastest of all memory. Secondary cache memory either stored on the CPU chip or built on the motherboard is called **Level 2 (L2) cache**. L2 cache feeds the L1 cache. A third level of cache memory, called **Level 3 (L3) cache**, is usually built on the motherboard and feeds the L2 cache. The amount of L1, L2, and L3 cache affect performance since the CPU accesses cache memory faster than other memory.

Memory   On the motherboard are two types of memory: **read-only memory (ROM)** and random access memory (RAM). ROM is used for storing instructions that the computer uses that do not change. For example, the programming code with the instructions used when starting a computer is often stored on a ROM chip, which is called the ROM BIOS, where **BIOS** stands for **Basic Input Output System**.

Recall from Chapter 1 that RAM is temporary memory where data and instructions are stored while processing and is erased when power is turned off. RAM is configured in modules that plug into slots on the motherboard (see Figure 3.2). Since all of the software and the data you are creating or editing while working on the computer must reside in RAM to access the CPU, the size and type of RAM in a computer affects its performance.

Today's desktop and notebook computers often have DDR3 SDRAM, which is the fastest RAM available at the time of writing; however, expect DDR4 RAM

A memory module used in a notebook includes DDR3 SDRAM chips on a smaller circuit board than one used in a desktop.

to crop up soon. DDR stands for Double Data Rate and refers to the ability to transfer data twice as often with 3 representing third generation DDR, which is twice as fast as DDR2. SDRAM means Synchronous Dynamic Random Access Memory and refers to a type of RAM that operates at higher clock speeds than older RAM technologies.

Installing additional RAM into an empty module slot can improve a computer's performance, extending the life of an older system.

Motherboards also house other components such as drive controllers and interfaces used to connect a system's hard drive and DVD drive to the motherboard via cables.

Did You Know?

USB 3.0 (known as SuperSpeed USB) can operate approximately 10 times faster than a USB 2.0 device.

Ports

Ports are the connectors located at the back of a desktop PC or at the sides, back, and sometimes the front of a notebook or other mobile device. Ports are used to plug in external devices. The most common type of port is the **universal serial bus (USB) port**, which is used to connect an external device such as a keyboard, mouse, printer, smartphone, or external storage media to name a few.

Most computers today provide several USB ports to accommodate multiple USB devices being used simultaneously. A USB hub can be used to increase the number of USB ports if your computer does not provide enough to meet your needs.

Plug in a USB hub to add more USB devices if you do not have enough USB ports.

A typical notebook also includes ports for plugging in an external monitor, connecting to a network using an Ethernet cable, connecting a telephone line for accessing a dialup network, an HDMI port for connecting to a high-definition TV, and a high-speed FireWire port to connect a digital camcorder or other device (Figure 3.3). Ports will also be found along the side or front of a notebook or other mobile device to plug in headphones, external speakers, or a microphone.

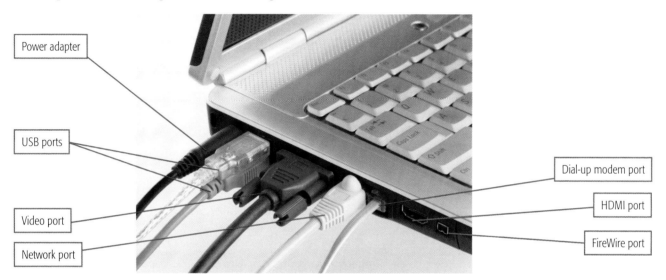

Figure 3.3 Ports at the sides, back, and sometimes front of a notebook are used to plug in external devices.

In desktop PCs, the ports are often color coded to make it easy for someone to plug in a device with a similar end to the correct port. For example, on older desktop PCs the keyboard and mouse connectors are colored purple for the keyboard and green for the mouse so that the devices are not mixed up.

EXPLORE   FURTHER

What is a Thunderbolt port?

Apple's MacBook and iMac feature a new high-speed port named Thunderbolt. What is a Thunderbolt port? How fast does it operate? What kinds of Thunderbolt devices are available? Are there Thunderbolt devices available for a PC?

1. Go to apple.com/thunderbolt and read the information about Thunderbolt presented by Apple.
2. Next, find out if Thunderbolt is available for Windows-compatible computers and if so, for what kinds of devices.
3. Create a document that provides answers in your own words to the above questions. Include the URL of the article(s) you read about Thunderbolt devices for PCs.
4. Save the document as **C3-Hardware-Thunderbolt-Your Name**.
5. Submit the document to your instructor in the manner she or he has requested.

TOPIC 3.2

Input Devices

As stated in Chapter 1, any device used to enter raw data or communicate instructions to the computer is an input device. Several input devices exist with the most common being a keyboard and mouse. Other devices used for input are also described in this topic.

Keyboards and Mice

While wired keyboards and mice were the standard for traditional desktop PCs, today's computer users prefer to be untethered from their computer. A wireless **keyboard** and/or mouse can be used with any computer device. Wireless keyboards and mice use batteries as a source of power. A wireless receiver is plugged into a computer's USB port and connects with the wireless keyboard and mouse. Electronic signals from the keyboard are interpreted by the keyboard's device controller and sent to the computer's operating system via the wireless receiver, which in turn sends the keystrokes to the active running program for display on the screen.

Wireless keyboards and mice are popular for traditional PCs and as peripherals for mobile devices.

In addition to the alphabetic and numeric keys on a keyboard, special purpose keys such as Esc, Insert, Delete, function keys labeled F1 through F12, the Start key on a Windows-compatible computer, and the command key on an Apple computer allow commands to be sent to a program. Directional movement keys such as the up, down, left, and right arrow keys, and the Home, End, Page Up, and Page Down keys provide the ability to move around a screen. Finally, keys labeled Ctrl, Alt, and Shift allow you to use a combination of one or more of these keys with letters, numbers, and function keys to send instructions to the active program.

Notebooks include a built-in keyboard while some tablets and smartphones may or may not have integrated keyboards that are built in or slide out. Some tablets include a keyboard that you can use by plugging the tablet into a dock port on the keyboard. Finally, some tablets and smartphones with touch-enabled screens display a keyboard onscreen that you use by tapping the onscreen keys with your fingers or a stylus.

Today's tablets and smartphones offer onscreen keyboards, which you tap using your fingers or a stylus (digital pen).

A **mouse** is a device used to point, select, and manipulate objects on the screen. The mouse works by detecting the motion of the mouse in relation to the surface beneath it as you move the mouse. Most mice in use today track the movement using light technology, while older mice used a trackball to sense movement. As you move the mouse, the pointer on the screen moves in the same direction. Buttons on the mouse provide the ability to send a command when the pointer is resting on the target that you wish to manipulate. A wheel on the mouse facilitates scrolling.

On notebooks, a **touchpad** is located below the keyboard. This rectangular surface with buttons is used in place of a mouse to move the pointer on the screen and manipulate objects. The touchpad senses finger movement and taps similarly to a mouse. Depending on the touchpad device, multi-finger gestures and pinch and zoom movements can be used to scroll and zoom the display. Some notebooks and smartphones include a track pointer, which senses finger pressure for moving the pointer.

On a notebook, a touchpad is used to move the pointer on the screen using finger movements, while taps and buttons allow you to manipulate objects.

Touch-Enabled Devices

Many of today's mobile devices such as tablets, smartphones, and some portable media players include **touch-enabled displays**, also called **touchscreens**, for accepting input. A touch-enabled device has a layer of capacitive material below a protective screen. When you touch the screen with your finger or with a digital pen called a **stylus**, an electrical signal is sensed by the capacitive layer, which sends data about the location you touched and any gesture you used to the computer's touch processor and software that interpret the touch gesture.

Self-serve kiosks such as an airline check-in station or an ATM use touchscreens in combination with other input devices such as keypads, buttons, and magnetic strip readers to accept input.

Many mobile devices and self-serve kiosks are touch-enabled or can be operated with a stylus.

Scanners and Readers

A **scanner** is a device that uses optical technology to analyze text and/or images and convert them into data that can be used by a computer. Scanners can be a separate input device such as a flatbed scanner (a scanner that sits on a desk) or a handheld scanner. Many printers and photocopiers used today are multi-purpose devices that also incorporate scanners.

Bar code readers optically scan barcodes to identify products in warehouses or at checkout counters. Even smartphones include the ability to scan **QR (Quick Response) codes**, a type of barcode that looks like a matrix of black square dots. The smartphone reads the QR code that usually directs the device to display a website. **Magnetic strip readers** can read data from the magnetic strip on the backs of cards such as debit cards, credit cards, or cards used to open doors or parking gates. **Biometric scanners** are used to identify people by individual human characteristics such as a fingerprint, iris, or voice pattern. Finally, **Radio Frequency Identification (RFID) readers** scan an embedded RFID tag to identify an object. RFID readers and tags use tiny chips with antennas that are

Check This Out

www.rfidjournal.com
Go here to read the latest news on RFID technology innovation in various industries.

readable when the reader and tag are within range of each other. Typically, RFID technology is used to read tags up to 300 feet away.

Many different types of scanners and readers are used to generate input from documents, images, barcodes, biometrics, or wireless tags.

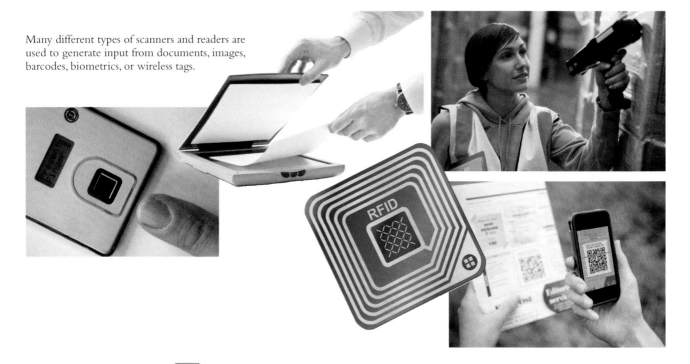

Keep Your Eyes on Your Cards

Protect cards with a magnetic strip that store personal data. These cards are targets for criminals who use skimmers to read the data. If you hand over a debit or credit card to a store clerk when making a purchase make sure you keep the card in your line of sight at all times.

Digital Cameras, Digital Camcorders, and Webcams

Digital cameras, camcorders, and webcams are used to convert images and live video into a digital format.

Digital cameras capture still images, while digital video cameras called **camcorders** capture live video and audio. Many of these devices are multi-purpose, meaning some digital cameras could be used to capture short live video segments and some camcorders double as digital cameras.

A **webcam** is a video camera built into a video display screen (mounted at the top center of the screen's edge), or plugged in as a peripheral and used to provide images to the computer during live web conferencing or chatting using a program such as Skype.

Smartphones and tablets have digital camera capabilities that allow you to snap pictures and record video and send them via messaging applications directly from the device.

Microphones and Voice Recognition

A **microphone** can be used in conjunction with software to create a digital audio file from voice input or other sounds captured by the device. You may also use a microphone to chat with someone online. Some games played online or with game systems accept voice commands. **Voice recognition technology** (also called **speech recognition technology**) is used to recognize voice commands as input for hands-free operation at work, with your car's navigation and communications system, or with your mobile device. Apple's Siri on the iPhone 4 uses voice recognition to send messages, schedule meetings, or make a call. A program such as Dragon NaturallySpeaking converts input you speak into your microphone into text and commands in documents or messaging applications.

Microphones provide voice input used with voice recording or voice recognition software.

Microphones are built into notebooks and mobile devices. An external microphone or a headset with a microphone attached can also be plugged in as a peripheral.

Entertainment Controllers

Gaming systems accept input using a variety of methods such as wired or wireless game controllers, joysticks, and motion sensors. Some games have controllers such as guitars, other musical instruments, or a tennis racket. Some exercise games use pressure sensitive mats or boards.

Other devices such as keypads and magnetic ink character recognition systems are used in specialized applications to provide input. Futuristic input devices such as wearable keyboards and holographic inputs are already being developed and tested. Imagine in the future wearing your keyboard on your sleeve or entering data using a hologram!

Entertainment systems such as game consoles use various types of controllers for input.

EXPLORE FURTHER

Virtual Reality Devices

Virtual reality devices are used with games and in commercial applications to train workers, such as simulating flights for pilots. Devices are worn on the body as headsets or as data gloves that detect input.

1. Research a virtual reality device for a game or training purpose.
2. Create a brief presentation that describes in your own words what you learned about the virtual reality device. Include a slide with a picture of the virtual reality device that you researched. Include the URL(s) of the sites from which you obtained information.
3. Save the presentation as **C3-Hardware-VirtualReality-Your Name**.
4. Submit the presentation to your instructor in the manner she or he has requested.

TOPIC 3.3

Output Devices

In Chapter 1 you learned that devices used to view the information processed and organized by the computer are output devices. The most commonly used output device is a monitor or other type of screen or display in a mobile device. Computer output can also be connected to high-definition televisions, projectors, or interactive whiteboards. Other types of output devices explored in this topic include speakers, headsets, printers, and copiers.

Video Displays

Video displays are electronic devices that present information from a computer visually. Desktop PCs connect a device called a **monitor** to the computer's video port. Notebooks and other mobile devices have a built-in video display screen. Other electronic devices with built-in display screens include eReaders and portable media players.

Video displays come in many different sizes, where the size is the diagonal length of the viewing area. For a mobile device, the size of the video display is constrained by the size of the notebook, tablet, or smartphone. Smaller notebooks may have a screen as small as 11 inches, while larger notebook screens can be as large as 21 inches. Tablet screens are typically in the range of 7 to 11 inches, while a smartphone screen can be as small as a few inches with newer phones breaking in near 5 inches.

Notebooks are often connected to external video displays such as a computer monitor or a high-definition television screen to take advantage of larger viewing areas or to use two screens at the same time. Newer monitors for a desktop PC are typically widescreen **Liquid Crystal Displays (LCD)**, which is a flat-panel technology in various sizes upward from 20 inches. LCDs are popular because they do not experience flicker or glare. Older PCs may have rectangular-shaped LCD screens from 14 to 17 inches.

The size of display screens varies by device with some smartphones as small as a few inches, and notebooks with display screens that could rival a desktop monitor.

Connecting two display screens to a PC or notebook is becoming more common as well as watching movies or images from a computer on a high-definition television.

Other flat-panel display screens are **Light-Emitting Diode (LED)** displays and **plasma** displays. These types of flat panel technology are more expensive and often used for televisions. Each has its advantages, with LED screens consuming less energy and plasma providing truer color representation.

A newer technology known as **Organic Light-Emitting Diode (OLED)** may eventually replace LCD display screens in mobile devices because this technology does not require backlighting like LCDs do, making them far more energy efficient for any device that runs off battery power.

Video Display Resolution A video display's **resolution** setting will affect the quality of output viewed on the display screen. Resolution refers to the number of picture elements, called **pixels**, that make up the image shown on the display screen. A pixel is square with red, green, and blue color values (called RGB) that represent each color needed to form the image. A resolution setting is expressed as the number of horizontal pixels by the number of vertical pixels. For example, a typical 20-inch widescreen monitor would have a resolution of 1600 x 900 pixels. The more pixels used to render the output, the sharper the image as shown in Figure 3.4. Also, at higher resolutions more content can be displayed on the screen than at lower resolutions. While displays typically default to recommended settings, the resolution can be changed using the operating system software to a higher or lower resolution.

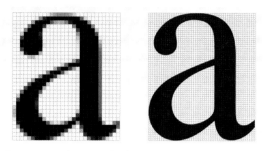

Figure 3.4 A character displayed at a low resolution using fewer pixels to form the character appears fuzzy (left) compared to the same character at a higher resolution using more pixels (right).

Video Display Projectors and Interactive Whiteboards

A **video display projector (VDP)** is used when a computer's output needs to be projected on a large screen when making presentations to groups. VDPs are often ceiling mounted in classrooms and boardrooms, while portable projectors are available for other venues. A PC or notebook connects to the projector via a video output cable.

An **interactive whiteboard** displays the computer's output on a large whiteboard. Special pens are used to annotate on the whiteboard while the image is displayed, making it easier for a presenter to make notes or draw attention to objects on the display. In these instances, the whiteboard is acting as both an output and an input device since the annotations can be saved with the images as electronic files that can be viewed at a later time. Interactive whiteboards also include tools that allow touch gestures for interaction with the computer while the display is being viewed.

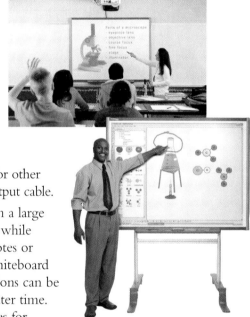

A computer's image can be directed to display on a video display projector or an interactive whiteboard when making presentations to groups.

Speakers and Headphones

Audio output from the computer such as music, voice, or sound effects is heard through the computer's internal speakers, external speakers, or headphones. PC monitors generally include built-in speakers. Notebooks and other mobile devices have speakers integrated into the device. Plug the headphones or earbuds into the audio port of a computer or mobile device to redirect the audio output to your headset when others are around you. High-quality headphones reduce background noise to improve the audio experience. Headsets are headphones that include a microphone.

Often when playing games, watching movies, or playing music on a computing device, higher-quality external speakers are used to achieve home theater quality sound. External speakers can be wired or wireless.

A **Bluetooth headset** can be paired with a smartphone to enable the user to hear a conversation when making and receiving voice calls.

External speakers, earbud headphones, and a Bluetooth headset are common ways to hear audio output from a computing device.

Printers and Copiers

Video displays provide output that is temporary. When the computer is turned off, the output disappears. Often, a printed copy of a document or an image is desired. Printed copies of computer output are called **hard copy**. Hard copy can be generated by a laser printer, inkjet printer, photo printer, thermal printer, plotter, or digital photocopier.

Laser Printers **Laser printers** are a popular choice for producing hard copy in offices and homes. A laser beam electrostatically charges a drum with the text and images sent for printing. A dry powder called toner sticks to the drum and is transferred to the paper as the paper passes through the printer. Paper feels warm when it comes out of a laser printer since heat is applied to the page to permanently adhere the toner to the paper. Although expensive, color laser printers are starting to increase in popularity.

A laser printer is a popular choice for high volume output.

Inkjet Printers The most common type of printer found in a home is an **inkjet printer**. These printers form text and images on the page by spraying drops of ink from one or more ink cartridges that move back and forth across the page. Inkjet printers allow home users to print in color relatively inexpensively.

Inkjet printers spray drops of ink on the page to form text and images.

Photo Printers A **photo printer** generally connects directly to a digital camera to print high-quality photos on photo paper usually using inkjet technology. Professional photo-printing service companies use higher-end photo printers that produce a high-quality image on specially treated paper for prints that last longer than those produced by inkjet printers.

Photo printers print directly from your camera or your camera's memory card.

Thermal Printers Most receipts you receive from retail stores or services are printed on **thermal printers**. These printers produce output by heating coated paper as the paper passes over the print head. These printers produce receipts quickly; however, the image fades away over time.

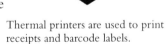

Thermal printers are used to print receipts and barcode labels.

Plotters Blueprints and technical drawings are often produced on **plotters**. A plotter moves one or more pens across the surface of the paper to produce the drawing. Plotters are slow as the movement of the pen or pens across the page takes a longer time.

Plotters are used to print blueprints or other large technical drawings.

Digital Copiers A **digital copier** in an office can now double as both a traditional paper photocopier and, by being connected to a network, can also accept output from computers for printing. Often these copiers are used to share color printing capabilities in a workplace.

Digital copiers in modern offices are connected to a network to print computer output.

All-in-One Printers Many laser and inkjet printer models are multipurpose, meaning that in addition to printing, the device can be used for scanning, photocopying, and sending/receiving faxes. Having a multipurpose printer saves desktop space, cuts down on multiple supply costs, and means you only have to learn to operate one device. The downside is that you cannot do multiple functions at the same time. For example, you cannot copy a document while another one is printing.

Other special-purpose printers are also used such as label printers and portable printers for carrying out specific tasks. In addition, other output devices are available such as a document camera that displays an image from hard copy on a video display. Some virtual reality devices provide output, and 3-D technology for displaying and printing output is being further developed.

Many printers have multifunction capability for printing, copying, scanning, and faxing.

 Blog Topic

Are you 3-D-ready?

3-D technology is available for display and printing purposes but is not yet commonplace. As the technology improves and newer devices develop that become less expensive, 3-D is sure to find its way into our homes and offices. Do you already own 3-D glasses and a 3-D monitor? Will you embrace 3-D in your computer world?

1. Research the current offerings for either 3-D displays or 3-D printing technology.

2. Write and post a blog entry that briefly describes what you learned about 3-D displays or 3-D printers. Provide your opinion on whether you are ready to embrace 3-D technology and give your reasons.

3. Read at least two of your classmates' blogs and post one comment to each.

4. Submit your blog URL and the URLs of your classmates' blogs for which you provided a comment to your instructor in the manner she or he has requested.

EXPLORE FURTHER

What is a video card and do I need one?

A computer uses a **video card** to process the data needed to display text and images on your monitor, projector, or television. These cards are also referred to as graphics accelerators. Most computers integrate the video circuitry directly on the motherboard. What are the advantages and disadvantages of this? Do you need to add a video expansion card to a computer? Why or why not?

1. Research video cards to find out the answers to the above questions. Also find out what GPU means and how the amount of memory on video cards affects graphics performance.

2. Create a document that summarizes in your own words what you learned about video cards. Include the URLs of the websites you used for information.

3. Save the document as **C3-Hardware-VideoCards-Your Name**.

4. Submit the document to your instructor in the manner she or he has requested.

TOPIC 3.4

Network Adapters

Recall from Chapter 1 that the term *communications device* refers to any component or device used to facilitate the transmission of data. In Chapter 2, the various types of Internet connection options were explored, and you learned about hardware used for accessing the Internet such as cable modems, DSL modems, mobile broadband sticks, and so on. A communications device can be thought of as both an input and an output device since the device receives (input) and sends (output) data to/from the computing device and other computers via a network. In this topic you will examine further the hardware provided in a notebook, tablet, or mobile device that enables connectivity to a network.

Network Adapters

Any device used to connect a computer to a network is called a **network adapter** (also called a **network card**). The network adapter is the interface between your computer and the other networking equipment such as the modem or router that provides the pathway for data to travel to/from the network. All networking equipment communicates with each other using a set of standards called **protocols**. Protocols can be thought of as a set of rules that define how data is exchanged between two devices. A network adapter has to use the same protocols as the modem or router with which the adapter is trying to communicate for each device to "understand" the other. This usually becomes a factor when an older wireless network adapter does not work with a newer router that uses a faster data transfer protocol. In that case, a newer adapter that supports the faster protocol can be purchased.

Network Adapters for Wired Connectivity

A network adapter for a wired connection is called an Ethernet port (sometimes referred to as an RJ45 port). One end of a network cable is plugged into the network port on the computer or mobile device and the other end into a modem or router to provide the communications channel as shown in Figure 3.5.

Ethernet refers to the type of cable used to connect two devices and the data transfer speed that the media can support. Typical ads for a computer will state Ethernet 10/100 or 10/100/1000. The numbers after Ethernet refer to the data transfer speed the adapter can support with 10 indicating 10 Mbps, 100 indicating 100 Mbps, and 1000 indicating 1,000 Mbps (or 1 Gbps, called Gigabit Ethernet).

With a wired network adapter, plug one end of a network cable into the network port of a computer and the other end into a modem or router to provide the communications pathway.

Figure 3.5 With a wired network adapter, a network cable connects two devices in a network.

Network Adapters for Wireless Connectivity

Wireless connectivity is preferred by people who do not want their movements constrained by the length of a physical cable. At home, at work, or when you are on the go, a wireless network allows you the freedom to move around. Today's computers come equipped with a wireless interface card that is integrated into the system unit as either Wi-Fi or Bluetooth.

Check This Out

www.wirelessindustrynews.org

Go here to find articles on recent news in the wireless industry.

Use Wireless Wisely

Wi-Fi hotspots in public areas are not secure networks. Never enter personal data at a website, in a text, or in an email message sent from a public location. Do not perform any financial transactions in a public Wi-Fi network. At home, make sure your wireless network's identification name is not obvious to your household and is secured with a strong password.

A USB wireless adapter or a wireless ExpressCard are often used to provide wireless connectivity or upgrade an existing Wi-Fi adapter.

Wi-Fi Adapters A **Wi-Fi adapter** communicates with a wireless access point or wireless router using radio frequencies to transfer data. Wi-Fi is often referred to as the **802.11 protocol**, which is the name of the standard developed to facilitate wireless communication among several hardware providers. As the protocol was improved to transmit data at faster rates, version letters were added to the 802.11 standards. At the time of writing, the latest Wi-Fi standard is 802.11n. A computer ad may state that the integrated Wi-Fi adapter is 802.11 a/b/g/n, which means the adapter can communicate with older Wi-Fi networks as well as the newer wireless networks.

If the integrated wireless adapter does not support a newer wireless network, or you have a desktop PC that does not have a wireless interface, you can purchase an **external wireless adapter**. External wireless adapters have built-in radio transmitters and receivers to allow you to connect to a wireless modem or wireless router. The most common type of external wireless adapter is a **USB wireless adapter**, also referred to as a **USB dongle** or USB mobile broadband stick. A **wireless ExpressCard** adapter plugs into a narrow slot on a notebook or other mobile device.

Did You Know?

The name Bluetooth came from 10th Century King Harold Bluetooth who was instrumental in uniting warring countries in Europe. Bluetooth seemed an appropriate name as hardware competitors had to collaborate to make devices that work with each other.

Connecting with Bluetooth Bluetooth is a communications technology for short range distances. With Bluetooth, one device is paired to another Bluetooth-enabled device that is usually within a 30-foot range. When the adapter is activated and another Bluetooth device is turned on, the adapter detects the wireless signal and the two devices are paired, meaning they can exchange data. Bluetooth is a popular way of connecting a smartphone to a communications system inside a car; however, the technology is also used to provide network access on other mobile devices such as a notebook or tablet. Newer notebooks and mobile devices include an integrated Bluetooth adapter, but you can purchase a USB Bluetooth adapter if needed.

A USB Bluetooth adapter can be used to provide connectivity with another Bluetooth device.

EXPLORE FURTHER

Which network adapters do you have?

Do you know the type of network adapters installed on the computer you are using at home?

1. Find out the network adapters installed on the computer or tablet you use. If you do not own a computer or tablet, use a computer at your school or public library. On a Windows-compatible computer use Device Manager in the Control panel and expand the list of network adapters. On a Mac, open the System Profiler. *Note: Some schools and public libraries prevent users from viewing a computer's devices. If necessary, look up ads for a newer notebook or tablet and identify the network adapters supplied with the computer.*

2. Create a document with a list of the network adapters installed on the computer. If you have purchased an external adapter, include a description of the external adapter you use.

3. Save the document as **C3-Hardware-MyNetworkAdapters-Your Name**.

4. Submit the document to your instructor in the manner she or he has requested.

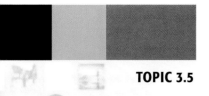

TOPIC 3.5

Digital Data

When you type a document on a computing device, you see the characters as you type them displayed on the video display screen. However, the digital data temporarily stored in RAM, processed by the CPU, and eventually saved to permanent storage when you save the document is stored using the **binary system**. In the binary system, only two possible values exist—0 and 1. Every document you save, picture on your camera, or message you send is really a series of 0s and 1s according to the computer. Understanding the way digital data is represented is helpful to put context to the speed of an Internet connection and the capacity of storage devices and memory.

Binary's Bits and Bytes

The smallest unit for digital data in the binary system is called a **bit**. Bit is derived from *bi*nary digi*t*. A bit is either 0 or 1. By itself, a single bit of 0 or 1 is not meaningful because only two possibilities exist. However, by adding additional bits to form a group, more possibilities to represent data are available because different combinations of 0s and 1s can be created to represent something. By grouping 8 bits together, 256 possibilities for combinations of 0s and 1s are created. This provides enough combinations to represent each letter of the alphabet in both upper and lower case, each number, and symbols such as $, ?, and !. Each group of eight bits is called a **byte** and represents one character. When you type the letter A on the keyboard and see A appear on the screen, one byte of RAM memory is being used to store the letter. Table 3.1 illustrates the binary equivalents for the two forms of the letter A, the number 4, and the $ symbol.

Table 3.1	Binary Equivalents for Letter a, Number 4, and Dollar Symbol
You type . . .	Computer stores in RAM . . .
a (lower case)	01100001
A (upper case)	01000001
4	01100100
$	00100100

Did You Know?

A coding system called Unicode based on binary was developed to accommodate every letter in every language. More than 100,000 characters are represented in Unicode, with some requiring two 16-bit groups to represent a character! Unicode is the standard for programming characters in browsers and operating systems.

Measuring Internet Speed and Data Caps

Bits are used to measure speed for transmitting data on the Internet. Recall in Chapter 2 when discussing broadband, average speeds were measured in mega*bits* per second (Mbps). One megabit was defined as 1 million bits. If it takes eight bits to represent one character, then one megabit transfers 125,000 characters. If your cable modem performs at an average speed of 20 Mbps, that means your cable modem is transmitting 2,500,000 characters per second.

Some ISPs put a limit on your monthly data transfer capacity. These limits are called data caps and are expressed in gigabytes. For example, a data cap of 100 GB means the ISP is limiting data transfer to 100 gigabytes in the billing period. Gigabytes are described in the next section.

Measuring File Size and Storage Capacity

A document such as an essay that you create in a program like Word is simply a collection of characters (bytes). When saved, the collection of bytes that comprise the document is called a **file**. The unique name that you assign to the document when you save it is called a **file name**, which allows you to identify one file from another on your storage medium. A file could potentially hold several thousand

An average speed of 20 Mbps means 2.5 million characters per second are being transmitted!

characters. Similarly, memory such as RAM and a permanent storage medium such as a hard disk drive can store several thousands of characters.

Prefixes added to the word byte describe progressively larger storage capacities. For example, adding *kilo* in front of byte creates the word **kilobyte**. One kilobyte, abbreviated as KB, is 1,024 bytes, but people use the approximated value of 1,000 characters when calculating storage capacity. The next prefix is *mega*, creating the term **megabyte**. One megabyte is approximately 1,000,000 bytes. Table 3.2 summarizes storage units including **gigabyte** and **terabyte** with their corresponding capacities for the types of storage mediums you would encounter at home or at work.

Storage capacities for USB flash drives such as this one are measured in megabytes or gigabytes.

Table 3.2	Storage Units and Capacities in Bytes		
Storage Unit	**Abbreviation**	**Popular Reference**	**Approximate capacity in bytes**
Kilobyte	KB	K	1,000 (one thousand)
Megabyte	MB	meg	1,000,000 (one million)
Gigabyte	GB	gig	1,000,000,000 (one billion)
Terabyte	TB	TByte	1,000,000,000,000 (one trillion)

Adding Context with Storage Capacity

Understanding that a megabyte is approximately 1 million characters is more helpful to you if you can put this value into some meaningful context. According to ehow.com, one megabyte equals approximately 500 typed pages of text with no images. However, most documents created today have some images or other graphics added to the text to make the documents more appealing to read. The picture shown of Balancing Rock uses 1.29 megabytes of storage space. One picture needs more space than 500 typed pages of text!

Many people like to download and store music and videos. It is not uncommon for one mp3 song to use more than 8 megabytes of storage and a movie file to require more than 4 gigabytes. If you like to use your computer to store pictures, music, and movies you will need a storage medium with a large capacity.

This picture of Balancing Rock in Nova Scotia, Canada, uses 1.29 MB of storage space.

Did You Know **?**

According to informationweek.com, storage used to house the data of top corporations requires many petabytes. One petabyte is approximately 1,000 terabytes!

EXPLORE FURTHER

Compressing Digital Photos

Picture files are large because of the number of bytes needed to digitize an image. Digital image sizes are measured in pixels. For example, a typical photo taken with a digital camera may be in the range of 3000 x 2000 pixels. Such a photo would be 6 million pixels, where each pixel needs to be represented by its RGB color values. RGB color information uses 24 bits for each pixel (or 3 bytes). Therefore, the file size is 18 million bytes or 18 MB (6 million pixels times 3 bytes per pixel). However, if you were to look at the file size of the picture on your digital camera's memory card, the file size would be much lower than 18 MB. This occurs because of the image file format's compression scheme.

1. Find out about the JPEG (pronounced *jay-peg*) file format used to store pictures for most digital cameras and for displaying pictures on websites. How does JPEG compression reduce file size? What is the sacrifice made to achieve the smaller file size? What are some other file formats used for digital images?

2. Create a document that describes in your own words what you learned about JPEG image files. Include the URLs for the articles you read.

3. Save the document as **C3-Hardware-JPEG-Your Name**.

4. Submit the document to your instructor in the manner she or he has requested.

Storage Options

TOPIC 3.6

Saving a document, spreadsheet, or presentation makes a permanent copy of the work in a file that is available after power to the computer is turned off. When saving, you identify the **storage device** upon which the file should be saved. A storage device is a piece of hardware with the means to write new data to and read existing data from storage media. Storage devices are often referred to as **drives**. Each drive is identified by a unique letter and label on a Windows-compatible computer (Figure 3.6). On a Mac computer, each storage device is assigned a name, such as Macintosh HD for a hard disk drive.

Several storage options for saving a permanent copy of a file are available, such as internal and external hard disk drives, solid-state drives, network storage, USB flash memory, optical discs, flash memory cards, and cloud storage. In this topic you will learn about each of these storage options.

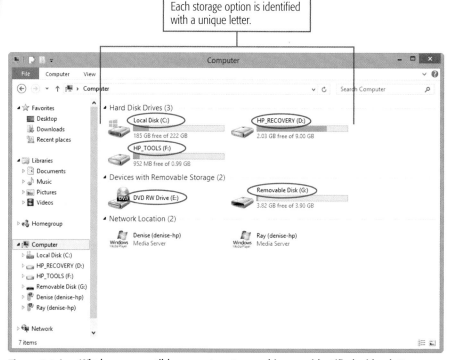

Each storage option is identified with a unique letter.

Figure 3.6 In a Windows-compatible computer, storage drives are identified with a letter.

Did You Know?

Notice the first drive letter used is C. Early PCs did not have hard disk drives and operated with one or two floppy disks (soft plastic disks that you inserted into a drive slot) that were assigned the letters A and B. When floppy disks became obsolete, A and B were not reused.

Hard Disk Drives

Inside the system unit of a PC is an internal **hard disk**, also called **hard drive** and **hard disk drive (HDD)**. The internal HDD is usually the largest storage device on a standalone PC and is assigned drive letter C on Windows-compatible computers. This is the storage medium upon which the operating system and application software programs are stored as well as data files. Hard disks are round pieces of metal called platters stacked inside a sealed unit with a magnetic coating on their surface. The disks spin and a read/write head moves across the surface of the disk magnetizing the data to the surface.

Internal hard disk with top cover plate removed to show platters and read/write head; a read/write head for each surface moves over the disks together as the platters spin.

An external hard disk drive is a storage device that you attach to the computer as a peripheral using a USB or FireWire port. External HDDs are a popular option for extending the storage capacity of a PC and/or for backing up documents, photos, videos, music, and other files.

Storage capacities for hard disk drives vary but are typically in the range of several hundred gigabytes with some newer computers having HDDs in the range of one to three terabytes.

External HDDs are often used to back up an entire computer.

Solid State Drives

A newer type of hard disk drive technology called **solid-state drive (SSD)** is increasingly being used in portable computers. SSDs use **flash memory**. Flash memory is chip-based technology where data is stored electronically on a chip instead of magnetically like a traditional HDD. With chip-based flash memory no mechanical parts are required inside the drive, making the device more durable. SSDs also weigh less than traditional HDDs, they make no noise when operating, and require less power. These qualities make SSDs popular for mobile devices. Internal and external SDDs are available in similar storage capacities as traditional HDDs.

Solid-state drives are popular in Ultrabooks because they weigh less and use less power than traditional HDDs.

Network Storage

In some workplaces, data is often required to be stored on a network drive for security and cost reasons. Network drives are hard disk drives installed in a network server and made available to users who have been granted access to the server's storage with their user name and password. A network drive will often have a letter assigned that is higher in the alphabet such as drive R or drive S. Networked storage is automatically backed up daily at the server. Centralized network storage is also considered more secure than leaving data on individual HDDs scattered about a workplace.

USB Flash Drives

A **USB flash drive** is a portable storage device that contains flash memory inside the case. USB as a storage option is popular because the drive is easy to use, small enough to carry easily, and inexpensive. The drive is powered through the USB port of the computer. When you plug in a USB flash drive, a drive letter is assigned to the device that is usually E, F, G, or another higher letter depending on the number of USB ports and other devices.

USB flash drives are made in all kinds of shapes, sizes, and colors. Some are disguised inside toys or cartoon characters. Storage capacities are available to meet several needs including 8 GB, 16 GB, 32 GB, 64 GB, and 128 GB. USB flash drives are called by many other names such as thumb drive, memory stick, jump drive, key drive, and pen drive.

USB flash drives come in all shapes, sizes, colors, and capacities.

With Blu-ray's higher storage capacity and better quality video and audio, Blu-ray media are fast replacing DVDs.

Optical Discs

An **optical disc** is a CD, DVD, or Blu-ray disc. Note that the spelling of this storage media is *disc* (not *disk*). An optical drive is internally mounted inside the system unit, though external drives are also available for plugging into a USB or FireWire port. Most PCs include an optical drive except netbooks and many ultrabooks. Optical drives are usually identified with the letter E or F, although this could vary depending on the number of other installed devices. A laser beam is used to read and write data on optical discs. Recording to an optical disc is referred to as *burning a disc.*

Optical discs are sometimes used to back up important data or for making copies of music, pictures, or movies since the removable media can be used in other devices and players and is relatively inexpensive. Optical disc types and storage capacities are listed in Table 3.3.

Table 3.3	Recordable Optical Discs and Storage Capacities	
Type of Optical Disc	**Media Options**	**Storage Capacity**
Compact Disc (CD)	CD-R (write once) CD-RW (rewritable up to 1000 times)	700 MB
Digital Versatile Disc/Digital Video Disc (DVD)	DVD +R or –R (write once) DVD +RW or –RW (rewriteable up to 1000 times)	4.7 GB for single-layer 8.5 GB for dual-layer
Blu-ray disc (BD)	BD –R (write once) BD –RE (erase and re-record multiple times)	25 GB for single-layer 50 GB for double-layer

Flash memory cards are used for storage in digital cameras, smartphones, and other portable devices.

Flash Memory Cards

The most common type of storage for a digital camera, smartphone, or other portable device is a **flash memory card**. A flash memory card is a small card that contains one or more flash memory chips (similar to SSDs and USB flash drives). Flash memory cards come in a variety of formats such as Secure Digital (SD), CompactFlash (CF) and proprietary formats made by Sony and Olympus for their digital cameras. Capacities for flash memory cards can range from 1 GB to more than 60 GB. The type of flash memory card you would buy for a device is dependent on the formats the device can read.

Some computers and notebooks have a card reader built in for easy transfer of files stored on a flash memory card's portable device (such as a digital camera) and the PC. Some USB hubs also contain readers.

Cloud Storage

Recall from Chapter 1 that cloud computing involves accessing software and storage services from the Internet. Some cloud computing providers allow you access to free storage with subscription plans available for those with higher capacity level needs. For example, at both Google Drive and Microsoft's SkyDrive you can store files for free up to a specified capacity limit (5 GB at Google and 7 GB at Microsoft at the time of writing). The main advantage with storing your documents using a cloud provider is the ability to access the files using a web browser from any location at which you have an Internet connection. You can also sync documents between multiple devices and easily share files with others. Transferring files via an Internet connection is fast and easy and you no longer need to buy, organize, and store media such as USB flash drives, CDs, DVDs, or BDs. Popular cloud storage providers besides Google and Microsoft are Dropbox and Box.net.

Storing files using a cloud storage provider is one way to access documents from multiple devices and easily share pictures or other files.

Storage capacities continue to grow to meet demands by consumers and businesses to store increasing amounts of data. The typical storage capacities mentioned here are likely soon to be replaced by higher capacity drives or media.

Career Connection

Computer Technician

If you like hardware and are a good communicator you may want to consider a career in computer hardware repair. Computer technicians troubleshoot and repair PCs and mobile devices. To succeed as a computer systems technician you need to like working with customers as well as hardware. CompTIA's A+ certification validates entry-level knowledge and skills for computer support. Consider also enrolling in a program at a community college in PC/Desktop Support or PC Support Technician.

EXPLORE FURTHER

Comparing Cloud Storage Providers

Using a cloud storage provider to keep a copy of important documents or other media files such as pictures, music, and videos has many advantages, but which provider offers the best deal?

1. Research at least five cloud storage providers besides Google and Microsoft. Find out how much, if any, free storage space is offered and the costs to purchase additional storage. Also learn the limit imposed on the file size that can be transferred to their servers.

2. Create a presentation with one slide per provider. Describe the features, benefits, costs, and file size limit for each provider. Include the URL at the provider's website where you found the information described. Conclude the presentation with a slide that states your recommendation for a cloud storage provider and give your reasons.

3. Save the presentation as **C3-Hardware-CloudStorage-Your Name**.

4. Submit the presentation to your instructor in the manner she or he has requested.

Concepts Review

Topic	Key Concepts	Key Terms
The System Unit	A peripheral device is hardware used for input, output, connectivity, or storage. The power supply is where you plug in the power cord. A cooling fan near the CPU prevents the CPU from overheating. A motherboard is the main circuit board into which all other devices connect. Expansion cards are plugged into expansion slots on the motherboard to provide or improve functionality. Data travels between components on the motherboard and the CPU via data buses. Parallel processing means the CPU can execute multiple instructions simultaneously. The instruction cycle is the process the CPU goes through to retrieve, decode, execute, and store an instruction. Clock speed refers to the speed at which the CPU operates and is measured in gigahertz. L1, L2, and L3 cache affect system performance since the CPU accesses cache memory faster than RAM. Read-only memory stores instructions that do not change, such as the BIOS instructions used to start up a computer. RAM is configured in modules that plug into the motherboard. The size and type of RAM affects system performance. External devices plug into a port attached to the motherboard. USB ports are the most common type of port.	Peripheral device Motherboard Expansion cards Data buses Parallel processing Instruction cycle Clock speed Gigahertz (GHz) Level 1 (L1) cache Level 2 (L2) cache Level 3 (L3) cache Read-only memory (ROM) BIOS (Basic Input Output System) Ports Universal Serial Bus (USB) port
Input Devices	Wireless keyboards and mice communicate with a wireless receiver plugged into a USB port. Special purpose keys on the keyboard are used to send commands to the computer. Some tablets and smartphones display an onscreen keyboard. A mouse detects movement using light technology and moves the pointer in the same direction you move the mouse. Buttons and a scroll wheel on a mouse are used to manipulate objects or send commands. On notebooks, a touchpad or track pointer senses finger movement and taps or finger pressure in place of a mouse. A touch-enabled device accepts input from finger gestures or a stylus (digital pen). A scanner uses optical technology to convert text and images into data. Other readers used for input are bar code, QR code, magnetic strip, and RFID readers, and biometric scanners. Digital cameras, camcorders, and webcams are input devices used to provide pictures or live video to the computer. Microphones combined with voice recognition technology are used to create data from audio sources. Various game controllers provide a means to input commands to entertainment systems.	Keyboard Mouse Touchpad Touch-enabled displays Touchscreens Stylus Scanner Bar code readers QR (Quick Response) codes Magnetic strip readers Biometric scanners Radio Frequency Identification (RFID) readers Camcorders Webcam Microphone Voice recognition technology Speech recognition technology

continued....

Output Devices	Video display screens connect to a video port on a PC or are integrated into a notebook or mobile device.	Video displays
	Newer monitors for PCs are widescreen LCD displays.	Monitor
	LED and plasma displays are often used for televisions.	Liquid Crystal Displays (LCD)
	OLED displays do not require backlighting and are expected to eventually replace LCD screens in mobile devices.	Light-Emitting Diode (LED)
		Plasma
	Resolution is the measurement of horizontal and vertical pixels used to render an image on a video display.	Organic Light-Emitting Diode (OLED)
	Video display projectors and interactive whiteboards are used to display computer output on large screens.	Resolution
		Pixels
	Audio output is heard from speakers, headphones, or headsets.	Video display projector (VDP)
	A Bluetooth headset is used with a smartphone to hear a conversation when making a voice call.	Interactive whiteboard
		Bluetooth headset
	Printed copy of computer output is called hard copy.	Hard copy
	A laser printer uses a laser beam to charge a drum to which toner is applied and then heated as the paper passes through the printer.	Laser printer
		Inkjet printer
	Inkjet printers form text and images by spraying drops of ink from ink cartridges onto a page.	Photo printer
	Photo printers are used to print high-quality pictures from digital cameras.	Thermal printer
		Plotter
	Thermal printers heat coated paper and are often used to print receipts at retail stores.	Digital copier
		Video card
	Blueprints and technical drawings are printed on plotters that move a pen across the page.	
	Digital copiers connected to a network can be used to print output.	
	Multipurpose printers include printing, scanning, copying, and faxing capabilities in one device.	
	A video card processes the data needed to display text and images on your screen.	
Network Adapters	A network adapter is any device used to connect to a network.	Network adapter
	The network adapter is the interface between a computer and a modem or router that allows data to be exchanged.	Network card
		Protocols
	Data is exchanged in a network using a system of rules called protocols.	Wi-Fi adapter
	A network connection for a wired connection is called an Ethernet port.	802.11 protocol
		External wireless adapter
	Ethernet refers to the physical cable used for the connection.	USB wireless adapter
	Wi-Fi adapters are used to communicate with a wireless network.	USB dongle
		Wireless ExpressCard
	The 802.11 protocol is the name of the standard used for wireless communications in Wi-Fi networks.	
	A USB wireless adapter or a wireless ExpressCard are external wireless adapters used to connect to a wireless network.	
	A Bluetooth adapter is used to provide connectivity to other Bluetooth-enabled devices.	

continued....

Topic	Key Concepts	Key Terms
Digital Data	Computers understand the binary system, which uses only 0s and 1s. The smallest unit in the binary system is a bit, which can have one of two values: either 0 or 1. A group of 8 bits equals a byte and represents one character, number, or symbol. Internet speed is measured in megabits per second, which is 1 million bits transferred per second. Files are permanent copies of documents, photos, or videos assigned a file name and measured in bytes. A kilobyte is approximately 1,000 bytes. A megabyte is approximately 1 million bytes. A gigabyte is approximately 1 billion bytes. A terabyte is approximately 1 trillion bytes. One megabyte can store approximately 500 pages of text. Images, music, and videos require many megabytes of storage space.	Binary system Bit Byte File File name Kilobyte Megabyte Gigabyte Terabyte
Storage Options	A storage device provides the means to read data from and write data to a permanent storage medium. Storage devices are referred to as drives. An internal hard disk drive is usually the largest storage device on a standalone PC. Traditional hard disk drives are magnetic storage mediums. External hard disk drives can be connected via a USB or FireWire port. Solid-state drives use chip-based flash memory to store data, are more durable, and use less power than HDDs. Some workplaces require data to be stored on network servers. USB flash drives are portable, easy to use, and come in all shapes, sizes, and storage capacities. CDs, DVDs, and Blu-ray discs use optical technology to read and write data to recordable discs. Flash memory cards are used in portable devices such as digital cameras. Some computers have a card reader built in for easy transfer of data from portable flash memory cards. Cloud storage providers allow you to store and share files that are accessible from any device with an Internet connection. Some cloud providers allow you access to free storage space, with higher capacities available for a subscription fee.	Storage device Drives Hard disk Hard drive Hard disk drive (HDD) Solid-state drive (SSD) Flash memory USB flash drive Optical disc Flash memory card

Multiple Choice

1. Which of the following is NOT found inside a system unit?
   a. Motherboard
   b. Power supply
   c. RAM
   d. USB flash drive

2. Additional circuit boards that add functionality are plugged into the motherboard in these slots.
   a. Data bus
   b. Expansion
   c. Parallel processing
   d. BIOS

3. A notebook computer senses finger movement from this device and moves the pointer.
   a. Touchpad
   b. Special purpose keys
   c. Biometric scanner
   d. Stylus

4. A smartphone can scan this type of matrix of black dots that usually directs the computer to display a website.
   a. UPC code
   b. QR code
   c. Magnetic strip
   d. RFID tag

5. This newer technology is expected to eventually replace screens in portable devices because it does not require backlighting.
   a. LED
   b. Plasma
   c. OLED
   d. LCD

6. This term refers to the measurement of horizontal and vertical pixels used to make up an image on a video display screen.
   a. Plasma
   b. Bytes
   c. Pixelation
   d. Resolution

7. A wired network adapter is referred to as this type of port.
   a. USB
   b. Wi-Fi
   c. ExpressCard
   d. Ethernet

8. A wireless USB adapter is sometimes referred to by this term.
   a. USB dongle
   b. USB pendrive
   c. USB memory stick
   d. USB flash drive

9. This is the term used to refer to data represented as a series of 0s and 1s.
   a. Microprocessing
   b. Binary system
   c. Character recognition
   d. Random access memory

10. Internet speed is measured in this type of unit.
    a. Bytes per second
    b. Megabits per second
    c. Terabytes per second
    d. Kilobytes per second

11. An internal hard disk drive is usually referred to by this drive letter in a standalone PC.
    a. A
    b. B
    c. C
    d. G

12. Solid-state drives use this type of technology.
    a. Flash memory
    b. Laser memory
    c. Optical memory
    d. Magnetic memory

Crossword Puzzle

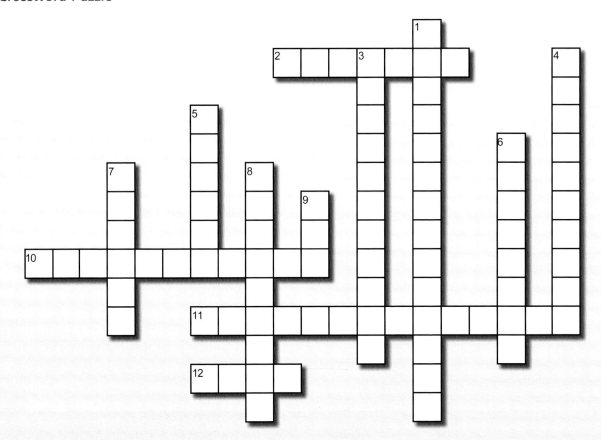

ACROSS

2 Term for network connectivity device
10 External wireless adapter
11 Prints on coated paper
12 A group of 8 bits

DOWN

1 Workplace storage requirement
3 Power cord plug
4 Reads embedded tags with antennas
5 Digital pen
6 Approximately 1,000 characters
7 Optical disc replacing DVDs
8 Measures clock speed
9 Typical monitor for PC

Matching

Match the term with the statement or definition.

_____ 1. Wi-Fi standard
_____ 2. Networked photocopier
_____ 3. Fingerprint reader
_____ 4. SkyDrive
_____ 5. Two CPU chips
_____ 6. Charged drum
_____ 7. Digital pen
_____ 8. Main circuit board

a. Parallel processing
b. Motherboard
c. Stylus
d. Biometric scanner
e. Laser printer
f. Digital copier
g. 802.11
h. Cloud Storage

Project 1 My Computer's Hardware

Individual

Deliverable: Document

Find out the specifications for all of the hardware and peripherals on the computer or mobile device that you use for school or personal use. Organize the information into the following categories: CPU, RAM, Input Devices, Output Devices, Ports, and Storage Options. If you do not own a computer, use one in a computer lab at school or in a public library. List all of the devices and any information you can learn about each device's capacity or speed. *Hint: In a Windows-compatible computer you can find storage options by opening a Computer window, and other hardware by exploring the System category in the Control Panel. In a Mac computer, open System Preferences.* If necessary, find a computer ad for a new notebook computer and use the ad to complete this project.

1. Create a document in a table format that describes all of the hardware you were able to identify in your computing device. Include as many specifications as possible such as CPU clock speed, amount of RAM, and so on.
2. Save the document as **C3-Project1-MyComputerSpecs-Your Name**.
3. Submit the document to your instructor in the manner she or he has requested.

Project 2 Adaptive/Assistive Technologies

Pairs or Team

Deliverable: Presentation

Adaptive technologies are also referred to by the term assistive technologies and refer to devices used by persons with disabilities to interact with a computer or mobile device. For example, technology exists to read text from a screen to an individual who is visually impaired. Choose the category of adaptive input devices or adaptive output devices and research a minimum of two technologies that are available to assist individuals with disabilities.

1. Create a presentation that describes the technologies you researched. Include the URLs of the websites from which you obtained information.
2. Save the presentation as **C3-Project2-AdaptiveTechnology-Your Name**.
3. Submit the presentation to your instructor in the manner she or he has requested.

Project 3 Laser or InkJet?

Individual or Pairs

Deliverable: Comparison Table in a Document or Presentation

You have been asked by the office manager at a small travel agency to research the costs of a laser printer versus an inkjet printer. The office manager is planning to replace all of the printers in the office and your analysis will help her decide the type of printer to buy.

1. Choose a manufacturer of printers such as HP, Canon, Epson, or another supplier and pick one laser printer and one inkjet printer from the company's website to compare for this project. Compare the features of each printer and the specifications for print speed. Compare the current cost to buy the printer as well as the cost of replacement toner and ink cartridges. Based on what you have researched, choose the laser or the inkjet printer as your recommendation.
2. Create a comparison table in a document or presentation with a summary of your work including your recommendation along with your reasons. Include the URLs of the websites you used for this project.
3. Save the document or presentation as **C3-Project3-LaserOrInkJet-Your Name**.
4. Submit the document or presentation to your instructor in the manner she or he has requested.

Project 4 Connecting Your Notebook to HDTV

Individual or Pairs
Deliverable: Instructional Handout

Your family just purchased a new high-definition television. You decide you want to watch movies from your notebook on the television video display, but you do not know how to connect the notebook to the television. Your notebook has an HDMI port and you have bought an HDMI cable. Now all you need to do is figure out how to connect the two devices.

1. Go to YouTube, and find and watch at least two videos that demonstrate how to connect a laptop computer to a high-definition television using HDMI.
2. Create a step-by-step instructional document for your family so that each person will be able to connect the notebook to the HDTV without difficulty. Make sure the instructions are written in your own words in clear language. Include graphics to illustrate your instructions to ensure the steps could be followed by anyone in your family.
3. Save the document as **C3-Project4-NotebookToTV-Your Name**.
4. Submit the document to your instructor in the manner she or he has requested.

Project 5 Upgrading Laptop RAM

Individual or Pairs
Deliverable: Presentation

Assume that a friend has asked for your help to upgrade RAM in her laptop. She has an IBM ThinkPad T60 laptop with 1 GB of RAM. She wants to add another 2 GB to improve the computer's performance. She has asked you to help her determine what type of RAM to buy and how to install the new RAM module.

1. Research RAM upgrades for an IBM ThinkPad T60. Find a website that advertises the RAM upgrade module and the current price.
2. Go to YouTube, and find and watch at least two videos that demonstrate how to replace the RAM module in an IBM ThinkPad.
3. Create a presentation with one slide that describes the type of RAM module, price, and company website URL for the RAM module you found. On the next slide, link to the YouTube video you thought best showed the process for upgrading the RAM module.
4. Save the presentation as **C3-Project5-RAMUpgrade-Your Name**.
5. Submit the presentation to your instructor in the manner she or he has requested.

Project 6 Storage Options

Team
Deliverable: Document, Blog Entry, or Presentation

Your team has been asked by a local accountant to educate him on storage options for his accounting firm. The accountant runs a small office with three staff members who currently save all clients' accounting work on individual internal hard drives. The accountant would like to move to a centralized storage system so that each person has access to all client files in case someone is absent. The accountant has heard of cloud storage and network storage and would like to know more about these options. Since the accountant stores the personal financial data of his clients, security and backup of data is a main concern for him.

1. Within your team discuss cloud storage and network storage options for the accountant. What are the advantages and disadvantages of each type of storage? Which option would best meet the security and backup needs or do both options adequately meet those needs? Which option might be more cost-effective? What would be the team's recommendation to the accountant? If necessary, conduct research to answer the questions posed.

2. Prepare a summary of your team's discussion in a document, blog entry, or presentation.
3. Save the document or presentation as **C3-Project6-Storage-Your Name**.
4. Submit the document, presentation, or blog entry to your instructor in the manner she or he has requested.

Project 7 Greener Computing

Individual, Pairs, or Team
Deliverable: Blog Entry

You are ready to purchase a new notebook computer and want to buy one that will have a minimal impact on the environment. A friend has told you about epeat.net, a rating system/registry for green electronics. Go to epeat.net and learn about the criteria by which products are rated for the EPEAT registry. Next, click the link to Search the Registry and choose the option to search by Manufacturer/Country (the list defaults to the United States). Click the number in the Notebooks column next to a manufacturer's name you recognize. Then, click the link to a product that has been evaluated with a Gold rating. Read the information on the next screen about the product and its individual scores by criteria.

1. Write and post a blog entry that describes what you learned about EPEAT. Would you use this registry to help you choose a new notebook? Why or why not? Were you surprised by any of the individual scores on the product you reviewed? Why or why not? (For example, a product can receive a Gold rating but score 0 on an individual criterion such as materials selection.)
2. Submit your blog URL to your instructor in the manner she or he has requested.

Optional

Read the blog entry for this project of at least two other classmates and post a comment to each. Submit the URLs of your classmates' blogs with Step 2.

Project 8 Ethics Discussion on Using Color Copier for Personal Use

Team
Deliverable: Document, Blog Entry, or Presentation

A coworker's daughter is getting married and you learned recently that your coworker used the company's high-quality color digital copier to print 200 wedding invitations.

1. Within your team discuss the ethics involved in using the company's high-quality color digital copier for personal use. Is it acceptable or not? If she only printed one copy, would that be acceptable? What should you do? Should you confront her and demand she reimburse the company for the cost of the paper and color toner? Should you tell her manager? Would any of your answers change if you knew you were going to be invited to the wedding?
2. Prepare a summary of your team's discussion in a document, blog entry, or presentation.
3. Save the document or presentation as **C3-Project8-PersonalUsePrinting-Your Name**.
4. Submit the document, presentation, or blog entry to your instructor in the manner she or he has requested.

Chapter 4

The Operating System and Utility Programs

After successfully completing this chapter, you will be able to:

- Identify system software and describe the role an operating system fulfills in computer operations

- List and describe the major functions of operating system software

- Identify the operating systems in use for personal computers and mobile devices

- Explain the purpose of an embedded operating system and a cloud operating system

- Describe and explain common utility programs used to maintain a computer

- Use troubleshooting tools found in the operating system to solve computer problems

A computing device needs software installed on it for the device to work. Software is the term that describes the set of programs that contains instructions that tell the computer what to do and how to perform each task. **System software** includes the operating system that is designed to work with the hardware that is present as well as a set of utility programs that are used to maintain the computer and its devices. The **operating system (OS)** program provides the user interface that allows you to work with the computer, manages all of the hardware resources, and provides the platform for managing files and application programs (the programs you use to perform tasks). It is the most important software on your computer because without an operating system, the hardware and other software programs you want to use would not work.

For example, most people go to their computing device because they have a specific task they want to do. Assume you want to log in to Facebook to check for updates on your friends. To do this, you start your computer and connect to the Facebook website. The computer first has to start the operating system before you see the interface that allows you to launch the Internet browser program such as Internet Explorer. Without the operating system, the interface would not appear and the browser would not be able to connect to the Internet to load the Facebook page. In this chapter, you will learn the various operating systems available for computers, the typical tasks that operating systems perform, and how to use a few utility programs to maintain and troubleshoot your computer.

Introduction to the Operating System (OS) and the OS Functions

TOPIC 4.1

The operating system manages all of the activities within the computer. The OS routes data between the hardware resources and the application programs as shown in Figure 4.1. The OS also starts the user interface and properly shuts down the hardware. Files that are stored on devices are managed by the OS, and while you are working the OS controls the flow of data between memory and the CPU. If you plug a new device into the computer, the OS looks for and installs the software that allows the device to work. Consider the OS as the conductor of a symphony; each instrument (hardware component and application program) needs the conductor (the OS) to direct when and how to "play" its individual piece so that the song plays correctly.

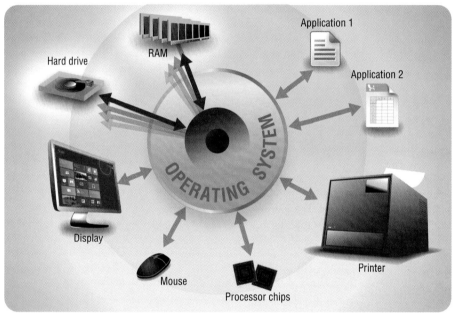

Figure 4.1 The operating system controls the flow of data and manages programs and memory.

Starting a Computer

Starting a computer is called **booting**. If you are turning on a computer that has been shut off, you are doing a **cold boot**. If you are restarting a computer without turning off the power, you are doing a **warm boot**. The instructions for booting are stored on the BIOS chip that resides on the motherboard. These instructions load the OS's **kernel** (the core of the OS that manages memory, devices, and programs and assigns resources) into RAM where it remains until you power off. Other parts of the OS are copied into RAM only when needed.

As the computer is booting, a series of messages may appear on the screen depending on the OS you are using. When the boot process is completed, the screen will display the user interface or the login screen. For example, on a computer running the Windows OS, the user interface is the Start Screen shown in Figure 4.2 (Windows 8) or the Desktop (Windows 7 and earlier).

Shutting Down a Computer If you decide to turn off the power to your computer, you should always perform a proper shut down command so that programs and files are properly closed. Depending on the OS, you can choose to *Shut Down*,

Figure 4.2 The Windows 8 Start Screen shown after booting and logging in to the system

which means you want to power off the computer, or invoke a power-saving mode such as *Sleep* where open documents and programs are saved but unnecessary functions and devices are turned off.

Functions of the Operating System

Although different operating systems are available for computers, most OS's perform similar functions. Most of these functions are performed automatically in the background, often without the user's awareness.

Providing a User Interface The **user interface (UI)** is the means with which you interact with the computer. For example, in Windows 8 with a touch-enabled computer, you tap a tile to launch an app; on a computer that is not touch-enabled, you click the tile to launch the app. In Windows 7 or earlier, you click or double-click an icon on the desktop or use the Start menu system to start an application. Most OS's provide the user with a **graphical user interface** (**GUI**, pronounced *gooey*) that presents visual images such as tiles, icons, or buttons that you tap or click to tell the OS what you want to do.

Sometimes a **command-line interface** similar to the one shown in Figure 4.3 is used to interact with an OS, where you type commands on the keyboard at a prompt to tell the OS what to do. Network specialists will sometimes use a command-line interface to configure or troubleshoot a network device.

Figure 4.3 A command-line interface requires that you type commands from the keyboard at a prompt such as C:\Users\Firstname> shown at the bottom of the window.

Figure 4.4 The Windows 8 Task Manager shows the many tasks the OS has to manage while you are working.

Managing Application Programs and Memory, and Coordinating the Flow of Data

The OS manages the installed application programs and provides you with the ability to run a program, install a new program, and uninstall a program no longer desired. When working at a computer, many people will have more than one program running at the same time. The OS manages the computer's resources (Figure 4.4), allocating data and software to/from the CPU and memory as needed, and determines the order in which tasks are performed. The OS manages the flow of data between the CPU, cache memory, RAM, and the input and output devices. If you exceed the capacity of RAM, the OS uses space on the hard disk to store overflow data. The hard disk space allocated to store RAM contents is called **virtual memory**.

Figure 4.5 When new hardware has been plugged in and a device driver has been installed, the OS displays a message indicating the device is ready for use.

Configuring Hardware and Peripheral Devices

The OS configures all devices that are installed or connected to the computer. Small programs called **drivers** contain the instructions the OS uses to communicate and route data to/from the device. When the computer is booted, the OS loads each device driver. If you plug in a new device after the computer is started, the OS searches the device for the driver, loads it automatically, and displays a message when the device is ready to use (Figure 4.5). This is called **Plug and Play**. If a device driver is not found, the OS will prompt you to install the driver from another source.

Providing a File System The OS keeps track of the files stored on a computer's storage devices and provides tools with which you can find and then manage those files by moving, copying, deleting, or renaming. In addition, utility programs to search, back up, restore, clean up, and defragment storage devices are also included in the OS package. Figure 4.6 shows the Windows 8 ribbon in a Pictures window with buttons shown to perform file management tasks.

Software Updates and Security Software often needs to be updated as program fixes, security enhancements, and new or modified device drivers become available. By default, the OS is generally set up to download updates automatically, as shown in Figure 4.7, free of charge to registered users who have activated the software.

Figure 4.6 The Windows 8 Pictures Window shows the ribbon's Home tab buttons used to manage files and folders.

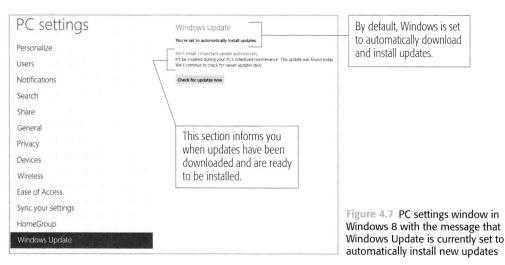

Figure 4.7 PC settings window in Windows 8 with the message that Windows Update is currently set to automatically install new updates

EXPLORE FURTHER

Look up the steps in the boot process

1. Using your favorite search engine, look up an article on the Web that explains the steps involved in the boot process when you turn on a computer.

2. Draw a flow chart or create a table that lists each step and explains what occurs in your own words.

3. Save the document as **C4-OS-BootProcess-Your Name** and submit it to your instructor in the manner she or he has requested.

TOPIC 4.2

**Check
This Out**

www.windows.microsoft.com/
en-us/windows/history

Go here to read the history of
Windows developments from
1975 to today.

**Did You
Know**

*Microsoft will stop provid-
ing support to Windows
XP in 2014. Home and
business users are
advised to upgrade to
Windows 7 or Windows
8 beforehand to avoid
problems that occur when
updates are no longer
provided.*

Popular Operating Systems for Computing Systems

When you purchase a new computing device, an operating system is preinstalled so that the device will work when you turn it on. The OS that is preinstalled may depend on the hardware since some hardware is designed specifically for a particular OS. This is known as a **computing platform**, which refers to the combination of hardware architecture and software design that allows applications to run. For example, buying an iMac computer means you will have the Mac OS installed since Apple computers are not designed to run Windows software. Four operating systems that you may encounter in your work or personal life are Windows, Mac OS, Unix, and Linux.

Windows

Windows, created by Microsoft Corporation, is the most popular OS because a wide variety of hardware is designed to run the Windows OS, and software applications designed for Windows are plentiful. Windows has evolved from Windows 1.0, released in 1985, to Windows 8, released in 2012. You will encounter a variety of Windows OS's since the Windows brand is so prevalent and not everyone upgrades to the most current release.

Windows is updated every few years as Microsoft develops new versions to keep up with hardware innovations, adds new functionality and/or redesigns existing functions, and overall strives to make the OS faster and more user-friendly. Generally, a new release is assigned a version number to differentiate the OS from earlier editions.

Each Windows version generally comes in a variety of editions for various home and business environments. In addition, Windows Server editions are available to provide advanced security and management needed for networks.

Windows 7, released in 2009, and Windows 8 are shown side-by-side in Figure 4.8. You can see the vast difference in the user interface between these two releases. While prior updates to Windows typically involved a fairly fast learning curve for users, Windows 8 is definitely a game changer. Windows 8 is focused on touch-enabled mobile devices, meaning the OS runs faster and integrates more easily with other apps and devices. The cloud is a major factor with Windows 8 since the OS is designed to store your favorite online services accounts (such as Facebook, Twitter, or Flickr) so that when you sign in to a Windows 8 device, these services are automatically connected. The tiles on your Start screen stream live updates so you instantly know when someone posts on your wall in Facebook, for example.

Figure 4.8 Windows 7 Desktop (left) and Windows 8 Start Screen (right)

Mac OS

The **Mac OS** is a proprietary OS created by Apple, Inc. with the first release in 1984 for Apple's Macintosh computer. The first Macintosh computer used a GUI interface and became the basis for the design of other GUI OS's down the road.

The Mac OS X family is the most recent OS, with the Mountain Lion version released in July 2012 shown in Figure 4.9. Apple uses a unique naming convention for Mac OS X with each version sporting an animal's name such as Leopard (2007), Snow Leopard (2009), and Mountain Lion (2012). Like Microsoft, Apple releases new versions to update functionality, responsiveness, and efficiencies to strive for faster, more user-friendly experiences. Server versions of Mac OS X are also available.

Historically, Macs were less prone to viruses since hackers went after Windows software because of its prevalence in the marketplace; however, with the rise in Mac sales in the past few years, virus attacks are now hitting the Mac world.

Mac computers have always been popular with graphic artists and those working in multimedia environments since the hardware is designed with high-end graphics processing capability. Consumer demand for Apple's iPod, iPad, and products that allow you to run Windows software on Mac computers has resulted in an increased Mac brand presence in the marketplace.

Figure 4.9 Mac OS X Mountain Lion, released in July 2012

UNIX

UNIX is an operating system that has been around since the late 1960s and is designed for servers. Originally designed to be multi-user and multitasking, the OS is often used for web servers because of the OS's robust ability to support many users. UNIX is available in several versions and is able to run on a variety of devices, including hardware built for Windows and Macs. In fact, Apple's Mac OS is based on the UNIX OS. Although UNIX is a highly stable OS, the cost and higher level of skill required to install and maintain a UNIX computer make it less prevalent for typical computer users.

UNIX was designed as a server operating system.

Linux

Linux was created by Linus Torvalds in 1991 and is based on UNIX. Linux can be used as a standalone OS or as a server OS. What makes Linux preferable to some users is that the OS is an **open source program**, meaning that the source code is available to the public and can be freely modified or customized. Linux, like UNIX, can run on a variety of devices and is available as a free download on the Web as well as by purchase from Linux vendors. Linux, because of its open source design, is available in many distributions (versions) such as Red Hat and Ubuntu. Figure 4.10 illustrates PCLinuxOS. You can order some computers with Linux preinstalled upon request.

Figure 4.10 PCLinuxOS, one of the many distributions available for this open source operating system

The open source software movement is increasing in large part due to the lower costs associated with using free software. Linux can be found in use at companies such as IBM and HP, and a popular mobile OS is based on Linux.

www.webopedia.com/ TERM/N/network_ operating_system_NOS.html
Go here to read a definition of a network operating system (NOS).

Blog Topic

To upgrade or not to upgrade—which side are you on?

When a newer version of an operating system is released, some people jump on the bandwagon and immediately upgrade, relishing the opportunity to be on the leading edge and experience what's new. Others prefer to wait a while and stick with the tried and true, assuming that it is more prudent to wait for the manufacturer to work out all of the bugs.

1. Assuming that cost is not a factor in the decision to upgrade, write and post a blog entry that supports immediately upgrading or taking the wait-and-see approach. Give your reasons for your position.

2. Read at least two of your classmate's blogs and post a comment to each.

3. Submit your blog URL and the URLs of the two classmates' blogs for which you provided a comment to your instructor in the manner she or he has requested.

EXPLORE FURTHER

Conduct a survey and look up statistics on OS usage

1. Survey a minimum of 10 friends, family, or classmates outside your class to find out which OS they use on their primary computing device.

2. Next, using your favorite search engine, look up current statistics on OS market share on the Web.

3. Create two charts in a new document or presentation that show the compiled results of your personal survey and the results you found on the Web.

4. Add a short paragraph that describes the comparisons you found. Include the URL of the site you used for your web research.

5. Save the document or presentation as **C4-OS-OSStats-Your Name** and submit it to your instructor in the manner she or he has requested.

TOPIC 4.3

Popular Operating Systems for Mobile Devices

A variety of mobile devices such as smartphones and tablets use a **mobile operating system**, an operating system designed specifically for a mobile device. The OS is stored on a ROM chip. These operating systems are designed to manage hardware and applications with less memory than a personal computer operating system yet run fast and efficiently. The mobile OS often manages input from a touchscreen and/or voice command and routes data to/from wireless connections including web browsing. Mobile devices also generally include cameras that can be used for video calling or taking pictures. Mobile OS's manage small application programs, called **apps**, with support for multitasking contacts, messages, calendars, music, video, social media updates, and numerous other mobile tools. Several hardware manufacturers produce mobile devices, and some have developed their own operating systems for use on their hardware. The most common mobile operating systems include Android, iOS, BlackBerry OS, and Windows Phone.

The mobile market changes rapidly as wireless technologies and software develop to take full advantage of faster speeds and capabilities. Competition in the industry is fierce and companies that lag in new development quickly run into trouble. For example, Symbian, a mobile operating system once used on most Nokia phones that was popular in Europe, has seen significant decline after Nokia announced a new partnership with Windows Phone. Consider also the struggle by Research in Motion's BlackBerry to remain viable. RIM's predicament is largely attributed to a failure to keep up with touch-enabled multimedia, web browsing, and apps consumers love on Apple and Android phones.

Secure Your Mobile Device!

Imagine your lost smartphone or tablet resulting in someone posting embarrassing updates or photos on your Facebook account! Secure your device by locking it in case it falls into the wrong hands. Some devices provide for a touch or swipe motion to unlock; others require a typed password.

Android is the operating system of choice for mobile devices.

Android

Android is the mobile operating system of choice for many smartphones and tablets. The OS is based on Linux, making it an open source OS. In 2007 Android was released by the **Open Handset Alliance**, which is a consortium of several mobile technology companies of which Google is a member. The goal of the alliance is to develop open standards for mobile devices. Android is now maintained and developed by the **Android Open Source Project (AOSP)**, which is led by Google.

Android currently enjoys the highest market share for mobile devices, and Google Play, the website where you download apps for Android devices, lists more than 450,000 apps.

iOS

Apple developed **iOS** as the mobile operating system for its iPhone, iPod Touch, and iPad. The OS is based on the Mac OS X operating system and is a proprietary OS. Users can only download apps for their Apple devices from the App store in iTunes. Development of new apps for Apple devices is tightly controlled by Apple, meaning that that new apps are generally virus-free, stable, and reliable. The Apple website indicates that more than 500,000 apps and games are available in iTunes for Apple devices.

Apple's iPad 3

BlackBerry OS

Research in Motion (RIM) developed the BlackBerry and the **BlackBerry OS**, which is the operating system designed for BlackBerry devices. Although known for its superior messaging security and its popular BlackBerry Messenger (BBM) tool, this smartphone has been experiencing a market decline. BlackBerry OS, like iOS, is proprietary. Apps available at BlackBerry's App World number more than 70,000.

Windows Phone

Windows Phone is the mobile operating system developed by Microsoft that replaced its earlier OS, Windows Mobile, which was used on Windows smartphones. Windows Phone introduced the tile interface, which is the basis for Windows 8 for standalone computers in which live tiles stream updates to the user's mail, calendar, and web apps.

BlackBerry was popular with businesses because of its superior security and popular BBM messenger tool; however, recently it has experienced declining sales.

Windows Phone uses a live tile interface.

EXPLORE FURTHER

Which smartphone would you choose?

1. Assume you have just won a contest where the prize is to buy any smartphone you want with a fully paid talk, text, and data plan for one year that more than meets your needs. Visit your preferred smartphone provider store or use the Internet to conduct your survey of smartphone providers.

2. Once you have made your selection, create a new document that explains your smartphone choice, the features of the smartphone, and your rationale. Include in your rationale the mobile OS that resides on the smartphone and whether the mobile OS had any influence on your choice.

3. At the end of the document, include the URL(s) of any websites you used and/or the name and location of the store you visited.

4. Save the document as **C4-OS-Smartphone-Your Name** and submit it to your instructor in the manner she or he has requested.

Embedded Operating Systems and Cloud Operating Systems

TOPIC 4.4

Computing consoles such as automated tellers, GPS navigation systems, smart appliances, video game controllers, medical equipment devices, point-of-sale cash registers, digital cameras, and a multitude of other consumer and commercial electronics need a specialized operating system designed for the device's limited use. In these computing devices, an **embedded operating system** is installed. Embedded operating systems are smaller and interact with fewer resources to perform specific tasks fast and reliably.

Windows Embedded

Windows Embedded is a family of operating systems based on the familiar Windows operating system designed for use in a variety of devices. For example, Windows Embedded, Windows Embedded POSReady, and Windows Embedded Compact are all variations recommended by Microsoft for an ATM, a kiosk, or a digital picture frame.

Embedded Linux

Embedded Linux applications can be found running smart appliances, in-flight entertainment systems, personal navigation systems, and a variety of other consumer and commercial electronics. Similar to the standalone Linux operating system, embedded Linux is available in many different distributions since it is an open source program.

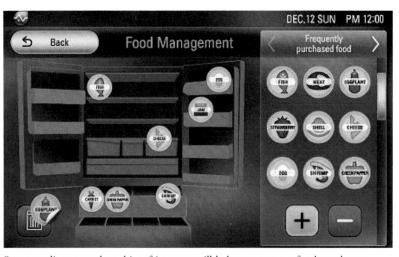

Smart appliances, such as this refrigerator, will help you manage food purchases.

ATMs are just one of many electronic devices that require an embedded operating system.

In-flight entertainment systems are popular with travelers.

Android is the operating system used on some netbooks.

Android

Android, an operating system based on Linux, is a popular choice for electronic devices beyond smartphones such as tablets, set-top boxes, and netbooks. Recently, Google announced its Android@Home project with the goal of controlling household objects such as your dishwasher, lighting, heating, and air conditioning systems using an Android device.

Cloud Operating Systems

Some companies, such as Google, are developing operating systems that operate like a virtual desktop. The interface may look and feel like a traditional desktop, but your settings, documents, pictures, contacts, and other files are stored in the cloud. This means you can access the objects from any device anywhere you have an Internet connection. These **web-based operating systems** are not true operating systems like Windows since you still need a standalone operating system on the computer you are using to access the web browser. However, the appeal of these systems is that extra software for applications does not have to be installed, and the ability to synchronize documents among multiple devices seamlessly is worthwhile as more people use multiple computers.

Cloud operating systems are like a virtual desktop with all settings, applications, and documents stored on cloud servers.

Protect Your Documents in the Cloud

Storing all your files in the cloud is not without risk of hackers or other unwanted intrusions into your personal data. Make sure the service provider encrypts data and choose a password that is difficult to hack. See Chapter 7 for information on encryption and creating strong passwords.

Figure 4.11 After logging in with your Apple ID, the iCloud website connects you to Mail, Contacts, Calendar, Find My iPhone, and Documents from any other Apple device or PC.

iCloud   Apple's **iCloud** is built into every new iOS device. Once set up, the iCloud provides access to your email, contacts, calendar, documents, and more as shown in Figure 4.11. You can work on documents in the cloud and have access to them on any device—including a Windows-based PC. If you download an app on one device, you have access to it on your other devices too. Apple includes 5 GB of free storage when you sign up for iCloud.

Chrome OS   Google's **Chrome OS** is a Linux-based operating system available on specific hardware called Chromebooks. Chromebooks boasts fast startup with built-in virus protection, automatic updates that promise not to slow down your device over time, and cloud-based applications such as Google Docs, Gmail, Google Drive, and Cloud Print. You also have the ability to sync your favorite websites, documents, and settings with other devices that use the Chrome browser.

Google is constantly updating Chrome OS as it receives feedback from users and reviewers. Figure 4.12 shows the desktop available in version 19 for an operating system that was first released in 2009!

Did You Know ?
Chrome OS led to the establishment of the Chromium projects with the goal to develop a fast, simple, and secure open-source OS for people who spend most of their time on the Web.

Check This Out

www.jolicloud.com/jolios
Go here to learn about Joli OS, a free cloud-based operating system.

Figure 4.12 A desktop image from version 19 of Google's Chrome OS

Career Connection

Careers in the Cloud

Cloud computing is a growing trend and businesses that use and supply cloud services are looking for IT professionals with the right cloud technology skill sets. These skills include knowledge of networks, security, data migration, and web programming languages. The Global Science and Technology Forum has created three certifications to demonstrate mastery of cloud computing and its applications: Certified Cloud Computing Associate (CCCA), Certified Cloud Computing Specialist (CCCS), and Certified Cloud Computing Professional (CCCP).

Blog Topic

Is there a future for cloud-based operating systems?

Within a team discuss the following question: *Will cloud-based operating systems eventually take over from traditional computing environments where all of the software and files are stored on a local hard drive?* Consider the advantages and disadvantages of using a system where all settings and files are stored in the cloud. What, if any, barriers will prevent these working environments from becoming commonplace?

1. Write and post a blog entry for your team with a summary of your team's position.
2. Read at least two of your classmates' team blogs and post one comment from your team to each.
3. Submit your team's blog URL and the URLs of the two classmates' team blogs for which you provided a comment to your instructor in the manner she or he has requested.

EXPLORE   FURTHER

Favorite Electronic Devices

1. Ask at least 10 family or friends to name their favorite electronic device other than a smartphone or tablet. Examples can include mp3 player, GPS, gaming system, digital camera, and so on.
2. Compare the results of your informal survey with a classmate's results and discuss the following questions: Which devices seem to be the most popular? Were there devices that were unique in each list? Was there a response that surprised you?
3. Create a document that summarizes the two survey results and the discussion.
4. Save the document as **C4-OS-FavoriteDevices-Your Name** and submit it to your instructor in the manner she or he has requested.

Utilities in Your OS Package for Maintaining System Performance

TOPIC 4.5   Just as a car needs regular tune-ups to keep the vehicle running smoothly and efficiently, so do computers. Files on the computer should be regularly maintained to remove unwanted files, and regular backups should be done to prevent loss of data. Most operating systems provide a utility that allows you to schedule regular maintenance. File maintenance utilities often include a file manager, a utility to clean up unwanted files, a disk defragmenter, and a backup and restore program.

Utilities that protect your computer from malware such as viruses and spyware are discussed in Chapter 7, *Computer Security and Privacy*.

File Manager

In Windows 7 you open **Windows Explorer** (Figure 4.13), and in Windows 8 open **File Explorer** (Figure 4.13) to perform file management tasks such as moving, copying, deleting, and renaming files. You can also set up your filing system by creating a new **folder**, which is a placeholder name for where you want to store related files. A folder on a computer is similar to a paper file folder you would use in an office for paper documents you want to keep together.

In Mac OS X, use the Finder utility to perform file management routines.

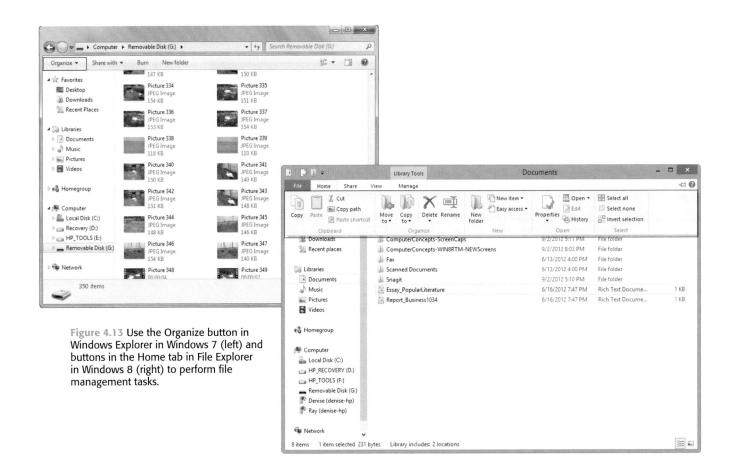

Figure 4.13 Use the Organize button in Windows Explorer in Windows 7 (left) and buttons in the Home tab in File Explorer in Windows 8 (right) to perform file management tasks.

Disk Cleanup

The Windows **Disk Cleanup** utility (Figure 4.14) allows you to scan a particular storage device or drive to select various types of files to be deleted. Files the utility will flag for deletion include temporary Internet files, temporary application files, downloaded files, files moved to the Recycle Bin, and offline web pages.

In Mac OS X, use the Repair Disk utility to clean up unwanted files.

First choose the drive you want to clean up and then choose the types of files to be removed. The first two options are selected by default.

Figure 4.14 In Windows 7 and Windows 8, the Disk Cleanup Utility first requires you to select the Drive and then choose the types of files you want to remove.

Disk Defragmenter

As time passes, a disk can become fragmented as a result of files being moved or deleted. Files are stored on a disk in groups called clusters, and several clusters are sometimes needed to store one document. Sometimes, the clusters needed for a document are not stored adjacent to each other. This is called a **fragmentation**. When you reopen a document that has been fragmented, the OS has to gather back together all of the fragmented clusters and arrange them in the correct order. As more fragmentation occurs, disk efficiency decreases. A **disk defragmenter** rearranges the fragmented files back together to improve file retrieval speed and efficiency. Figure 4.15 shows the Windows 7 Disk Defragmenter window and the Windows 8 **Optimize Drives** window, both of which are opened from the System and Security section of the Control Panel.

In Mac OS X, use Disk Utility to defragment a disk.

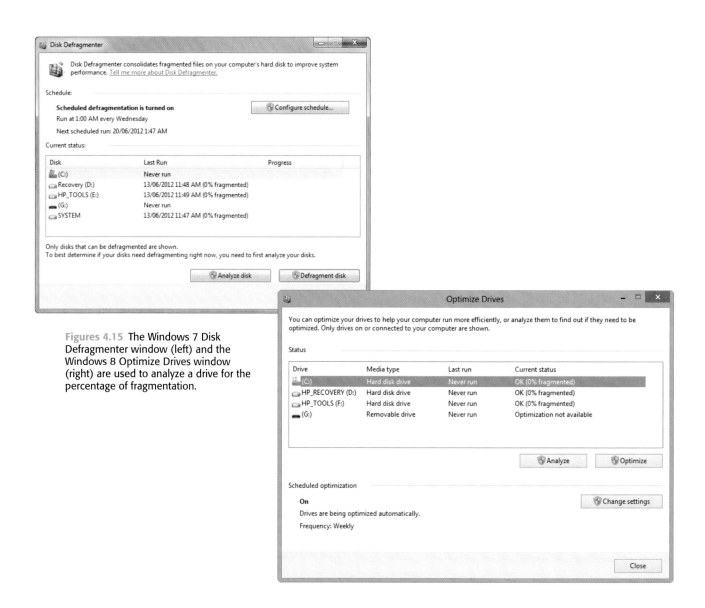

Figures 4.15 The Windows 7 Disk Defragmenter window (left) and the Windows 8 Optimize Drives window (right) are used to analyze a drive for the percentage of fragmentation.

Back Up and Restore

Regular backing up of important files is something all computer users should do to prevent loss of data from disk corruption, accidental deletion, or other damage that prevents the files from being usable. A **backup utility** is a program that allows you to back up selected files or an entire disk to a removable storage medium. To begin a backup, in the System and Security section of the Control Panel open **Windows Backup** (in Windows 7) or **File History** (in Windows 8) as shown in Figure 4.16.

Files backed up using a backup utility are not stored in a readable format since the files are compressed to save space. Open the operating system **restore utility** if you need to copy files from a backup back to a disk drive in their original state.

In Mac OS X, use Time Machine to back up and restore files.

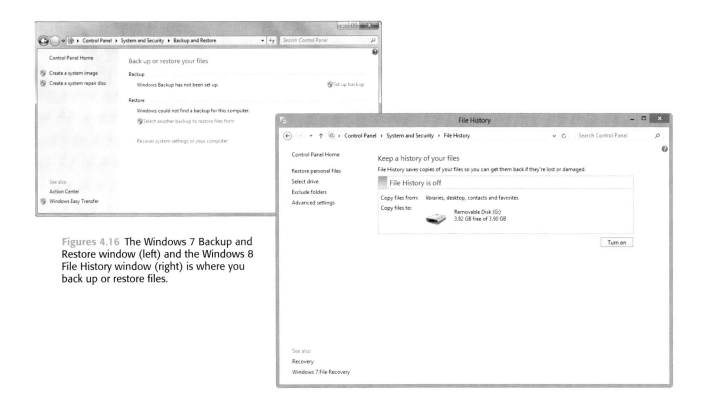

Figures 4.16 The Windows 7 Backup and Restore window (left) and the Windows 8 File History window (right) is where you back up or restore files.

EXPLORE FURTHER

Develop a Computer Maintenance Checklist

1. In this topic you have seen a sampling of a few common utility programs provided with the operating system that are used to perform computer maintenance. A comprehensive computer maintenance plan includes other tasks such as wiping clean the screen and other peripherals. Search the Web for articles on computer maintenance to learn about other tasks recommended by computer experts.

2. Individually or in pairs, develop a computer maintenance checklist that you could use at home or at work to maintain your computer. Consider grouping tasks by frequency such as Daily, Weekly, Monthly, and Yearly.

3. Create the checklist in a document or in a spreadsheet. Set the checklist up to be easy to follow and user-friendly such as by providing check boxes you can check off when the task is completed.

4. Save the document as **C4-OS-MaintenanceChecklist-Your Name** and submit it to your instructor in the manner she or he has requested.

Using Operating System Tools to Troubleshoot Computer Problems

TOPIC 4.6

In a perfect world the printer would always print, the connection to the Internet would always work, and your computer would always operate at blazing fast speed! Causes of computer problems can be complex and not easily resolved; however, knowing how to use a few of the tools provided in the operating system package can help you fix the problem and get back to work.

Windows Action Center

The **Action Center** (available in Windows 7 and Windows 8) shown in Figure 4.17 is a good place to begin when something is not working. Open the Control Panel to find the Action Center utility in the System and Security category. The window displays messages when the OS has detected potential issues that need your attention. If the problem you are experiencing is not listed in one of the messages, tap or click the Troubleshooting link to open the Troubleshooting window. Tap or click the link that most closely describes the problem you are having to open tools to help you resolve the problem. The prompts that display vary depending on the issue you are troubleshooting.

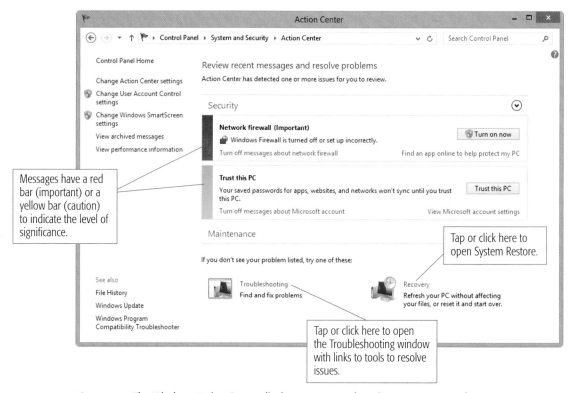

Messages have a red bar (important) or a yellow bar (caution) to indicate the level of significance.

Tap or click here to open System Restore.

Tap or click here to open the Troubleshooting window with links to tools to resolve issues.

Figure 4.17 The Windows Action Center displays messages about issues encountered on your computer and provides buttons and links to tools that can be used to resolve the issues.

System Restore

Sometimes a problem will occur after you have installed something new like a device driver, a new application, or have run updates that inadvertently caused a problem with something else. Or you may have accidentally deleted or overwritten a system file that has rendered a program or device unusable. In these cases, **System Restore** is a way for you to turn back the clock to when the computer was functioning normally. System Restore will undo a recent change while leaving all documents intact. You will find System Restore in Windows 7 and Windows 8 in the Action Center. Tap or click the Recovery link located at the bottom right of the window. The System Restore window in Windows 7 and Windows 8 is the same in both versions (Figure 4.18). You select an event from a list of changes that have been made to your system (Figure 4.19 shows Windows 7 restore points) and then follow the prompts that appear.

Figures 4.18 Windows 8 System Restore window used to undo changes made to your computer

Figure 4.19 In both Windows 7 (shown) and Windows 8 System Restore, you can select the restore point from the event list and then click Next to begin the undo process.

Help and Support

Operating systems offer extensive help and support that you can search to find answers to most questions and issues. In Windows 8, you can access **Help and Support** by tapping or clicking the Search charm and typing *Help* in the Search Apps text box or by clicking Help and Support in the Apps list. In Windows 7, click the Start button and then click Help and Support at the Start menu. In the Help and Support window, type a short phrase to describe the issue in the *Search* text box and then press Enter or tap or click the Search button. Navigate through Help information by tapping or clicking the links that appear in the Search results list. Figure 4.20 shows a list of help topics associated with a search in Help using the phrase *fix sound* in the Windows 7 and Windows 8 Help and Support windows.

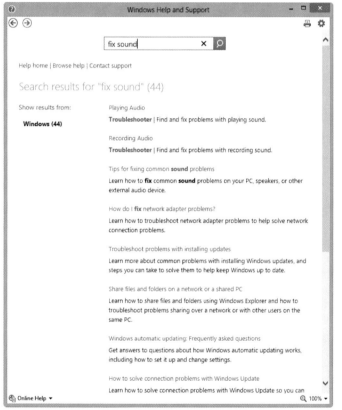

Figures 4.20 Windows 7 (left) and Windows 8 (right) Help and Support in which you can search for solutions to a computer issue in extensive online resources

Did You Know?

*Mac Help and
support.apple.com
contain extensive
resources to assist Mac
users with resolving
computer issues.*

Career Connection

Careers in Technical Support

Computer technicians and help desk technical support specialists that can solve computer problems are always in demand. In the Top IT Skills in Demand for 2012 Computerworld survey, IT executives reported that mobile devices have added complexity to this in-demand role. Certifications to demonstrate your ability to work well in this field include CompTia's A+ certification geared toward workers in desktop support, and Microsoft's MCTS (Microsoft Certified Technology Specialist), which validates your skills in troubleshooting Microsoft technology. Go to microsoft.com/learning to learn more about Microsoft certifications.

 ## Blog Topic

How I Fixed My Computer

Almost everyone has had to troubleshoot a computer issue at some point. Think about the last time you had a problem with your computer and how you resolved the problem. If you do not have an experience that you can recall, ask a family member or friend to describe his or her experience to you.

1. Write and post a blog entry that relates the issue and the resolution. Include tips or techniques learned from the experience to prevent the problem from reoccurring.
2. Read at least two of your classmates' blogs and post one comment to each.
3. Submit your blog URL and the URLs of the two classmates' blogs for which you provided a comment to your instructor in the manner she or he has requested.

EXPLORE FURTHER

Common Computer Problems

1. Look up articles on the Web that describe five common computer problems and how to fix them.
2. Create a presentation with one issue per slide and include the recommendations for how to fix the problem.
3. Add a slide to the end of the presentation that includes the URL(s) of any websites that you used.
4. Save the presentation as **C4-OS-ComputerProblems-Your Name** and submit it to your instructor in the manner she or he has requested.

Concepts Review

Topic	Key Concepts	Key Terms
Introduction to the Operating System (OS) and the OS Functions	The OS provides the user interface. The OS coordinates the data and activities between hardware resources and application programs. Starting a computer is called booting. The Shut Down command turns off the power to a computer, properly closing all files and programs. The user interface is what you use to interact with the computer. The OS manages all of the application programs and memory, and coordinates the flow of data. The OS configures hardware. The OS keeps track of files. Automatic updates ensure the OS has all program fixes, security enhancements, and new or modified drivers.	System software Operating system (OS) Booting Cold boot Warm boot Kernel User interface (UI) Graphical user interface (GUI) Command-line interface Virtual memory Drivers Plug and Play
Popular Operating Systems for Computing Systems	A computing platform is a combination of hardware architecture and software design. Windows is the most popular OS since a wide variety of hardware is designed to run Windows OS and Windows applications. Windows 8 is focused on touch-enabled mobile devices with a redesigned Start screen that contains live tiles and automatically connects to online accounts. Mac OS is the proprietary OS used for Apple computers such as the iMac and MacBooks. UNIX was developed in the 1960s for servers and is a popular choice for web servers. Linux was created in 1991 and is an open source program that can run on a variety of devices. Several versions of Linux are available because it is able to be freely modified and distributed.	Computing platform Windows Mac OS UNIX Linux Open source program
Popular Operating Systems for Mobile Devices	Mobile operating systems are designed specifically to handle smaller hardware and apps with less memory. Most mobile OS's include support for cameras, touch screen and/or voice commands, and video calling. Android is the mobile OS of choice for many smartphones and tablets. The Android Open Source Project is now tasked with maintaining and developing Android. iOS is the proprietary mobile OS developed by Apple for the iPhone, iPod Touch, and iPad. Research in Motion developed the proprietary BlackBerry OS to support its family of BlackBerry devices. Windows Phone is the mobile OS developed by Microsoft for Windows smartphones.	Mobile operating system Apps Android Open Handset Alliance Android Open Source Project (AOSP) iOS BlackBerry OS Windows Phone

continued….

Embedded Operating Systems and Cloud Operating Systems	Consumer and commercial electronic devices need a specialized OS designed for their limited use. Windows Embedded is a family of embedded OS's used on a variety of devices. Embedded Linux is similar to standalone Linux. Android is used for electronic devices beyond smartphones and tablets. Cloud OS's operate like a virtual desktop, providing access to files and apps anywhere you have Internet access. iCloud is built into every iOS device and syncs documents in the cloud to all devices, including PCs. Chrome OS is available on Chromebooks and supports Google's cloud-based apps.	Embedded operating system Windows Embedded Embedded Linux Web-based operating system iCloud Chrome OS
Utilities in Your OS Package for Maintaining System Performance	File Managers such as Windows Explorer in Windows 7 and File Explorer in Windows 8 provide file-maintenance tools. Disk Cleanup is a utility used to remove unwanted files. Disk Defragmenter is a utility used to increase disk speed and efficiency by rearranging files. Backup and Restore are utilities used to back up files and restore backed up files to their original state.	Windows Explorer File Explorer Folder Disk Cleanup Fragmentation Disk Defragmenter Optimize Drives Backup utility Windows Backup File History Restore Utility
Using Operating System Tools to Troubleshoot Computer Problems	The Action Center in Windows is used to view messages about issues and access tools to resolve problems. System Restore will undo a recent change leaving all documents intact. Windows Help and Support can be used to find answers to problems occurring on your computer.	Action Center System Restore Help and Support

Multiple Choice

1. Which of the following is NOT a function of the operating system?
   a. Provides a user interface
   b. Booting
   c. Configures hardware devices
   d. Manages memory

2. This term describes the process of automatically installing a device driver when new hardware is plugged into the computer.
   a. Soft boot
   b. Virtual memory
   c. Driver
   d. Plug and Play

3. Which of the following is NOT one of the popular operating systems for standalone computers?
   a. iOS
   b. Windows
   c. UNIX
   d. Linux

4. Linux is based on which other operating system?
   a. Windows
   b. Mac OS X
   c. UNIX
   d. Chrome OS

5. This mobile operating system currently enjoys the highest market share.
   a. iOS
   b. BlackBerry OS
   c. Windows Phone
   d. Android

6. This mobile operating system displays a live tile interface.
   a. Android
   b. Windows Phone
   c. BlackBerry OS
   d. iOS

7. This term describes an operating system designed for a device that performs a specific task such as an ATM or a GPS.
   a. Open source operating system
   b. Embedded operating system
   c. Cloud operating system
   d. Standalone operating system

8. This term describes an operating system that operates like a virtual desktop where you access all files and applications using a web browser.
   a. Server operating system
   b. Embedded operating system
   c. Standalone operating system
   d. Cloud operating system

9. This utility program is used to remove unwanted files from your computer.
   a. Windows Explorer
   b. Disk Defragmenter
   c. Optimize Drives
   d. Disk Cleanup

10. This utility program is used to increase disk efficiency by rearranging files that have been split up.
    a. Optimize Drives
    b. Disk Defragmenter
    c. Disk Cleanup
    d. Windows Explorer

11. Open this window to view messages that describe issues the OS has detected.
    a. Help and Support
    b. Action Center
    c. System Restore
    d. Windows Explorer

12. You can undo a recent change made to your computer, such as installing a new driver, by opening this window.
    a. Disk Cleanup
    b. Windows Explorer
    c. Help and Support
    d. System Restore

Crossword Puzzle

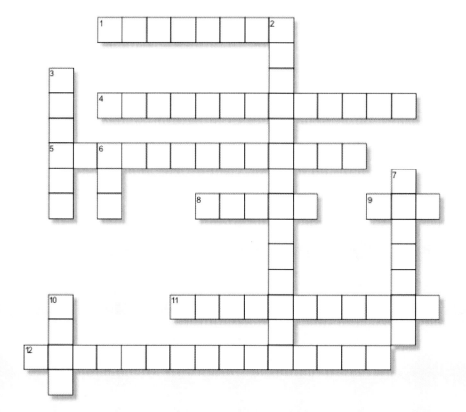

ACROSS

1 Cloud OS developed by Google
4 Term that describes a file broken up into nonadjacent clusters
5 RAM contents stored on the hard disk
8 Apple's OS for the iMac and MacBooks
9 Mobile OS for the iPhone
11 Interface where you type instructions at a prompt
12 Microsoft's family of OS's for consumer electronics

DOWN

2 Includes OS and utility programs
3 Small program used to configure hardware
6 BlackBerry manufacturer
7 Starting a computer
10 OS developed in the 1960s

Matching

Match the term with the statement or definition.

_____ 1. Kernel
_____ 2. Open source program
_____ 3. Open Handset Alliance
_____ 4. iCloud
_____ 5. Restore
_____ 6. Control Panel

a. Built into every new iOS device
b. Utility to copy files back to their original state
c. Window to open to find the Action Center utility
d. Source code that can be modified by anyone
e. Core of the OS loaded into RAM
f. Released Android in 2007

Project 1 Training for the Windows GUI

Individual, Pairs, or Team
Deliverable: Presentation

You work in the IT department of a local travel agency. The owner of the agency has asked you to prepare a training presentation for new employees who need to learn how to use the Windows interface. Specifically, consider that the new employees have never before used Windows software and need to know the basics of how to run application programs, open and close windows, switch between open programs, and properly shut down the computer system.

1. Create a presentation that could be used as a self-guided training program on how to use Windows 7 or Windows 8 to perform the basic tasks described. Include an introductory slide that explains the purpose of the Windows software. Be creative in your approach and make sure the information is presented in such a way that someone reading the slides could learn the material on his or her own.
2. Save the presentation as **C4-Project1-WindowsGUI-Your Name**.
3. Submit the presentation to your instructor in the manner she or he has requested.

Project 2 Comparison of Features in Mobile Operating Systems

Pairs or Team
Deliverable: Table in Word Processor or Spreadsheet

The business manager of a new documentary film-making company has asked your group to assist him with research for new mobile device purchasing decisions by developing a comparison of features available by mobile operating systems. He has asked your group to develop a table that compares the popular mobile operating systems by four criteria: Ease of Use, App Availability, Connectivity Options such as tethering and WiFi hotspots, and Security.

1. Create a table in a word processor or spreadsheet that shows a comparison of at least three popular mobile operating systems by the four criteria. Use the Web to research current features and standards for the mobile OSs you want to compare and to look up the definition of features you may not understand such as tethering and WiFi hotspots. Make sure the table is easy to read and understand and provides complete information for a comparison. Below the table, include the URLs of the main websites from which you obtained your information.
2. Save the document or spreadsheet as **C4-Project2-MobileOSComparison-Your Name**.
3. Submit the document or spreadsheet to your instructor in the manner she or he has requested.

Project 3 Utility Programs to Speed Up Computer Performance

Individual, Pairs, or Team
Deliverable: Document

You volunteer at a local senior citizen community center. Many of the seniors you meet ask you why their computer's performance declines over time and how they can improve the computer's speed. You explain that most computers slow down because of virus or spyware infections, too many programs included in the startup process, undersized RAM, and the hard disk running out of space and/or becoming fragmented. The manager of the community center has asked you to create a document that can be used by the seniors to help them tune up their computers.

1. Research utilities within the operating system package with which you are familiar that do the following: scan for viruses and spyware, remove unused programs from the computer, and increase disk space and efficiency. (Assume that the amount of RAM cannot be upgraded for most seniors so you decide to leave out this option for improving speed.)
2. Create a document that specifies the operating system and explains the utilities you researched and how to use each program. Make sure the document is presented in a style that can be easily read and understood by seniors.

3. Save the document as **C4-Project3-PerformanceUtilities-Your Name**.
4. Submit the document or spreadsheet to your instructor in the manner she or he has requested.

Project 4 Help! My Computer Will Not Start

Individual or Pairs
Deliverable: Flowchart, Table, or Decision Tree in a Document or Presentation

The manager at the IT call center where you work has asked you to prepare a flowchart or decision tree to be used for training new help desk employees on how to question callers to help resolve why their computer is not booting up properly.

1. Research on the Web possible problems with computers that will not boot properly.
2. Develop a progressive list of questions that a person could ask someone on the telephone to help guide him or her to the root of the startup problem. Begin with simple questions that gradually progress to more complex questions. Assume the caller begins with the statement, "*My computer turns on but the screen remains blank.*"
3. Create a document or presentation with a flowchart, table, or decision tree with the questions in the order the help desk specialist should ask callers.
4. Save the document or presentation as **C4-Project4-TroubleshootBoot-Your Name**.
5. Submit the document or presentation to your instructor in the manner she or he has requested.

Project 5 Virtualizing Your Desktop for Students

Pairs or Teams
Deliverable: Presentation including a Video

Your group wants to switch to a cloud operating system as a way to save money on upgrading your PC or Mac. Before you dispense with your comfortable standalone operating system, you decide it would be prudent to learn more about these systems.

1. Research on the Web free cloud operating systems. Choose three services and explore them further to learn as much as you can about how they work.
2. At YouTube, search and watch videos that describe and show the three cloud operating systems functioning on a computer.
3. Within your team, discuss the cloud operating system that you think best meets your needs as a student.
4. Create a presentation that includes a slide describing each cloud operating system, one slide with your team's recommendation and rationale for the recommendation, one slide with the link to the YouTube video that best showcases your team's choice, and one slide with the URLs of the websites you used for this project.
5. Save the presentation as **C4-Project5-CloudOSServices-Your Name**.
6. Submit the presentation to your instructor in the manner she or he has requested.

Project 6 Greener Computing

Individual
Deliverable: Blog Entry

All operating systems provide tools to manage power on your computing device. Changing power options, sleep settings, and adjusting your screen settings can help with conserving energy use. Adjusting power options on your notebook or tablet will help prolong the life of the battery.

1. Learn more about the power options in the operating system on your desktop, notebook, or tablet.
2. Read at least two articles on the Web that recommend the best power settings for your computer.
3. Write and post a blog entry with a summary of what you learned and what you will set your power options to for your computer.
4. Submit your blog URL to your instructor in the manner she or he has requested.

Optional
Read the blog entry for this project of at least two other classmates and post a comment to each. Submit the URLs of your classmates' blogs with Step 4.

Project 7 Ethics Discussion on Copying OS

Team
Deliverable: Document, Blog Entry, or Presentation

At a party recently you overheard your neighbor bragging to someone that she had upgraded her computer to Windows 8 by using her company's site license product key and Windows 8 DVD to install the software on her notebook. She stated that since she often worked at home on her personal time she felt there was nothing wrong with using her company's software and license. She admitted that her work from home involved using documents and spreadsheets that worked fine under Windows 7; however, she wanted the new Windows 8 interface.

1. Within your team discuss the ethics involved in the neighbor's behavior. If the company's site license covers enough installations, is the neighbor justified in installing the software on her personal device? If yes, what should the neighbor do at her workplace to make sure she is acting ethically? If no and if this practice is commonplace, does that make it OK? Would any of your answers change if the neighbor was copying the word processing and spreadsheet applications and not the OS?
2. Prepare a summary of your team's discussion in a document, blog entry, or presentation.
3. Save the document or presentation as **C4-Project7-CopyOSEthics-Your Name**.
4. Submit the document, presentation, or blog entry to your instructor in the manner she or he has requested.

Project 8 Ethics Discussion on Upgrade Resisters

Team
Deliverable: Document, Blog Entry, or Presentation

At your workplace, company training is currently being conducted for all employees on Windows 8. Some employees are resistant to change as they are comfortable with Windows 7 and do not want to upgrade since the new interface is quite different. These resisters are constantly complaining during the training sessions and always finding fault with the trainer's presentations. The mood in the training room is deteriorating. You and a few other colleagues have heard that these employees are telling their managers that the trainer is not competent and that the upgrade to Windows 8 should be delayed as they are not ready for the conversion.

1. Within your team discuss the ethics involved in the resisters' behavior. What should you and your colleagues do? Would it be wise to tell management of their tactics, or should you try to win them over to Windows 8 without turning them in? Would your strategy be different if you work closely with the resisters or if they were in another department? If you decide to win them over, how will you accomplish this if they are so resistant to changing their methods? What role should the trainer be playing in this scenario?
2. Prepare a summary of your team's discussion in a document, blog entry, or presentation.
3. Save the document or presentation as **C4-Project8-Win8ResistorsEthics-Your Name**.
4. Submit the document, presentation, or blog entry to your instructor in the manner she or he has requested.

Chapter 5

Application Software

After successfully completing this chapter, you will be able to:

- Identify productivity application programs used in workplaces
- Distinguish various multimedia applications
- List and explain types of applications used by individuals
- Recognize web-based and open source applications
- Explain how to acquire, install, uninstall, and upgrade software programs
- Describe a mobile application and provide examples of mobile apps

Whether you turn on a computing device for work, for school, for personal tasks, or for entertainment, it is **application software** that you are using. Application software, also called **apps**, are programs used by individuals to carry out tasks or otherwise get things done. For example, if you need to update your budget, you might open a financial program. If you have a photograph with red eye, you might open a graphics editing application to edit the picture. An application exists for just about any purpose. Software is what makes our computers useful to us since it is the programs that provide us with the ability to create, write, calculate, draw, edit, manipulate, and otherwise work with text, graphics, audio, and video.

In Chapter 4 you learned about system software and the role of the operating system to route and manage data between the hardware and the other programs that are running. Once a computer is started and the OS is loaded, you are ready to start the application in which you want to work. In this chapter you will learn about software applications commonly used in the workplace and by individuals. You will also learn how to manage the software on your computing device and survey mobile apps for a smartphone or tablet.

Productivity Applications for the Workplace

Software for the workplace generally includes word processing (working with text), spreadsheets (calculating and managing numbers), presentations (slide shows), and database management (keeping track of data). This group of software programs is referred to as **productivity software** because it is used in the workplace to efficiently perform a wide variety of business-related tasks.

A group of productivity software applications will typically be bundled together in what is called a **software suite** or **productivity suite**. For example, the Microsoft Office Suite includes Microsoft Word for word processing, Microsoft Excel for spreadsheets, Microsoft PowerPoint for presentations, and Microsoft Access for database management. Microsoft's suite is available in several different configurations (called editions) to provide bundles of programs needed in different office environments. Apple computer users have a software suite called iWork that runs on Apple computers.

Regardless of the suite you use, features available for each type of productivity application are generally the same. In this topic, you will learn the basic features and uses for four commonly used productivity applications.

Word Processing

A **word processing application** is software used to create documents containing mostly text, although images are also included to add visual appeal and promote understanding of content. Figure 5.1 presents a cottage rental agreement document in Microsoft Word. Apple's word processor is called Pages. With a word processing program, individuals create a variety of documents such as essays, reports, letters, memos, contracts, brochures, catalogs, menus, newsletters, mailings, labels, articles, blogs, and journals. Features of word processing programs generally include:

- text formatting options to change the typestyle, color, size, and style of text called fonts and font attributes
- bold, underline, italic, and other text effects such as shadow and strikethrough
- spelling and grammar checking as well as synonyms from a thesaurus
- paragraph alignment options, spacing, tabs, indents, borders, and shading
- page numbering, margins, columns, and page breaks for formatting pages
- bulleted or numbered lists, tables, images, charts, and other graphics

Buttons and tools used to format, edit, and manipulate the document layout

Figure 5.1 A word processor is used to create any kind of document that is mostly text such as this cottage rental agreement created in Microsoft Word.

- footnotes, endnotes, captions, and citations
- pre-formatted templates for cover pages, reports, letters, and other documents
- standard documents and labels for a mailing
- collaboration tools such as track changes, comments, share, and compare

Spreadsheet Programs

A software program in which you work primarily with numbers that you organize, calculate, and chart is called a **spreadsheet application**. Data is entered in a worksheet, which is a grid of columns and rows. Each intersection of a column and row is a placeholder for data called a cell and is addressed by the column letter and row number. For example, A1 is the cell for the intersection of column A and row number 1. You perform calculations on values stored in cells that can be simple mathematical operations or complex formula statements for advanced data analysis. Spreadsheets automatically recalculate whenever you change a number. People like to perform "what-if" analysis with spreadsheets, which involves changing a value or formula to see what will happen to another value. For example, you could increase your salary to see how much more money you will have after paying expenses. Spreadsheet programs also have charting capabilities so you can graph the values in a pie or column chart. Figure 5.2 illustrates a worksheet in Microsoft Excel. Apple's spreadsheet program is called Numbers.

Spreadsheets are used for any work that primarily tracks numbers such as budgets, revenue, expenses, asset tracking, inventory control, production control, gradebooks, research data, payroll, billing, costing, estimating, attendance recording, and scheduling. Features of spreadsheet programs generally include:

- pre-programmed functions for advanced formulas such as those used in statistics, finance, math, date, and logic analysis
- formatting options for text and numbers to change typestyle, color, size, alignment, and numeric options
- sorting and filtering options to organize large blocks of data
- various chart styles and options to graph data
- multiple worksheets for grouping, consolidating, and managing data
- shapes and other graphics to enhance a worksheet's appearance
- page layout and format options for printing large worksheets

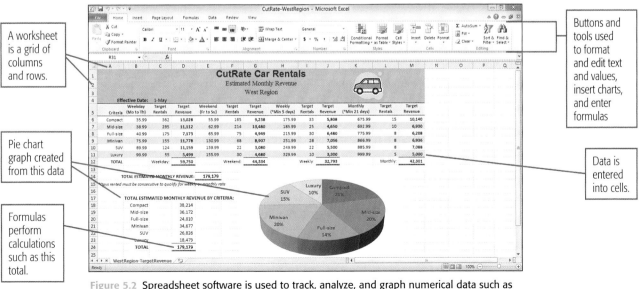

Figure 5.2 Spreadsheet software is used to track, analyze, and graph numerical data such as this car rental pricing worksheet shown in Microsoft Excel.

- tools to perform what-if analysis
- collaboration tools such as track changes, comments, and share

Presentation Software

Slides for an electronic slide show that may be projected on a screen during an oral presentation or on a video display at a self-running kiosk are created in a **presentation application** like Microsoft's PowerPoint or Apple's Keynote. Presentation software helps you organize, describe, and explain key points, facts, figures, messages, or ideas. Slides can have images, audio, and video as well as text to provide a dynamic presentation experience. Figure 5.3 shows a group of slides in a presentation created with Microsoft PowerPoint. Features of spreadsheet programs generally include:

- several slide layouts for arrangement of titles and content
- predesigned presentation designs and themes for backgrounds, colors, fonts, and effects
- formatting options to change typestyle, color, size, and alignment of content
- pictures, clipart, photos, shapes, charts, tables, and other graphics
- sound and video media options
- slide transition and animation schemes to enhance presentations
- options for customizing presentation slide shows
- collaboration tools such as track changes, comments, and share

Figure 5.3 Presentation software such as Microsoft PowerPoint is used to create a series of slides that are presented in a slide show.

Database Management Software

A **database management application** is a software program that organizes and keeps track of large amounts of data. The data is stored in such a way that information can be extracted in useful lists and reports. For example, a manager could request a list of all customers residing in a certain ZIP code, or all employees with no absences. With database software you set up the structure for storing data, input and maintain the data, and produce lists and reports to serve a variety of purposes. Businesses use databases to keep track of data such as customers, patients, clients, vendors, employees, products, inventory, assets, contacts, claims, equipment, and service records. Any data that needs to be organized and stored can be set up in a database. Figure 5.4 illustrates a database created in Microsoft Access to keep track of computer service work orders. Features of database applications generally include:

- tables for designing the structure of data in columns (called fields) and rows (called records)
- forms for entering and maintaining data in a user-friendly interface
- queries for extracting and displaying data by criteria
- reports for printing or displaying data with rich text formatting options
- the ability to join related tables for queries and reports that extract data from multiple objects

Did You Know?

In July 2012, Kurt DelBene, president of the Microsoft Office Division, announced at a worldwide partner conference that Microsoft Office was deployed on more than 1 billion users' desktops worldwide!

A database is composed of a series of tables, queries, forms, and report objects.

Each column in a table is called a field.

Buttons and tools used to create objects, format text, and perform database commands

Each row in a table is called a record.

Figure 5.4 Database management software helps a business track and organize data such as this computer service database shown in Microsoft Access.

Microsoft also publishes a version of Office designed for Mac computers. Alternatives to Microsoft Office and Apple iWork include OpenOffice, a free productivity suite made available by the open source community, and web-based productivity software offered by cloud providers such as Google and Zoho. These applications are introduced in a later topic.

EXPLORE FURTHER

Corel WordPerfect Office versus Microsoft Office

Corel is a software company that publishes the WordPerfect Office Productivity suite. How does WordPerfect Office compare to Microsoft's suite?

1. Research the features in the most recent professional editions of the Office suite offered by Corel and Microsoft. Find out what applications are included and the price for each suite.
2. Create a table in a document or spreadsheet that compares the features of the two productivity suites and the price for each. Below the table indicate which suite you think offers the better deal and give your reasons.
3. Save the document or spreadsheet as **C5-Apps-CorelvsOffice-Your Name**.
4. Submit the document or spreadsheet to your instructor in the manner she or he has requested.

Other Workplace-Oriented Productivity Applications

Businesses need applications beyond the basic word processing, spreadsheet, presentation, and database management programs. Software applications to manage communications, calendars, contacts, financial information, projects, and documents are also used. In some industries, specialized software is designed to complete tasks unique to the industry, and large companies use enterprise-wide software programs to manage large-scale operations. In this topic, you will be introduced to a sampling of other types of applications found in a workplace.

Personal Information Management Software

Managing one's messages, schedule, contacts, and tasks can be onerous with the volume of emails, appointments, contacts, and to-do lists a typical worker encounters. **Personal information management (PIM) software** helps you organize this type of information. Reminders and flags help you remember and follow up on important emails, appointments, events, or tasks. Figure 5.5 displays the Calendar in Microsoft Outlook. Microsoft Outlook is part of the Microsoft Office suite. Outlook can be used by individuals at home to manage personal information or, when Outlook is used in a workplace, an Exchange server allows you to send and track meeting requests and tasks to other employees. Lotus Notes by IBM is another PIM application. Apple devices include iCal, Contacts, and Mail programs. PIM apps are also included on smartphones. Syncing of calendars, contacts, and emails on multiple devices is important so that you have access to the latest information wherever you may be. Some PIMs also provide the ability to share your calendar or contact information with other people outside your workplace.

Buttons and tools used to create, navigate, arrange, and manage Outlook items

The day's appointments are displayed with the outstanding tasks shown below the schedule.

Navigate to e-mails, calendar, contacts, or tasks with these buttons.

Figure 5.5 Microsoft Outlook is an application in which you can manage messages, schedules, contacts, and tasks. Here, the Calendar is displayed in Day view with tasks displayed below the day's appointments.

Accounting Software

All businesses need an **accounting software application** to record and report financial information related to assets, liabilities, equity, revenue, and expenses. These programs provide the basis for financial reporting and tax calculations. Accounting software is generally organized by accounting activity such as invoicing, purchasing, inventory, payroll, banking, paying bills, receiving payments, and processing memos. Accounting programs also support costing and estimating features for customer and vendor-related functions. Several accounting software programs are designed for small, medium, and large businesses. Figure 5.6 shows the home screen for QuickBooks, an accounting program used by many small businesses.

In QuickBooks use the menu system, buttons on the toolbar, or icons to open forms in which you enter financial transactions or display reports.

Figure 5.6 QuickBooks is a popular accounting software application for recording and reporting the financial activities for a business.

Project Management Software

Large projects that need several resources and are to be completed on a schedule and within a budget are often managed using **project management software**. Project management software such as Microsoft Project shown in Figure 5.7 allows you to enter all of the tasks needed to get a project done, establish time frames, assign resources, and allocate budget money to each task. Once the project is created, the program develops a project schedule and shows you interdependencies between tasks. A typical way to display a schedule is in a Gantt chart, which plots tasks in time lines as shown in Figure 5.7. Maintaining the data also allows you to view the impact on the schedule or budget if changes are made to tasks, resources, or time lines. Several project management software programs are available including the popular web-based application called Basecamp.

The project schedule is shown as a Gantt chart.

A project's tasks, durations, and dependencies are entered here to create a project schedule.

Figure 5.7 With project management software such as Microsoft Project you can manage a project's schedule, resources, and budget to finish on time and within budget.

Document Management Software

A **document management system (DMS)** is a program that manages the creation, storage, retrieval, history, and eventual disposal of information stored in a central repository. Paper documents are scanned, coded or tagged, and stored electronically in the DMS. DMS programs provide advanced search tools for retrieval as well as sharing of documents. A document's life cycle is managed through the DMS, and all documents are stored in a common file format such as PDF. DMS systems use secure servers and controlled access to ensure privacy and security. Some industries, such as the legal industry, use DMS systems to manage the thousands of documents that are exchanged between lawyers in litigation cases. A DMS is the cornerstone of a paperless office. The DMS called Dokmee is shown in Figure 5.8.

All documents are stored electronically in a DMS.

Search tools for finding electronic documents

Figure 5.8 Companies use Document Management Software such as Dokmee to electronically manage all documents, including paper documents that are scanned, coded, and stored on central servers.

Other Specialized Software

Industries such as automotive, construction, manufacturing, and engineering firms use industry-specific software such as computer-aided design (CAD) or computer-aided manufacturing (CAM) programs to create complex designs and drawings. Medical establishments use medical software programs to track patient records, billings, and insurance claims. Hotels and travel agencies use programs to manage bookings, guests, and resources. These are just a few examples of industry-specific software applications.

Large companies, referred to as enterprises, have higher-level needs to manage the multitude of activities and processes involved in transactions with customers, vendors, inventories, and human resources. These companies often use a category of software called **enterprise resource planning (ERP)**, which is a software solution designed for large-scale organizations. Companies such as SAP and Oracle provide ERP software for these environments, which often involve extensive customization, training, and support.

Career Connection

Project Management Skills in Demand for All Sectors

Any organization that launches a large project involving many resources and multiple teams needs to have a skilled project manager to keep the project on time and on budget. According to WANTED Analytics (a company that provides business intelligence for talent supply and demand), in May 2012 there were more than 235,000 online job listings that included a need for project management skills. The Project Management Professional (PMP) certification is recognized by industry as providing evidence of one's competency to lead large project teams. Consider investigating what it takes to be a project manager if you like to be well-organized, lead groups of diverse teams, and have excellent communication skills.

EXPLORE FURTHER

Which industry-specific software will you use?

Chances are industry-specific software is used in your field of study. For example, contractors use materials and labor estimating software, restaurants use meal service software, and airlines use reservation systems. What industry-specific software will you be required to use in your future career?

1. Research industry-specific software applications used in your field of study. If possible, interview someone who works in your field and ask him or her to describe specialized software used in the workplace.
2. Create a document that describes the software applications used in your field and how they are used to track, manage, and report information.
3. Save the document as **C5-Apps-IndustrySpecificSoftware-Your Name**.
4. Submit the document to your instructor in the manner she or he has requested.

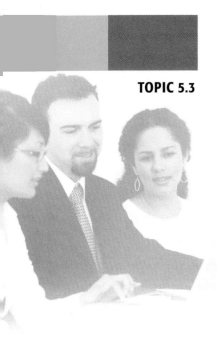

Applications for Working with Graphics, Multimedia, and the Web

TOPIC 5.3

Software programs for creating, editing, and manipulating drawings, photos, clip art, and scanned images are called **graphics software**. **Desktop publishing software** is an application that incorporates text, graphics, and the use of colors for creating high-quality documents for marketing, communication, or other commercial purposes. **Multimedia software** includes programs that use text and images with video, audio, and animations to create engaging and interactive applications that market products or services, educate, or entertain users. **Web authoring software** is a program designed to create content to be provided over the Internet.

In this topic you will be introduced to applications used by businesses and individuals to work with graphics, audio, video, animations, and for creating web pages.

Graphics Software

Graphic artists, illustrators, photographers, and other professionals use specialized software to create and edit images. Painting and drawing programs provide tools for artists to draw pictures, shapes, and other images to which they can add special effects. Adobe Illustrator is an example of a graphics program used to create, edit, and manipulate illustrations.

Photo editing software is used by photographers and others to edit pictures and add special effects and text to pictures taken with a digital camera. Adobe Photoshop is a popular choice for editing photos by professionals and individuals. Tools are available in Photoshop to crop out unwanted portions of a picture, remove red eye, retouch areas, correct color brightness and contrast, add text, add special effects, and even add in a person or object copied from another photo. Figure 5.9 shows an artistic filter effect applied to a photo using Adobe Photoshop.

Figure 5.9 An artistic filter effect called Poster Edges is applied to a picture in Adobe Photoshop.

Desktop Publishing Software

Although word processing software provides tools to arrange text and graphics in a document, these programs do not let you precisely position objects and control text flow around objects. For professional publications, desktop publishing (DTP) software is used for producing a print-based document such as a corporate newsletter, annual report, price list, restaurant menu, catalog, brochure, or book. Programs such as Adobe's InDesign or Microsoft's Publisher are popular choices for advanced page layout. DTP programs use rulers, grids, and guides as well as other tools and features that allow DTP professionals to precisely place text and graphics on a page. In addition, the software provides more control over spacing between and around objects and text, and a wider range of fonts, sizes, and colors for text formatting. Figure 5.10 illustrates a newsletter in Adobe's InDesign application.

Figure 5.10 Adobe's InDesign application is used by desktop publishers to do page layout for professional publications such as this technical newsletter.

Multimedia Software

For content delivered via the Web or distributed on CD, DVD, or Blu-ray discs, multimedia programs are used by professionals to create animations, add audio and video, and author multimedia applications. **Animation software** is used to create images or objects that have movement or otherwise interact with users. Adobe's Flash application is often used to create interactive applications delivered over the Web. In Flash, the designer works with a time line and a stage in which text, graphics, and other objects are placed in the sequence for which the movement or interaction is to occur.

Video editing software such as Apple's Final Cut Pro (Figure 5.11) or Adobe's Premiere Elements provides tools to create videos referred to as clips. Video shot with a camcorder can be manipulated by cutting, adding, or moving scenes, creating split screens, or adding music, audio effects, or text for titles or credits. Some audio editing capability generally is also included as well as the capability to organize content on DVD and Blu-ray discs. For example, video editing programs also create the menus and burn the content to a DVD or Blu-ray disc. **Audio recording and editing software** such as free, open source Audacity or Adobe's Audition include tools for recording and editing music, sound clips, and podcasts (audio clips posted on the Web).

Other multimedia applications capture screen images and computer activity for creating training segments and demonstrations.

Figure 5.11 Apple's Final Cut Pro video editing software is a package used by some professional multimedia producers.

Web Authoring Software

Web authoring programs such as Adobe's Dreamweaver and Microsoft's Expression Web are two applications used to create and maintain today's interactive websites. Web pages are stored in programming code that is interpreted by browsers. Web authoring software provides tools for individuals to create and manage all of the pages and external resources for a website by working in either Design view or Code view. Non-programmers can create a web page in Design view and let the software generate the programming code needed for browsers. Experienced web developers can choose to work in Code view and often switch between views as pages are fine-tuned. Figure 5.12 is a web page with a reservation form with Design view and Code view shown side by side in Adobe Dreamweaver.

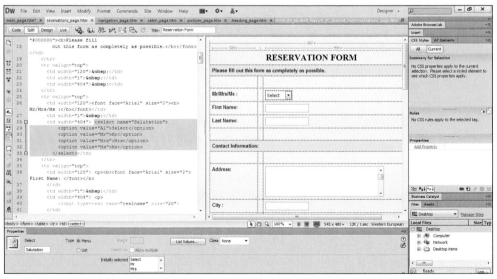

Figure 5.12 A reservation form for a website created in Adobe's Dreamweaver software is shown with Design view and Code view displayed.

Multimedia for the Non-Professional

A variety of graphics and multimedia programs are available to meet the needs of both professional and non-professional users. The Adobe and Apple programs showcased in this topic are more expensive software programs geared toward professionals or hobby enthusiasts. Less expensive or free programs are used by non-professionals or individuals who want to work with multimedia at home. For example, Windows Live Essentials is a free suite offered to Windows users that includes a program to work with video (Windows Live Movie Maker) and photos (Windows Live Photo Gallery). The Windows OS also includes programs for drawing (Windows Paint) and recording sound (Windows Sound Recorder). In Figure 5.13, a photograph's color is shown being adjusted using Windows Live Photo Gallery. Apple devices are packaged with the iLife suite that includes iPhoto, iMovie, and GarageBand for working with photos, video, and audio.

Check This Out

www.windows.microsoft. com/en-US/windows-live/ essentials-home

Go here to download Windows Live Essentials for free.

Figure 5.13 A photo's color is adjusted using Windows Live Photo Gallery, part of the free Windows Live Essentials suite from Microsoft.

EXPLORE FURTHER

Are you a skilled photo editor?

Web-based photo editing software programs allow you to edit photos without downloading and installing software on your computer. Tools may vary between services, but each offers a basic set of tools that do an adequate job for non-professionals.

1. Do a search for free online image editing programs and choose one with which to experiment for this activity.

2. Take a picture with a digital camera of something related to your field of study. For example, take a picture of a park if you are going to be a landscape designer or a house if you are going to work in construction. Upload the photo to the image editing website and experiment with the software's editing tools to edit the image. For example, crop out a part of the picture, change the color, retouch the photo, add shapes, special effects, text, and so on.

3. Save the revised image as **C5-Apps-EditedPhoto-Your Name**.

4. Submit the original photo and the edited photo to your instructor in the manner she or he has requested.

TOPIC 5.4

Software Applications for Personal Use

Software programs for personal use include a wide range of applications that cover every hobby, interest, and need. For example, you can install software to help you manage personal notes, ideas, and thoughts at work, at school, or at home, manage your personal finances, prepare tax returns, play games, design a garden, and create a genealogy map. Programs help you organize recipes and plan trips as well as educate and provide reference information. In this topic you will survey a variety of applications for personal use.

Note-Taking Software

While in meetings, classes, or at home you often need a place to record notes, thoughts, or ideas. **Note-taking software** such as Microsoft's OneNote (Figure 5.14) is used to store, organize, search, and share notes of any type. Notes can be entered by clicking anywhere on the screen and typing or writing by hand using a stylus. Documents, audio, video, images, emails, appointments, contacts, and web links can be attached to a note to collect everything related to a topic in one place. You can organize notes into notebooks and tabs and use search and share tools.

Organize notes into tabs.

Text is typed free-form and can be marked up with highlight or drawing tools. You can click anywhere on the page and start typing.

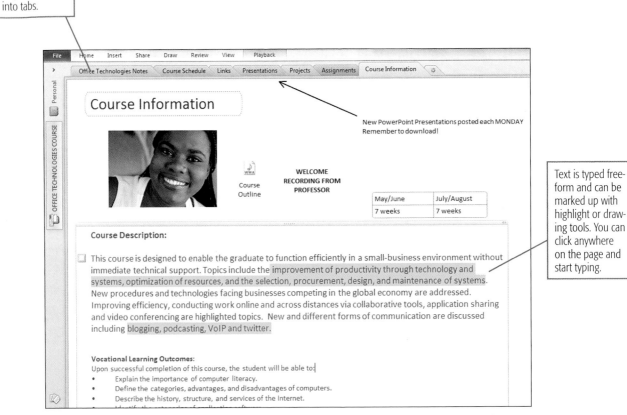

Figure 5.14 Microsoft's OneNote application is a useful tool to organize notes on any topic related to school, work, or home.

Software to Manage Personal Finances and Taxes

Keeping track of a checking or savings account and personal investments is accomplished with **personal finance software**. Most personal finance software programs allow you to download activity from your banking account directly into the personal finance program. You can balance your checking account, analyze home expenses, and track investments. Quicken is a popular program used for managing finances.

Tax preparation software guides you through the completion of the complex forms required to file your income taxes with the government. These programs generally estimate your tax bill using an interview-style series of questions and input boxes. Programs generally alert you to missing information and/or deductions that can help minimize taxes. Tax forms can be printed or, with some programs, filed with the government electronically.

Personal finance and tax preparation software help you manage your money.

Legal Software

Legal software such as Quicken's WillMaker, MyAttorney, or Family Lawyer help you prepare legal documents such as wills, contracts, leases, loan agreements, and living trusts. Standard contracts and other legal documents are provided that you customize for your purposes through a series of questions, forms, or dialog boxes that prompt you for input.

Legal software programs help individuals create legal documents such as this contract.

Hobby Software

Software applications for creating a family tree; scrapbooking; planning trips; managing recipes and meal planning; designing homes, decks, and gardens; and creating and printing custom greeting cards are just a few **hobby software applications** you can use to pursue your favorite leisure activities.

Entertainment and Games

Entertainment software includes programs for playing interactive games and videos. Some games are designed to be played individually while others involve subscribing to online services where you can join hundreds of thousands of other game enthusiasts and play against others online. For example, with more than 10 million subscribers, World of Warcraft (WoW) is a highly successful online multiplayer role-playing game.

Software is available to help individuals with just about any hobby imaginable.

Angry Birds is an example of entertainment software that is available in multiple versions.

Games are often available in multiple versions such as an edition for a PC, a version that can be played online through a browser, or as a smaller app for downloading to a smartphone. Angry Birds is one example of a game that is available in all of these flavors.

Education and Reference

Educational software designed for children and adults to learn about subjects such as math, spelling, grammar, geography, and history are available as interactive references or games. You can also find software to help you learn a foreign language and teach you how to type. **Reference software** programs use multimedia tools to provide rich content information in encyclopedias, dictionaries, translation guides, atlases, and other reference resources.

If you have an interest or a hobby that has not been mentioned here, chances are that a software program has been created that is related to your area of interest. Use the Web to search for an application if you have not already found one.

Education and reference software use multimedia to help with understanding complex information.

Be Cautious with Free Software!

The lure of free software can be enticing. Be cautious with offers found on the Internet for free software of any type but especially those that offer to manage personal finances for free. Read the details including the fine print before downloading or submitting your email address or any other personal information to obtain free software. Often these programs are used to collect personal information for resale or they may contain malicious code such as viruses.

Blog Topic

What is your favorite game?

Do you play Facebook games? If yes, which game is your favorite? Do you play other games online? If yes, which game do you find most challenging? Most relaxing? How much time per week do you spend playing games?

1. Write and post a blog entry with your answers to the above questions. If you do not play computer games, ask someone you know who does to describe a favorite game for you.

2. Read at least two of your classmates' blog entries and post one comment to each.

3. Submit your blog URL and the URLs of the two classmates' blogs to your instructor in the manner she or he has requested.

EXPLORE   FURTHER

Survey note-taking software

The ability to organize, store, sort, and search notes electronically can save you time finding information. Is there a free note-taking software application that you might like to use?

1. Search for free note-taking software reviews and read at least two articles.

2. Decide on one program that you think would work best for you as a note-taking application. Consider the program's features and ease of use while considering your preference.

3. Create a document that describes the note-taking application you selected and give your reasons. Include the URLs of the articles you read for this topic.

4. Save the document as **C5-Apps-NoteTakingSoftware-Your Name**.

5. Submit the document to your instructor in the manner she or he has requested.

TOPIC 5.5

Cloud and Open Source Applications

In Chapter 1 you were introduced to Cloud Computing and the SaaS delivery model for software applications. Recall that SaaS stands for software-as-a-service and means that the software you are using is not installed on your computing device. SaaS applications are hosted by a third party and made available to you from a web browser. Open source programs are often provided for free, meaning that one can download and install the software on a computer without paying a license fee. In this topic you will survey three web-based and three open source software alternatives for productivity applications.

Web-Based Productivity Applications

The main advantage to using web-based applications is that you have access to the software application and your documents from any location at which you have an Internet connection. Table 5.1 provides a summary of three popular web-based productivity application alternatives. If you decide to use a cloud application, consider spending time working with a few different suites until you find the one with the features and interface that works best for you. In Figure 5.15 the same text is shown in the word processing application from each of the three providers summarized in Table 5.1.

Table 5.1	Summary of Three Popular Web-Based Productivity Applications		
Criterion	**Google Drive**	**Microsoft Web Apps**	**Zoho**
Free storage offered at time of writing	5 GB	7 GB	1 GB
Applications	Documents Spreadsheets Presentations Drawings	Word Excel PowerPoint OneNote	Calendar Notebook Planner Sheet (Spreadsheet) Show (Presentation) Writer (Word Processor) Plus several apps for collaboration and business processes
URL and sign-in for applications	google.com Sign in with your Gmail account, then click Documents.	skydrive.live.com Sign in with your Windows Live ID, then click the icon for Word, Excel, PowerPoint, or OneNote.	zoho.com Sign in with your Zoho account, then click the Application you want to work in (you may need to scroll down the page to see the list of applications).

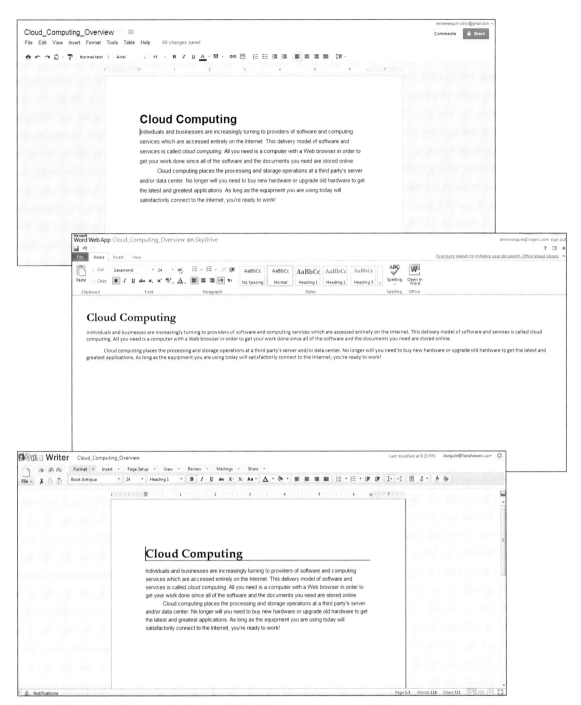

Figure 5.15 Each web-based application is slightly different as shown here with the same text formatted in Google's (top), Microsoft's (middle), and Zoho's (bottom) cloud word processor.

Open Source Applications

www.openoffice.org

Go here to learn more about OpenOffice.

Apache OpenOffice is a free productivity suite that includes word processor, spreadsheet, presentation, graphics, and database programs. OpenOffice is a project of The Apache Software Foundation that provides support for open source software initiatives. In Figure 5.16 you see the opening screen of OpenOffice, which lists the available applications and the window for OpenOffice.org Writer. The interface for OpenOffice is intuitive for people who have experience with Microsoft Word 2003 and earlier versions (before the ribbon interface). OpenOffice is updated and maintained by volunteers.

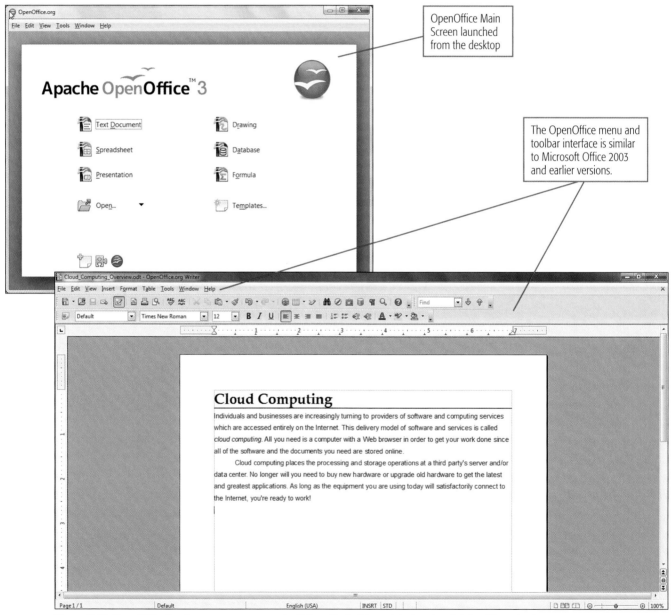

Figure 5.16 OpenOffice is a free open-source productivity suite that is updated and maintained by volunteers.

OpenOffice has been modified and packaged under the name Lotus Symphony offered by IBM at ibm.com/software/lotus/symphony. Lotus Symphony includes documents, presentations, and spreadsheets in a free download.

Another free open-source productivity suite is LibreOffice. LibreOffice runs on Windows, Macintosh, and Linux computers and includes the applications Writer, Calc, Impress, Draw, and Base. LibreOffice is a project of The Document Foundation.

Several other web-based and open source applications are available. Consider searching for a free cloud or open source application the next time you need to acquire new software for your computing device.

Check This Out

www.libreoffice.org

Go here to learn more about LibreOffice.

EXPLORE FURTHER

Discover Zoho

Zoho is a popular web-based applications provider with several programs beyond the standard word processor, spreadsheet, and presentation software. Try out Zoho and compare it to what you are using now for productivity applications. *Note: If you are already a Zoho user, complete this activity using another web-based productivity application.*

1. Go to zoho.com, sign up, and activate a free account.

2. Once signed in, launch one of the productivity applications that you want to use for your comparison. Experiment with the program to see how it works and the features that are available. For example, enter some sample text and try formatting options and spell check features.

3. Create a document that compares your Zoho experience with the equivalent productivity application that you normally use. Consider doing the comparison in a table or chart to compare each program that you tested feature by feature.

4. Save the document or spreadsheet as **C5-Apps-ZohoComparison-Your Name**.

5. Submit the document or spreadsheet to your instructor in the manner she or he has requested.

TOPIC 5.6

Acquiring, Installing, Uninstalling, and Upgrading Software

Software applications can be acquired in various ways such as purchasing an application from a retailer either in the store or online, buying directly from the publisher, or buying from software download websites such as Tucows where people look for software that is low cost or free (Figure 5.17). Software is a licensed product, meaning that when you install software you have paid for the right to use the product while ownership remains with the publisher that created the software. In this topic you will learn the various models for distributing software and the general steps that you take to install, uninstall, or upgrade an application.

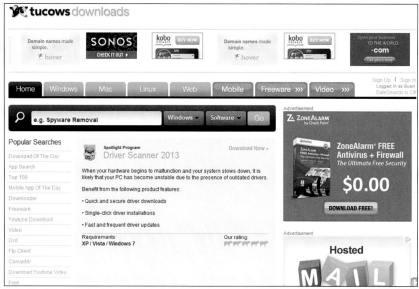

Figure 5.17 Tucows downloads has been a popular site for finding low-cost and free software since 1994.

Software Distribution Models

Traditional software suites like Microsoft Office or Adobe Creative Suite can be purchased as **packaged software** at a retailer's store or from several e-commerce websites. You can also buy the software online directly from the company that published it. Pricing for software suites can vary, so it is wise to check out a few options before making a purchase.

Other ways to acquire software include the following:

■ **Shareware** software is available to download for a free trial period. Once the trial period expires, you need to pay a fee to the software publisher to unlock the application. Other forms of shareware continue to work beyond the trial period but generally have features made inaccessible until the fee payment is made.

■ **Freeware** software can be downloaded and installed at no cost and without restrictions. An example of a popular freeware program is Apple's iTunes.

■ Open source software is generally available for free and downloaded from a website.

■ **Subscription software** is purchased from cloud computing providers who generally charge a monthly fee per user for access to the provider's software and storage services. Fees vary based on the number of users and the amount of storage space required.

Did You Know ?

You should check the system requirements before paying for packaged software to make sure the software will work with your PC's hardware and with your OS. Software packages that have been opened are generally not returnable.

Installing Software

When you buy packaged software at a retail store, you receive a DVD inside the package. Insert the DVD into the appropriate drive on your computing device and the software will automatically begin the installation process. Follow the prompts that appear to complete the installation routine.

If you have downloaded software from a website, you generally have two methods for installing the software:

Packaged software purchased at a retailer generally includes a DVD that you use to install the software.

- You can opt to run the installation program directly from the website. After clicking the download link, you'll be presented with the option to Run or Save the installation file. Click Run to run the program directly from the source website and then follow the prompts that appear. In the Windows OS you will be prompted with a security warning message and will have to allow the installation to proceed.

- Alternatively, you may opt to save the downloaded file to your hard drive and run the installation later. After clicking the download link, select the option to Save or to Save As and navigate to the drive and folder in which to store the file. When the download is complete, open the window that you use to view files and display the location where you saved the downloaded file name. Double-click the file name to start the installation routine (Figure 5.18). Follow the prompts that appear. In the Windows OS you need to

Software installers generally provide a series of prompts in dialog boxes to guide you through the installation process.

Figure 5.18 Installing software you have downloaded generally involves proceeding through an installer wizard that prompts you along the way.

click the option to allow the installation to proceed at the security warning message. Generally, you choose this method if you want to make sure you have the software program's installation file saved in case you need to reinstall it again at a later date.

Software License Agreements When you install software you are required to accept a license agreement (unless the software product is open source) similar to the one shown in Figure 5.19. License agreements, called **Software License Agreements (SLAs)** or **End User License Agreements (EULAs)**, vary by software publisher. Although the terms and conditions are generally long and filled with legal terminology, you

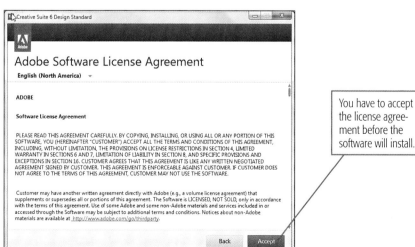

You have to accept the license agreement before the software will install.

Figure 5.19 Proprietary software such as Adobe requires that you accept a license agreement for the software installation to proceed.

should read the agreement and not just blindly click I accept/I agree to move on. The SLA or EULA specifies the number of computers upon which you can legally install the software. For example, some publishers will allow installation on up to three computers while others may restrict you to one.

Download Beware!

Exercise caution at software review websites that provide links to download free software. Many of these sites have ads that look deceptively similar to the actual download link you are supposed to click. Clicking the ad by mistake means you often end up with other software on your PC that you do not want and that is difficult to remove completely. To be safe, download a program from the actual company's website to make sure you are getting only the software you want and the latest release.

Uninstalling Software

If you have installed a software application that you no longer use, uninstall the program from the hard drive to free up resources. To do this on a Windows-compatible computer, open the Control Panel and click the link to Uninstall a Program in the Programs category (Figure 5.20). At the Programs and Features window, click to select the program you want to remove in the list of software applications and then click the Uninstall button. An uninstall routine will automatically run. Close the Control Panel when finished. In some cases, programs are not completely removed until you restart your computer.

On a Mac computer, you uninstall an application by finding the application icon (in the Finder window) and dragging the icon to the Trash. The icon is a shortcut to the program's installation bundle, which includes all related program files. To remove a program's shortcut icon from the dock, simply drag the icon off the dock.

Figure 5.20 Open the Control Panel on a Windows-compatible computer and click Uninstall a program to open the Programs and Features window and remove software you no longer want.

Upgrading Software

Upgrading software simply means installing a newer version of a program you are already licensed to use (not to be confused with updating, which simply installs fixes or patches to the existing version). Usually, when you install an upgrade, the older version is replaced; however, in some applications, you can opt to keep the older version and the newer version on the same computer. Some software applications prompt you when an upgrade is available, and clicking the prompt will take you to the website where you can download the newer version (Figure 5.21). Some upgrades are free, while others require payment for the upgrade at a price lower than the original purchase. Registering software when you buy it is a good idea so that you are notified of upgrades and qualify for reduced pricing.

⚠ A new version of AnyDVD is available! ✕
Your current Version: 7.0.4.0
New version available for download: 7.0.6.0

Click here to visit the SlySoft download page!

Figure 5.21 Software usually installs with a setting that checks automatically for newer versions and prompts you to download the upgrade when it becomes available.

Blog Topic

Why pay for software?

As you have learned in this chapter, there are several alternatives to paying for a software license for a traditional packaged suite like Microsoft Office. Despite these free alternatives, software suites like Microsoft Office have loyal supporters that consistently buy upgrades. Why do you think people pay for software? What benefits do paying customers receive that users of freeware do not?

1. Write and post a blog entry with your thoughts on why people prefer to pay for software like Microsoft Office instead of using OpenOffice or free web-based applications.

2. Read at least two of your classmates' blog entries and post one comment to each.

3. Submit your blog URL and the URLs of the two classmates' blogs to your instructor in the manner she or he has requested.

EXPLORE FURTHER

EULAs for Retail Editions of MS Office and Apple Software

Do you know the usage rights in the Microsoft Office retail edition EULA? For example, if you purchased the Home and Student edition of Microsoft Office, can you legally install the software on more than one computer? Does Apple's SLA have the same terms and conditions as Microsoft?

1. On your home computer in the Help screen of Microsoft Word or at microsoft.com, find and read the software license terms section titled *Installation and Use Rights*. Next, find the application software license agreement for Pages at apple.com. Read the section titled *Permitted License Uses and Restrictions*.

2. Compare and contrast the two license agreements. Are they the same or do they specify different terms? How do the two license agreements vary for the specified sections?

3. Create a document with a brief summary in your own words of the specified sections and your answers to the above questions.

4. Save the document as **C5-Apps-MSandAppleEULAs-Your Name**.

5. Submit the document to your instructor in the manner she or he has requested.

TOPIC 5.7

Mobile Apps

Mobile devices such as smartphones require a different edition of software that is designed specifically for mobile use. These programs are **mobile applications**, or more generally referred to as *apps*. Apps are designed to work on smaller screens and accept touch input from finger gestures. Functionality for on-screen keyboards, handwriting recognition, and speech recognition capabilities are also part of app design. Other important features include compatibility and synchronization with PC software and sharing information from the smartphone with other programs and users.

Apps by the thousands are available for Android, Apple, BlackBerry, and Windows devices for just about any type of task you can imagine. For example, built-in or downloadable apps are available for mail, scheduling, contacts, maps, GPS, weather, news, travel, games, mobile banking, calculators, currency conversion, messaging, and connecting with social media such as Facebook and Twitter. These are just a few of the categories of apps you will find at the Android, Apple, BlackBerry, and Windows Phone stores (Figure 5.22). In this topic you will survey a sampling of built-in and productivity apps for mobile devices.

Figure 5.22 Apps for smartphones are downloaded from app stores such as Windows Phone Marketplace shown here. New apps are added frequently, with many offered for free or at a low cost.

Built-in Apps

Apple, Android, BlackBerry, and Windows smartphones and tablets come equipped with several built-in apps such as the ones shown on the iPhone 4 in Figure 5.23. Typically, personal information management apps for keeping track of appointments, contacts, to-do lists, reminders, and notes are standard as well as apps for mail, messaging, maps, music, and games.

Figure 5.23 Smartphones and tablets come equipped with several built-in apps such as the ones shown here that are included with Apple's iPhone4.

Mobile Productivity Apps

Microsoft Office Mobile has Word, Excel, PowerPoint, and OneNote editions designed for a smartphone. You can review, edit, and sync documents to and from email, SkyDrive, Sharepoint, or other web-based services. Apple's iWork for iOS is the mobile edition of Pages, Keynote, and Numbers. Zoho provides mobile editions of Mail, Calendar, Creator, Writer, Sheet, and Show at m.zoho.com. Google Mobile is a suite of productivity apps for Android devices. Figure 5.24 shows the app screen for Excel Mobile and Zoho Mobile Writer.

Figure 5.24 Microsoft Excel Mobile (left) and Zoho Writer Mobile (right) allow you to view, edit, and create spreadsheets and documents on your smartphone.

 Blog Topic

My Favorite App

What is your favorite smartphone or tablet app? Why? How often do you use the app in a typical day?

1. Write and post a blog entry that describes your favorite app, why it is your favorite, and how often you use it in a typical day.

2. Read at least two of your classmates' blog entries and post one comment to each.

3. Submit your blog URL and the URLs of the two classmates' blogs to your instructor in the manner she or he has requested.

Did You Know?

Quickoffice, a mobile productivity suite with Quickword, Quicksheet, and Quickpoint apps that are compatible with Google Docs and Microsoft Office, was acquired by Google in June 2012. Watch for changes to Quickoffice that involve rebranding within Google Apps.

EXPLORE FURTHER

Popular Apps for Android, Apple, BlackBerry, or Windows Devices

With thousands of apps available for mobile devices, finding the most useful apps for one's smartphone or tablet might not be an easy task.

1. Find and read at least two articles that rate the top five apps for an Android, Apple, BlackBerry, or Windows mobile device.

2. Create a presentation that describes the five apps (one app per slide) you found most interesting. Include a sixth slide with the URLs of the articles you used.

3. Save the presentation as **C5-Apps-Top5Mobile-Your Name**.

4. Submit the presentation to your instructor in the manner she or he has requested.

Concepts Review

Topic	Key Concepts	Key Terms
Productivity Applications for the Workplace	Application software, or apps, are programs used by individuals to carry out tasks or otherwise get things done.	Application software
	A productivity suite generally includes a word processor, spreadsheet program, presentations program, and database management program.	Apps
		Productivity software
	The Microsoft Office suite includes Microsoft Word, Microsoft Excel, Microsoft PowerPoint, and Microsoft Access.	Software suite
		Productivity suite
	A word processing program is used to create, edit, and format documents that are mostly text.	Word processing application
	Spreadsheet applications are used to organize, calculate, edit, format, and chart numbers that are entered in cells within a worksheet grid of columns and rows.	Spreadsheet application
		Presentation application
	Spreadsheets are often used to perform what-if analysis where a value is changed to view the impact on other values.	Database management application
	Presentation software is used to create slides for an electronic slide show that communicate key points, facts, figures, messages, or other ideas.	
	Large amounts of data are organized, stored, and maintained in software called database management applications.	
	In database software you set up the structure to store data, input data, maintain data, and produce lists and reports for various purposes.	
	Microsoft publishes a productivity suite used on Apple computers.	
Other Workplace-Oriented Productivity Applications	Personal information management (PIM) software is used to organize emails, appointments, contacts, and to-do lists.	Personal information management (PIM) software
	Accounting software applications are used to record and report the financial activities of a business related to assets, liabilities, equity, revenue, and expenses.	Accounting software application
	A business will use project management software to create and maintain a project schedule and budget.	Project management software
	Document management software is used for managing the storage, retrieval, history, and eventual disposal of documents stored in a central repository.	Document management system (DMS)
	Industry-specific software applications are programs used to perform tasks unique to a specific business environment.	Enterprise resource planning (ERP)
	Enterprise resource planning (ERP) software is designed to support large-scale operations with higher level needs.	

continued....

Applications for Working with Graphics, Multimedia, and the Web	Painting and drawing software provides tools for artists to create, edit, and apply special effects to pictures, shapes, or other images.	Graphics software
	Photo editing software is used to edit pictures and add special effects and text.	Desktop publishing software
	Desktop publishing (DTP) software provides tools to place text and graphics on a page with more control over spacing and a wider range of fonts, sizes, and colors for professional publications.	Multimedia software
		Web authoring software
		Photo editing software
	Animation software applications allow a multimedia professional to create images with movement or otherwise interact with users.	Animation software
		Video editing software
	Video editing software is used to manipulate video recorded with a camcorder and add music, audio effects, and text to create videos called clips.	Audio recording and editing software
	Recording and editing music clips, sound clips, or podcasts is done using audio recording and editing software.	
	Websites and web pages are created and maintained using web authoring programs.	
	Non-programmers can create a web page in web authoring software without having to know the programming code used by browsers.	
	Low-cost or free multimedia programs are available for non-professionals to work with graphics, pictures, video, and sound.	
Software Applications for Personal Use	Note-taking software provides a way to store, organize into notebooks and tabs, search, and share notes of any type.	Note-taking software
	Personal finance software allows you to balance your bank accounts and manage personal investments.	Personal finance software
		Tax preparation software
	Prepare and file your tax returns using tax preparation software.	Legal software
	Legal documents such as wills and contracts can be prepared using legal software, which contains forms for completing legal documents.	Hobby software applications
		Entertainment software
	Hobby software applications are available to help you with just about any type of leisure activity such as scrapbooking, meal planning, or genealogy.	Educational software
		Reference software
	Programs for playing games and videos are referred to as entertainment software.	
	Learning about subjects such as math and geography is made easier using educational software programs that use multimedia to incorporate interactivity and games.	
	Reference software programs use multimedia tools to provide rich content in encyclopedias, translation guides, and other references.	

continued....

Topic	Key Concepts	Key Terms
Cloud and Open Source Applications	The main advantage to using web-based applications is that you have access to the software and your documents from any location with an Internet connection.	
	Google Drive, Microsoft Web Apps, and Zoho are all cloud providers that offer free storage space and a suite of productivity applications for free.	
	Apache OpenOffice is a free, open source productivity suite updated and maintained by volunteers.	
	IBM's Lotus Symphony is a free suite with word processing, spreadsheets, and presentations based upon the OpenOffice package.	
	LibreOffice, a project of The Document Foundation, includes Writer, Calc, Impress, Draw, and Base.	
Acquiring, Installing, Uninstalling, and Upgrading Software	Software is a licensed product, meaning that you pay for the right to use the software but you do not own the program code.	Packaged software Shareware Freeware Subscription software Software License Agreement (SLA) End User License Agreement (EULA)
	Packaged software can be purchased in a retail store, at e-commerce websites, or directly from the software publisher.	
	Shareware is downloadable software for which you pay a small fee if you decide to keep the program after a trial period.	
	Freeware is software provided for your use without restrictions such as Apple's iTunes program.	
	Subscription-based software is generally purchased from cloud computing providers, and there is a monthly charge per user.	
	Packaged software contains a DVD inside the package with which you install the software application.	
	Download and install software directly from a website by running the install program at the source website, or by saving the install program on your hard disk drive and then installing it at a later time.	
	To install all software programs except open source applications, you are required to accept a Software License Agreement (SLA) or End User License Agreement (EULA).	
	The EULA will specify the number of computers upon which you can legally install the software program.	
	Remove software from the computer when you are no longer using it to free up computer resources.	
	In a Windows-compatible computer, open the Control Panel to uninstall a software program.	
	On a Mac computer, drag the program's icon and dock shortcut to the trash.	
	Installing a newer version of a software program is called upgrading; upgrades are available free or at a price lower than purchasing the software new.	

continued....

Mobile Apps	Mobile applications specifically designed for use on a mobile device such as a smartphone are designed to work on smaller screens. They accept input from touch, handwriting, and voice, and include compatibility with PC software.	Mobile applications
	All smartphones and tablets come equipped with several built-in apps that typically include PIM, communication, music, and game apps.	
	Microsoft Office Mobile, iWork for the iOS, Zoho, and Google Mobile all have separate mobile apps for smartphones.	

Multiple Choice

1. Which of the following applications is NOT generally included in a productivity suite?
   a. Word processor
   b. Tax preparation
   c. Database management program
   d. Spreadsheet

2. This software application included with a productivity suite is used for organizing, storing, and maintaining large amounts of data.
   a. Presentation
   b. Word processor
   c. Personal information management
   d. Database management

3. A business will use this type of application to keep a project on time and on budget.
   a. Project management
   b. ERP
   c. Accounting software
   d. Industry-specific software

4. Outlook is an example of this type of application.
   a. Personal finance
   b. Personal information management
   c. Spreadsheet
   d. Database management

5. This type of software is used to create images with movement.
   a. Web authoring applications
   b. Desktop publishing applications
   c. Animation software applications
   d. Video editing software applications

6. Adobe Dreamweaver is an application used for this type of work.
   a. Web authoring
   b. Graphics editing
   c. Desktop publishing
   d. Audio recording and editing

7. This is the note-taking software application published by Microsoft.
   a. OneNote
   b. LibreOffice
   c. OpenNote
   d. OfficeNote

8. This type of software is used to manage personal investments.
   a. Reference software
   b. Tax preparation software
   c. Legal software
   d. Personal finance

9. Which of the following is NOT a cloud-based productivity suite?
   a. Zoho
   b. Microsoft Web Apps
   c. OpenOffice
   d. Google Drive

10. IBM's Lotus Symphony productivity suite is based on this open source application.
    a. OpenOffice
    b. OpenSuite
    c. LibreSuite
    d. Quickoffice

11. This type of software is made available for a trial period after which a license fee is paid to unlock the software.
    a. Shareware
    b. Freeware
    c. Subscription software
    d. Packaged software

12. Open this window on a Windows-compatible computer to remove a software application that you no longer use.
    a. Documents window
    b. Computer window
    c. Windows Explorer
    d. Control Panel

13. This is the name of the mobile application of Microsoft Office.
    a. Microsoft Office Mobile
    b. Microsoft Quickoffice
    c. Microsoft GoOffice
    d. Microsoft SmartOffice

14. Typically, a smartphone is preinstalled with built-in apps for everything except which type of software?
    a. Personal information management
    b. Communications
    c. Games
    d. Hobby apps

Crossword Puzzle

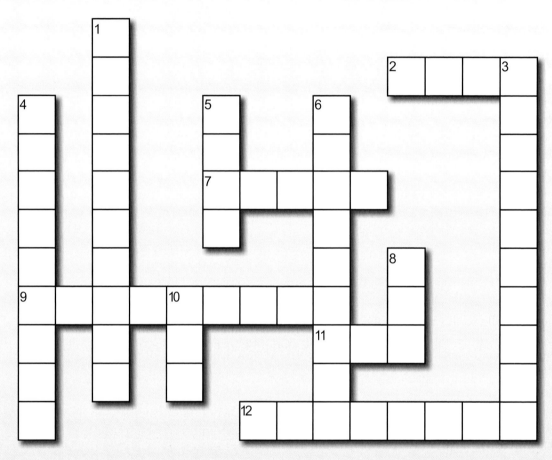

ACROSS

2 Cloud productivity suite
7 Category of software for wills or contracts
9 Created with Microsoft PowerPoint
11 Means mobile application
12 Software with no license restrictions

DOWN

1 Record and report financial activities in this type of application
3 Open source productivity suite
4 Photo editing program from Adobe
5 License agreement
6 Software with initial trial period
8 Used to do advanced page layout
10 Software used to manage large-scale operations

Matching

Match the term with the statement or definition.

_____	1. Productivity suite	a.	Manage large-scale operations
_____	2. Subscription-based software	b.	Designed for smaller screens
_____	3. ERP	c.	Open source software suite
_____	4. Multimedia	d.	Manage central document repository
_____	5. LibreOffice	e.	Multimedia-enriched encyclopedia
_____	6. Mobile apps	f.	Cloud computing
_____	7. Document management software	g.	Microsoft Office
_____	8. Reference software	h.	Text, graphics, video, and audio

Project 1 Learning Microsoft Office

Individual or Pairs
Deliverable: Document or Presentation

You have a friend who has asked for your help with learning how to use Microsoft Office. You want to provide her with a description of online learning tools available from Microsoft to help her learn how to use features in the software suite.

1. Go to www.office.microsoft.com and click the Support link. At the Support page, click a Training link to browse tutorials by application. Choose a tutorial that interests you and complete the course. Next, find and watch an Office video demo.
2. Create a document or presentation that describes each learning tool and provides an overview of how to access the resource. Include the features you liked the most about each resource as well as any weaknesses you noticed so that your friend can make an informed choice about which resource to use on her own. Be creative with the document or presentation to make the guide clear, interesting, and easy to follow. Include links to the tutorial and video that you watched.
3. Save the document or presentation as **C5-Project1-MSOfficeTraining-Your Name**.
4. Submit the document or presentation to your instructor in the manner she or he has requested.

Project 2 Managing Events Using Web-Based Software

Individual, Pairs, or Team
Deliverable: Document or Presentation

A charity at which you volunteer is planning a free seminar to promote awareness of the services that the charity provides to the general public. The seminar will be offered for free but you are requesting that people register in advance so that proper facilities are booked to accommodate everyone planning to attend. You will be assisting with the organization of the seminar and want to find an online event management software application that will help you manage online marketing, registrations, communications, and reports on participants.

1. Search for a free web-based event management application. Choose two programs to review, visit the websites and learn about the features and usability of each program.
2. Create a document or presentation that describes each program you reviewed, links to the source applications, and concludes with your recommendation and rationale for the application the charity should use to manage its seminar.
3. Save the document or presentation as **C5-Project2-EventManagement-Your Name**.
4. Submit the document or presentation to your instructor in the manner she or he has requested.

Project 3 Word Processor or Desktop Publisher?

Individual or Pairs
Deliverable: Document or Presentation

Word processing software includes many features that allow the formatting of text and placement of graphics to create documents such as newsletters, brochures, price lists, or catalogs. What distinguishes a word processing application from a desktop publishing application? Does a business need both programs? Assuming you are the creator of a monthly newsletter for a charity for which you volunteer, which program would you use to produce the newsletter each month? Why?

1. Search for information on the differences between desktop publishing and word processing software applications to find answers to the above questions.
2. Create a brief document or presentation that informs the reader as to the differences between the two types of software applications, states the application you would use for your monthly newsletter, and includes your rationale. Provide the URLs used for your research.
3. Save the document or presentation as **C5-Project3-WPvsDTP-Your Name**.
4. Submit the document or presentation to your instructor in the manner she or he has requested.

Project 4 Home or Hobby Software

Individual
Deliverable: Document, Presentation, or Blog Entry

You want to find software to help you with your personal finances, home, or hobby activities such as gardening, cooking, crafts, travel planning, genealogy, or other hobby.

1. Search for a personal, home, or hobby software application that is of interest to you that was not described in this textbook. Learn about the software application's system requirements, features, and cost. Find and read at least two reviews or articles about the application.
2. Create a document, presentation, or blog entry that provides a summary of what you learned at Step 1. Include a link to the page at the software company's website that features the product and the URLs of the reviews or articles you read.
3. Save the document or presentation as **C5-Project4-PersonalSoftware-Your Name**.
4. Submit the document, presentation, or blog URL to your instructor in the manner she or he has requested.

Project 5 Using Cloud Collaboration Tools to Evaluate Shareware Usefulness

Pairs or Team
Deliverable: Collaborative Presentation Using Cloud Software

Shareware has been a popular alternative to packaged software for many individuals and businesses that want to try out a software application before paying for a license. What are the advantages and disadvantages of shareware?

1. Each person will find and read at least two articles on the advantages and disadvantages of shareware.
2. Using a web-based presentation application such as Google Presentations, PowerPoint Web App, or Zoho's Show, one person in the pair or team will create the initial presentation that describes advantages and disadvantages of shareware. Save the presentation as **C5-Apps-Project5-Shareware-Your Name**.
3. The creator of the presentation will share the file with his or her partner or team members.
4. The partner, or each of the other team members, will modify the presentation to add additional advantages, disadvantages, or other information about shareware that is considered important to know. If no new advantages and disadvantages can be added, the individual will add information to the existing points already contributed or format the presentation to include graphics and other effects to make the presentation engaging and interesting to view.
5. Include a slide at the end of the presentation that has a table with each team member's name and the links to at least two articles he or she used for their contributions.
6. Share the final copy of the presentation by emailing a link to your instructor or by submitting the presentation in some other manner that she or he has requested.

Project 6 Podcast or Video Commercial for Mobile App

Individual, Pairs, or Team
Deliverable: Podcast or Video

Research free tools for creating and editing podcasts and videos to help you complete this project. Consider your favorite mobile app that could be used in a commercial by your smartphone manufacturer.

1. Write a storyboard for a one-minute commercial that promotes your favorite mobile app. Save the storyboard document as **C5-Apps-Project6-MobileAppStoryboard-Your Name**.
2. Use the storyboard to produce a one-minute podcast or video.

3. Upload the podcast to a free podcast-hosting website such as podbean.com or upload your video to YouTube.
4. Submit your storyboard document and the podcast or video link to your instructor in the manner she or he has requested.

Project 7 Greener Computing

Individual, Pairs, or Team
Deliverable: Presentation or Blog Entry

Assume you work in Marketing for a software company that publishes hobby software application packages that are sold primarily through electronics retail stores such as Best Buy. As a green computing initiative, you want to discontinue the packaged software model to stop the oversized box and plastic packaging and DVDs that are discarded in landfills. To do this, you have to convince management to move to a download-only software distribution model. Consider key points that support your initiative and also any barriers that may prevent management from approving the plan.

1. Create a presentation or write and post a blog entry that convinces management to approve the new software distribution model.
2. Save the presentation as **C5-Apps-Project7-GreenComputingSoftware-Your Name**.
3. Submit the presentation or your blog URL to your instructor in the manner she or he has requested.

Optional

Read the blog entry for this project of at least two other classmates and post a comment to each. Submit the URLs of your classmates' blogs with Step 2.

Project 8 Ethics Discussion on Downloading TV Shows and Movies

Team
Deliverable: Document, Blog Entry, or Presentation

A friend of yours regularly uses a bit torrent client program (a file sharing tool used to download large files on the Internet) to download television show episodes and movies. She has a large collection of her favorite television shows and movies stored on her PC. She has a copy of the most recent season of a television show you want to watch. Is it OK for you to copy her files to watch the season? Why or why not? Should you try to convince your friend to stop downloading television shows and movies? What are the ethics involved in bit torrent search engine and indexing websites that enable the sharing of copyrighted content? How should these companies ensure that individuals are not using their website to infringe on copyrighted content?

1. Within your team discuss the ethics involved in bit torrent file sharing of movies and television shows with respect to the above questions. If necessary, search for information on bit torrents and copyright infringement.
2. Prepare a summary of your team's discussion in a document, blog entry, or presentation.
3. Save the document or presentation as **C5-Project8-BitTorrentDiscussion-Your Name**.
4. Submit the document, presentation, or blog entry to your instructor in the manner she or he has requested.

Chapter 6

Using Social Media to Connect and Communicate

After successfully completing this chapter, you will be able to:

- List and describe popular social networking websites

- Explain how social bookmarking is used to track and share information

- List popular websites used for sharing music, videos, and photos

- Identify websites for blogging and know how to create a blog and blog post

- Describe how wikis generate content from users and list popular wiki websites

- Provide examples of social media strategies used by businesses

In Chapter 2 you learned that Web 2.0 refers to second-generation websites that provide for two-way communication, where individuals interact with organizations and with each other by sharing ideas, feedback, content, and multimedia. A large component of Web 2.0 involves social networking sites such as Facebook and Twitter that are used daily by millions of people of all ages all over the world. Businesses and other organizations also use social media technologies to connect with existing and potential customers or clients. Media sharing, blogs, and wikis are other components of Web 2.0 that focus on user-generated content.

In this chapter you will learn about social networking, social bookmarking, media sharing, blogging, and wikis. You will also be introduced to ways in which various organizations have incorporated social media technologies into their business strategies.

NOTE: The nature of social media websites is that they constantly evolve in response to innovation or new trends. The screens shown and instructions provided in this chapter are subject to change. Often, updates or changes to software mean that changes occur to the layout, design, or procedures. If necessary, use the Help function at a website if the screens shown or steps provided are no longer applicable.

TOPIC 6.1

Social Networking

Social media is a term used to describe any online tool in which users generate content and interact with others. A website that provides tools for people to connect with groups of people and interact is called a **social networking website**. Generally, social networking sites provide a means to build a list of friends with whom you share information and publish a profile that contains information about you. In this topic you will be introduced to three social networking sites: Facebook and Google+ to connect with friends and family, and LinkedIn to connect with business contacts.

Facebook

Facebook logo

Facebook is one of the most popular social networking sites used by people who want to connect with friends and family. A new user starts by creating an account, setting up his or her profile with personal information, and adding friends to his or her Friends list. To add friends, you search by the person's name and look at his or her profile page. If the person is someone you want to add to your Friends list, click the Add Friend button. A friend request is sent to the individual to accept or ignore. Once accepted as a friend, you and the other person can see each other's Facebook activity.

People post updates in Facebook about what they're doing and share interesting links, photos, videos, music, games, news items, quotes, or just about anything else that appears to be of interest. People comment on a person's wall (their Facebook page) or a photo and generally post messages back and forth to each other. You can chat with friends who are online or use Facebook's Message tool to send private messages.

Users can create or join Facebook groups to gather with people that share a similar interest or goal. Businesses and other organizations create Facebook pages to share information and interact with customers, clients, or other interested visitors. For example, in Figure 6.1 the Facebook page for the U.S. Department of Education is shown.

Did You Know?

Facebook reported 955 million monthly active users at the end of June 2012—that's more than three times the population of the United States in the same year!

Figure 6.1 Education news is shared and discussed in comments with the general public on the Facebook page for the U.S. Department of Education.

Google+

In 2011, Google launched a social networking site called **Google+**. Sign in at Google+ with your Gmail account or create a new account. Edit your profile and then start adding people to your circles.

Google+ logo

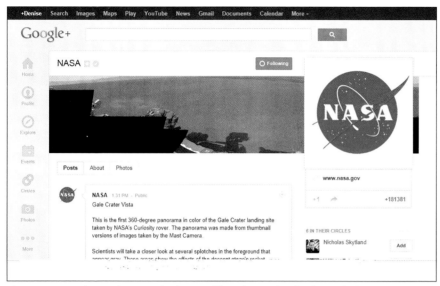

Figure 6.2 NASA's Google+ page is shown with a photo taken by the Curiosity rover on Mars and a post describing the photo.

Circles   In Google+, people or websites that you connect with are organized into categories called circles. The default circles are Family, Friends, Acquaintances, and Following. You can create your own new circles to group people with a similar interest. When you add someone you want to connect with in Google+, you are prompted to select the circle in which the individual should be associated. By maintaining your social network in separate circles you can share activity with only the people for whom the content is of interest. For example, you can post information about a family reunion and share it only with your Family circle. This is unlike Facebook, where a message you post is seen by everyone in your Friends list.

Add websites with which you want to keep up to date to your Following circle. For example, adding a news website will ensure current news articles are added to your Home page. Type a note, upload a photo or video, or enter a link at the *Share what's new* box at the top of your page and then choose how to share the activity by adding names, the names of circles, or email addresses. With Google+, you can also use the Chat feature to talk with others online or use the Hangout feature to conduct video chats.

As with Facebook, businesses and other organizations have created pages in Google+ to interact with interested users. Figure 6.2 shows the page for NASA in Google+.

LinkedIn

LinkedIn is the most visited business-related social networking site. It is a professional network where you connect with your business contacts. Creating an account with LinkedIn allows you to create a professional profile with your current and past employment positions, education credentials, and links to websites (such as your current company's website). Your profile can be expanded to represent in resume-like fashion a summary of your qualifications and prior work experiences. Once your profile is established, you begin connecting through LinkedIn with people in your workplace contacts list and with other professionals in your field and related fields. The Search tool in LinkedIn can be used to find people by name, job title, company name, or location. You can also join professional association groups to keep up with news in your field.

An Answers tool lets you post any type of question to the LinkedIn community so that experts can respond. A Jobs board shows current job listings and includes a search tool to search job listings by job title, keywords, or company name. Figure 6.3 shows the LinkedIn company page for Adobe.

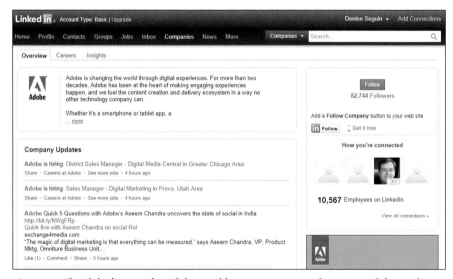

Figure 6.3 The LinkedIn page for Adobe provides a company overview, current job openings, and links to news, blogs, and articles related to Adobe products.

Mobile Apps for Social Networking

All of the popular social networking websites have free mobile apps that you download to your smartphone so that you can post messages, upload photos, or otherwise stay connected from your mobile device.

In this topic you have been introduced to three social networking websites. Table 6.1 lists three additional social networking websites that are also popular.

Social networking apps are free for your mobile device.

Table 6.1	Popular Social Networks
Social Network	**URL**
Bebo	bebo.com
Biznik	biznik.com
Facebook	facebook.com
Google+	plus.google.com
LinkedIn	linkedin.com
Tumblr	tumblr.com

Know Your Privacy Settings!

Make sure you check the privacy settings at the social networks that you use when you set up your account. You may be sharing more personal information than you intended. Ask your friends not to tag your name in photos they post if you don't want friends of friends to see what you've been up to.

EXPLORE FURTHER

Favorite Social Networking Websites

1. Conduct a survey with at least 10 relatives, friends, neighbors, or classmates to find out the social networking websites used by each individual and each person's estimate of the amount of time spent per week on social networking.

2. Compile the survey results in a table or chart in a document, spreadsheet, or presentation.

3. Save the document, spreadsheet, or presentation as **C6-SocialMedia-SocialNetworks-Your Name**.

4. Submit the document, spreadsheet, or presentation to your instructor in the manner she or he has requested.

TOPIC 6.2

Social Bookmarking

A category of social networking that provides tools with which you can organize, store, and share content with others is known as **social bookmarking**. You have probably saved a link that you visit frequently to Favorites within your browser. These links are stored in folders on your local hard drive. Social bookmarking is similar to your Favorites list except that the links are called **bookmarks** and are saved in your social network so that you have access to them from anywhere and can share the links with others. At social bookmarking sites, you can search bookmarks that others have created.

Bookmarks are created by **tagging** a website. A **tag** is a keyword that you assign to the content to describe or categorize the photo, article, or item from a web page. The tags help users at the social bookmarking site find content. For example, if you find a recipe for Greek Soulvaki that you want to share you would tag the recipe at the source website with keywords such as *recipe, greek soulvaki, greek, entrée*.

Social bookmarking site icons called **bookmarklets** allow you to bookmark the page instantly by clicking the icon. The icons are copied from the social bookmarking website to your Favorites or Bookmarks toolbar in the browser. Some web pages include the more popular icons near the top of their pages. The icons have programming code attached that captures the site's references for bookmarking. In this topic, you will explore three social bookmarking sites: Pinterest, StumbleUpon, and Delicious.

Pinterest

According to Pinterest.com, **Pinterest** is a virtual pinboard. People pin pictures of things they have seen on the Internet that they like and want to share using the Pin It button. Pinterest users add the Pin It button (bookmarklet) to their browser's Favorites or Bookmarks toolbar. Click the Pin It button at a website with an image you like, select the image to pin, choose the board to pin the image to, and then type a description to pin a picture to your board. You can also upload your own pictures to share on a board.

Pinterest logo

A board is a name you assign to a collection of related pictures. For example, you can create a board for technology and collect pictures of cool gadgets. You can browse and follow boards created by other Pinterest users to get ideas for yourself. If you like something you find on someone else's board, you can repin the item to your own. Figure 6.4 displays a Pinterest board with bookmarked items.

Pin It bookmarklet added to Favorites bar in IE9

Click Add to create a new board, or to pin items by typing a URL or uploading from your PC or mobile device.

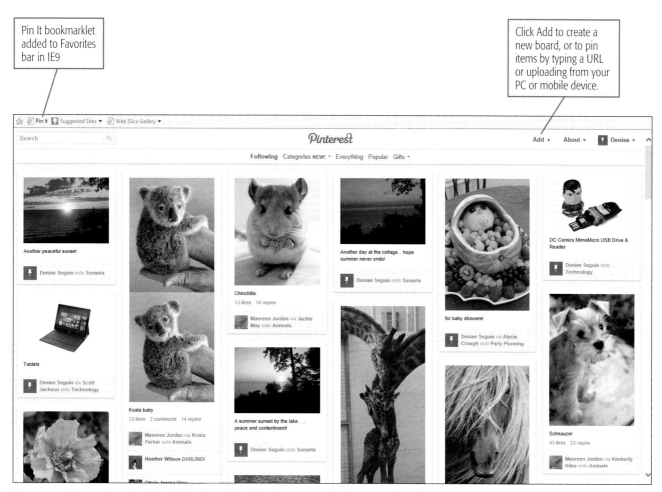

Figure 6.4 Pinterest is a visual social bookmarking site where users pin pictures to boards that link to items of interest.

StumbleUpon

By joining **StumbleUpon** you can browse recommended web pages and save the pages you like to your profile. When you join StumbleUpon, you choose categories for topics about which you want to see related content. Once your interests are established, navigate through various web pages StumbleUpon finds for you by clicking the Stumble! button in the black StumbleBar at the top of the screen (Figure 6.5). Use the like and dislike buttons on the StumbleBar as you view pages so that StumbleUpon can tailor the recommendations to your preferences. You can share a page you find with others and follow someone else if you like the same web pages as another StumbleUpon user (called a Stumbler). View web pages you have liked in the past using the History link in the left pane of your profile page.

StumbleUpon logo

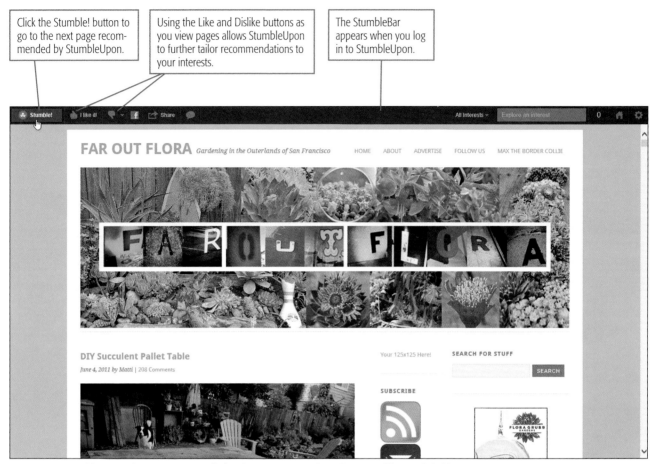

Click the Stumble! button to go to the next page recommended by StumbleUpon.

Using the Like and Dislike buttons as you view pages allows StumbleUpon to further tailor recommendations to your interests.

The StumbleBar appears when you log in to StumbleUpon.

Figure 6.5 StumbleUpon shows recommended web pages for you based on your likes and dislikes.

Delicious

Create an account at **Delicious** to save and share links to pages on the Web that have articles, pictures, videos, blogs, or some other content that you want to bookmark. Use the Delicious bookmarklet to save links to pages in your Delicious account. You will have to add the Delicious bookmarklet to your browser's Favorites or Bookmarks bar. Use the Add Link button on the Delicious toolbar to type a link directly that you want to save in Delicious. Delicious also has an import utility that will import bookmarks you have saved in your browser.

Delicious bookmarklet

When viewing a page on the Web that you want to save, click the Delicious bookmarklet, sign in to your account if you are not already logged in, enter tags or accept the default tags, type a description if desired, and click the Save button. You can mark links as private or public and follow other Delicious users.

Once you have a collection of links, you can sort and search through your personal collection or the collections of people you are following (use the Feed page). The Inbox contains private messages with links sent directly to you by other Delicious users. Figure 6.6 displays a Delicious page with saved bookmarks.

Some social bookmarking websites have connectors to Facebook and Twitter so that you can register using your existing Facebook or Twitter account instead of an email address.

Other popular social bookmarking sites are listed in Table 6.2.

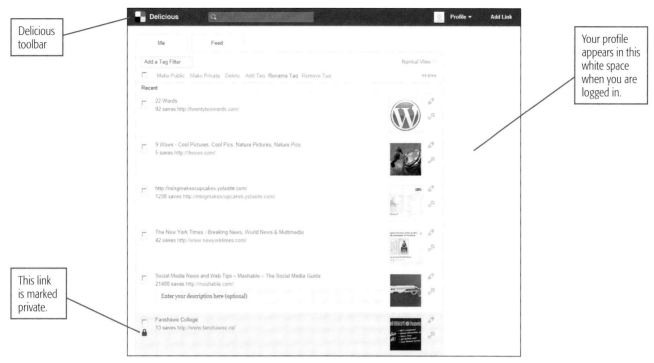

Figure 6.6 Use Delicious to collect pictures, videos, blog entries, articles, or anything else you have found that you want to save and/or share.

Table 6.2	Social Bookmarking Websites
Social Bookmark	**URL**
Clipboard	clipboard.com
Digg	digg.com
Delicious	delicious.com
Pinterest	pinterest.com
Reddit	reddit.com
StumbleUpon	stumbleupon.com

EXPLORE FURTHER

Start social bookmarking

As mentioned in the introduction to this topic, social bookmarks are available to you from any device, are searchable, and can be easily shared. If you have not yet experimented with social bookmarking, complete this activity to learn more about these websites.

1. Choose one of the social bookmarking websites listed in Table 6.2 and create an account at the website.

2. Experiment with the tools available at the site by adding at least 10 bookmarks to content that you like on the Web. Bookmark different types of content such as a blog, news article, picture, and video (unless you chose Pinterest, which bookmarks images only). Consider also customizing your profile and sharing some links with others.

3. Capture an image of your page at the social bookmarking website showing your saved links using a screen capture program such as Windows Snipping Tool or PrintScreen. Depending on the method used, save the image as a jpg file or paste the image into a document. Save the image or document as **C6-SocialMedia-Bookmarks-Your Name**.

4. Submit the image or document to your instructor in the manner she or he has requested.

TOPIC 6.3

Sharing Media

Photos, videos, music, and presentations are shared, viewed, and downloaded using sites referred to as **media sharing** websites. Popular media sharing sites are YouTube for videos, Flickr for photos, Last.fm for music, and Slideshare for presentations. Sharing media using social sharing sites allows you to publish, collaborate, and distribute content to several people more easily than sending files or links as message attachments. In this topic you will survey the popular media sharing sites YouTube, Flickr, and Last.fm. In addition, Instagram, a photo sharing app for mobile devices, is introduced.

YouTube

Most people have viewed videos on **YouTube** (youtube.com). YouTube, which is owned by Google, is the most popular video sharing website in the world. Some YouTube videos become **viral videos** (video clips that spread quickly via forwarded or shared links or word-of-mouth). With a YouTube account you can search or browse for videos, upload a video you have created, rent full-length films, subscribe to someone's YouTube channel, and share videos with friends. Figure 6.7 shows a page from YouTube EDU, which hosts educational videos, some of which are lessons from teachers or full courses from leading universities.

Did You Know?

Google's Larry Page wrote in April 2012 that YouTube had 800 million-plus monthly users uploading more than an hour of video per second!

Choose Primary & Secondary Education, University, or Lifelong Learning here and then pick a subcategory to browse or search educational videos by topic.

Click Browse, and then click Education or type *youtube.com/education* to find the education channel.

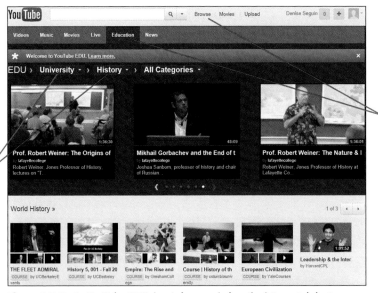

Figure 6.7 Go to YouTube EDU (youtube.com/education) to watch lectures, courses, or other educational videos.

Flickr

Sharing photos is one of the more popular media sharing activities on the Web since most people have digital photos they want to share with family and friends. Uploading photos to a sharing site lets you easily send a link to share your photo album with other people. Although social networking sites such as Facebook and Twitter let you upload and share photos, these sites generally have lower photo storage limits than dedicated photo sharing websites.

Many dedicated photo sharing websites are available, with **Flickr** being one of the popular choices. See Table 6.3 to review other photo sharing websites. Generally, photo sharing websites let you upload pictures organized into albums, sets, or folders; tag and comment on pictures; and share the photos with others. Sharing can be with other users of the site, or you can connect the photos to Facebook, Twitter, email, blogs, or other messaging tool. You can search for pictures uploaded by others, and sites such as Flickr include The Commons, which lets you search public photography archives. Figure 6.8 shows search results for *butterflies* in The Commons gallery in Flickr.

Some photo sharing websites such as Picasa include tools for editing photos.

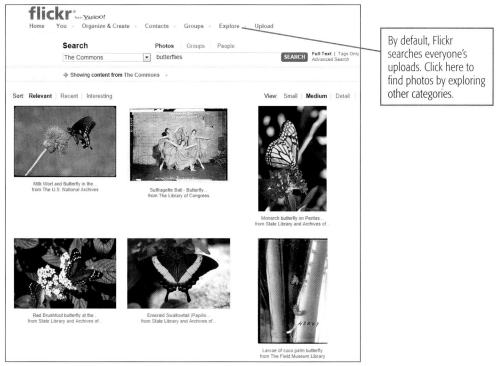

By default, Flickr searches everyone's uploads. Click here to find photos by exploring other categories.

Figure 6.8 Some of the search results for *butterflies* in The Commons public photography archive in Flickr

Table 6.3	Sampling of Photo Sharing Websites	
Photo Sharing Website	**Restrictions for Free Accounts**	**URL**
Flickr	300 MB of photos and 2 videos *per month*	flickr.com
Photobucket	Unlimited photos and 500 videos for non-commercial users	photobucket.com
Picasa	1 GB of free storage space for photos and videos	picasa.google.com
Shutterfly	Unlimited photos	shutterfly.com
Snapfish	Unlimited photos	snapfish.com

Last.fm

Music fans who want to share their music discoveries or search for new music artists use one of many music sharing websites such as **Last.fm** (www.last.fm). Last.fm is a popular music streaming service. Using the site's software app called the Scrobbler, recommendations for new music are presented to you based on the types of songs you currently play (Figure 6.9). You can search for an artist or song, add a track to your library, and share it with another Last.fm user via Facebook, Twitter, Google+, or email.

Music sharing sites are often the target of litigation by major music recording labels for copyright violations. For example, at the time of writing, Grooveshark, another popular music sharing website, is in the process of defending itself against litigation from four major music labels: EMI Music Publishing, Universal Music Group, Sony Music, and Warner Music Group.

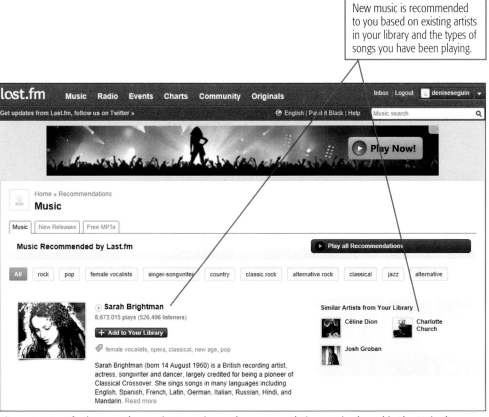

New music is recommended to you based on existing artists in your library and the types of songs you have been playing.

Figure 6.9 Last.fm is a popular music streaming and recommendation service based in the United Kingdom.

Sharing Photos from Mobile Devices

Instagram is a popular free app for sharing photos from your iPhone, iPad, iPod Touch, or Android phone. After taking a photo with your mobile device, you can use Instagram to add a special effect filter to the picture and then share the photo using your favorite social networking site. You can download the Instagram app from the iTune App store or Google Play. Instagram was purchased by Facebook in April 2012.

Instagram is a popular photo sharing app for mobile devices.

Check This Out

www.mashable.com
Go here for up-to-date news on digital culture, social media, and technology.

EXPLORE FURTHER

Sharing Presentations

Slideshare is a website at which you can upload and share presentations created in PowerPoint, PDF, Keynote, or OpenOffice. The slide hosting website also allows you to upload and share documents and videos. In 2012, Slideshare reported that 60 million people visited the site monthly.

1. Create a presentation with at least three slides that describes the methods or websites that you use to share media such as photos, videos, or music. If you do not share media, create one slide for each of the websites mentioned in this topic that summarizes what you learned.

2. Save the presentation as **C6-SocialMedia-MediaSharing-Your Name**.

3. Go to www.slideshare.net and sign up for a new account or log in if you already have an account.

4. Upload the C6-SocialMedia-MediaSharing-Your Name presentation. Add appropriate tags and a description and select the Education category.

5. Email the presentation to your instructor from slideshare.net or, alternatively, submit the presentation and a screen capture of your presentation uploaded in slideshare.net to your instructor in the manner she or he has requested.

TOPIC 6.4

Check This Out

www.technorati.com
Go here to find a blog. Technorati is a search engine that indexes more than a million blogs.

Blogging

Blogs are basically journals posted on a website with the most recent entry at the top of the page. Older blog entries are usually archived by month and can be displayed by clicking the month to expand the blog entry list. The word blog is derived from *web log*. The collection of all of the blogs on the Web is referred to as the **blogosphere**. Writing and maintaining a blog is called **blogging**. Entries in a blog are called **blog posts**, posts, or entries. The individual who writes the blog content is referred to as a **blogger**. Blogs exist on just about any topic one can think of and are mostly text and pictures; however, posts also contain links to other web pages and sometimes video and/or audio. Blog websites include tools that allow individuals to create, update, and maintain blogs without a programming background. Blogs are interactive, meaning that people can post comments below a blog post, and the author and his or her audience can have a conversation about the post.

Several popular blogs are viewed by millions of people every day. In this topic you will learn about two popular blog hosting websites: WordPress and Blogger. Twitter, a microblogging website, is also introduced.

WordPress

WordPress (wordpress.com) is a blog hosting website that uses the WordPress open source blogging software. Sign up for a free blog by providing a blog address, user name, password, and email address. A blog address begins with the domain you want to name your blog and ends with .wordpress.com. For example, if you type your name as the blog address, the URL you would give to people to find your blog would be *yourname.wordpress.com*. Once you activate the blog from the confirmation email message, choose a theme and start writing a post. A default post is created for you that you edit as your initial *About* entry, which generally describes you and the purpose of your blog. Click New Post to create a new blog post by typing a title and the body of the blog entry in a word processor-style window (Figure 6.10). Buttons are available to add a photo, video, quote, or link. Click the Publish Post button to add the entry to your blog.

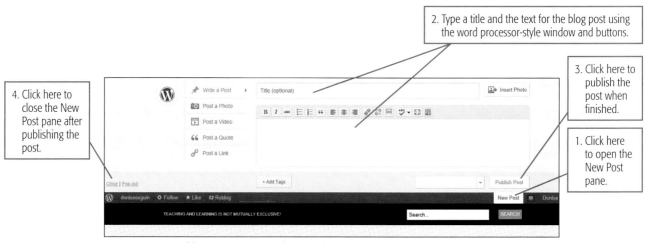

2. Type a title and the text for the blog post using the word processor-style window and buttons.

3. Click here to publish the post when finished.

4. Click here to close the New Post pane after publishing the post.

1. Click here to open the New Post pane.

Figure 6.10 New blog posts are created at Wordpress by typing inside a window similar to a word processor.

Blogger

Google's Blogger (blogger.com) is another popular choice for creating a blog. Sign up for the blog using your Gmail account. At the first screen, you can customize your profile or click the button to continue directly to Blogger. At the Blogger window, click the New Blog button to create a new blog. At the next screen, type a title for your blog, enter a blog address, choose the template with the colors and style you want to use, and then click Create blog! Blog addresses in Blogger end with .blogspot.com so the URL for your blog would be *yourblogaddress.blogspot.com* or *yourblogaddress.blogspot.ca* if you reside in Canada. Once the blog is created you can start publishing blog posts. Click the orange button with the icon of a pencil (Create a new post button) next to your blog title to create a new blog post. At the screen shown in Figure 6.11, type the post title and text in the word processor-style window. Add links, pictures, video, or quotes as needed and click Publish when finished.

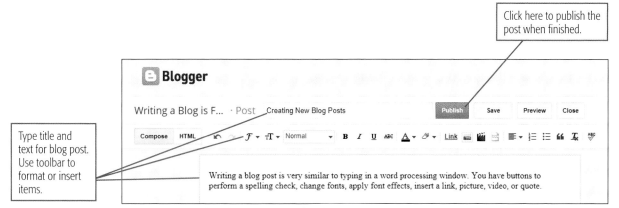

Click here to publish the post when finished.

Type title and text for blog post. Use toolbar to format or insert items.

Figure 6.11 Google's Blogger is a popular blog hosting service because the tools are easy to use and navigate for beginner bloggers.

Blogger is integrated with Google's other services and you may be prompted to share the blog on Google+ when you create it. Blogger uses a template design for blogs with a variety of colors for each template. You can change the template at any time in the Design window and see how the template will appear in both a PC and a mobile environment (Figure 6.12). Many other blog hosting websites are available such as those shown in Table 6.4.

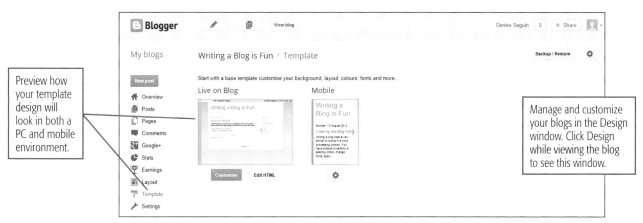

Preview how your template design will look in both a PC and mobile environment.

Manage and customize your blogs in the Design window. Click Design while viewing the blog to see this window.

Figure 6.12 The template design can be changed at any time and you can preview how the blog will look on both a PC and a mobile device.

Table 6.4	Blog Hosting Services
Blog Hosting Service	**URL**
Blog.com	blog.com
Blogger	blogger.com
LiveJournal	livejournal.com
Squarespace	squarespace.com
Tumblr	tumblr.com
Twitter	twitter.com
Wordpress	wordpress.com
Xanga	xanga.com

Microblogging

A few blog services such as Twitter and Tumblr are **microblogging** hosting services. A **microblog** is a blog that restricts posts to a smaller amount of text than a traditional blog. **Microbloggers** typically post about what they are doing, where they are, what they are thinking about at the moment, or links to interesting content (stories, pictures, videos) they have seen on the Web. The most popular microblog is Twitter, although Tumblr is another highly popular microblog that includes social networking and social bookmarking features. A post in Tumblr is called a tumblelog. Many Tumblr users use their blogs to bookmark videos or pictures they have found on the Web and share them with their followers. Tumblr users also frequently reblog items seen on someone else's page at their own pages.

Twitter

By far, **Twitter** is the most popular microblog with posts limited to 140 characters or less. A post in Twitter is called a **tweet** and contains a short update on a breaking news story, opinion, a status update, or other topic the author finds interesting. Because of the short nature of a tweet, many users post to Twitter from their mobile devices. Clicking Compose New Tweet opens a small window in which you type your post. Twitter users type the **hashtag symbol (#)** preceding a keyword or topic (with no space) in a tweet to categorize messages. Clicking a hashtagged word in any post will show you all of the other tweets categorized with the same keyword.

Twitter logo

Many people like to follow other Twitter users to see their daily tweets, including popular businesses to find out about deals or specials (Figure 6.13). Twitter followers for some people reach millions. According to Twitter, at the 2012 Olympics in London, Usain Bolt set a new conversation milestone with 80,000 tweets per minute during his 200-meter run!

Figure 6.13 Businesses are using Twitter to post tweets with daily deals or news about products.

Be Careful What You Post Online

What you write in a blog or in comments at social media websites reflects on your ethics and your personality. Poor spelling and grammar portray sloppiness. Be mindful of your digital persona at all times. Do not engage in conversations or blogs that potential employers might read and use to decide that you are not a good fit for their organizations.

EXPLORE   FURTHER

Tweet a social media fact

You may have been using blogs throughout this textbook but do you tweet? Complete this activity to post a tweet with an interesting fact about social media.

1. Search the Web for a fact about how Twitter has been used for social good.

2. Go to twitter.com and sign in or sign up for a new account if you do not already have one.

3. Compose a tweet to share the Twitter fact you found at Step 1. Precede your tweet with #courseidentifier so that your instructor can locate your tweet. Your instructor will provide you with the hashtag keyword to use for *courseidentifier*. For example, the hashtag keyword might be #comp100f2013.

4. In addition, or as an alternative, your instructor may request that you make a screen capture of your tweet and submit the screen capture as a jpg file or pasted in a document saved as **C6-SocialMedia-Tweet-Your Name**. In that case, submit the tweet in the manner she or he has requested.

TOPIC 6.5

Wikis for User-Generated Content

A **wiki** is a website with **wiki software** that allows anyone to create and edit content at the website. Clicking the edit tab, edit button, or edit link in a wiki opens the text in a word processor-style window where you can add, delete, or edit content. This type of open content is used for collaboration and knowledge sharing. Wikis that provide encyclopedic or other reference content have people that monitor postings to make sure entries are well written and accurate. In this topic you will explore two well-known wiki websites: Wikipedia and wikiHow.

Wikipedia

The most used online encyclopedia is **Wikipedia**, owned by the not-for-profit Wikimedia Foundation. Individuals looking for new information about a subject often start at Wikipedia. Content at Wikipedia can be created by anyone; however, thousands of editors regularly edit pages.

People who want to edit at Wikipedia are encouraged to create an account so that postings are identified with the individual either by name or alias. If you edit a page without being logged in to an account, the IP address for your PC is attributed to your content in the page history. New contributors to Wikipedia are encouraged to first post in the **Wikipedia Sandbox** (Figure 6.14).

At the time of writing, 4,027,065 articles were available on Wikipedia.

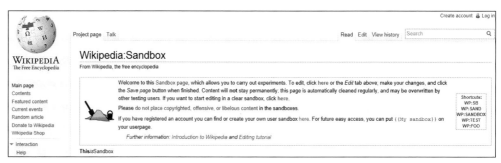

Figure 6.14 The Wikipedia Sandbox contains instructions on how to edit content and is where new contributors are encouraged to post a test edit before modifying a real article.

wikiHow

When a how-to instruction manual is needed, **wikiHow** is often where people look. The website contains more than 140,000 how-to articles. According to wikiHow, the mission of the website is to "build the world's largest, highest quality, how-to manual." You can search for the instructions you need using keywords or browse articles by category at the Home page. Figure 6.15 shows the beginnings of the how-to article titled "How to Change a Tire." wikiHow is a for-profit wiki that shows ads to users who are not registered to finance the operation of the website.

Other wikis that you might want to investigate are listed in Table 6.5.

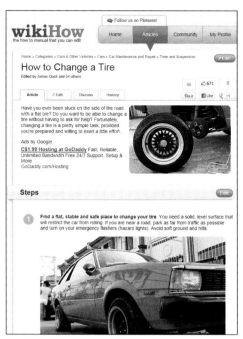

Figure 6.15 wikiHow's user-generated articles are how-to instructions such as this article that describes the steps for changing a tire.

Table 6.5	Popular Wiki Websites	
Wiki	**URL**	**Purpose**
Wikibooks	wikibooks.org	Free textbooks and manuals
Wikimedia Commons	commons.wikimedia.org	Freely usable images, photographs, or videos
wikiHow	wikihow.com	How-to instructions
Wikipedia	wikipedia.org	Encyclopedia
Wikiquote	wikiquote.org	Collection of quotations from notable people
Wiktionary	wiktionary.org	Dictionary for words in all languages
WikiTravel	wikitravel.org	Worldwide travel guide

EXPLORE FURTHER

Explore a new wiki

Most people have experience looking up information at Wikipedia. In this activity you will explore another wiki of your choice.

1. Choose a wiki website from Table 6.5 other than Wikipedia that you have not used before and look up information on a topic or subject of interest to you. For example, you may want to use WikiTravel to find an article on a destination that you want to visit.

2. Read the article at the wiki website.

3. Create a document that provides a brief summary of the wiki you used, the information you researched, and your perception of the content's usefulness to you. Include the URL of the article at the end of the document.

4. Save the document as **C6-SocialMedia-WikiArticle-Your Name**.

5. Submit the document to your instructor in the manner she or he has requested.

TOPIC 6.6

Social Media Strategies in Business

Business strategies for using social media incorporate a wide variety of techniques such as using Facebook pages to provide customer support, invite feedback from customers, offer opportunities for new ideas, allow customers to share tips, or promote products. Businesses also offer coupons or information on specials using social media. In this topic, a sampling of selected companies' social media strategies is shown.

Amazon.com

Amazon's Facebook page provides a space for customers to post comments about interesting topics, showcase photos posted from customers, run contests, and provide customer service. In Figure 6.16, Amazon.com's Customer Service Support page is illustrated.

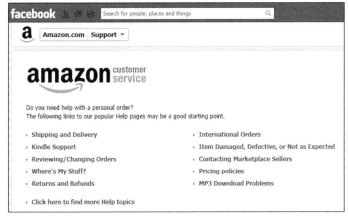

Figure 6.16 Amazon.com's Facebook page includes links to customer service Help pages.

Figure 6.17 Amtrak's Deals are advertised on its Facebook page.

Amtrak

Amtrak's Facebook page engages customers in a variety of ways, including providing a place to leave comments; post photos, videos, and questions; learn about deals (Figure 6.17) and rewards; and book trips.

Coffee Groundz

A coffee shop in Houston called Coffee Groundz uses Twitter to tweet specials and promotions (Figure 6.18) and also was one of the first businesses to accept takeout orders from its customers in tweets.

Figure 6.18 Coffee Groundz in Houston tweets promotions and lets customers tweet their takeout orders.

Southwest Airlines

Southwest Airlines publishes a blog titled *Nuts About Southwest* (blogsouthwest.com), which uses a variety of multimedia (videos and podcasts) to engage readers who visit with information designed to build brand loyalty (Figure 6.19). Readers can create an account at the blog and exchange travel experiences with each other. At the Downloads page, people can download wallpapers and screen savers for their computing devices and install an app that notifies the user when new airfare deals are posted.

Figure 6.19 Southwest Airlines uses a blog to publish articles about the airline designed to build brand loyalty and provide a place for customers to exchange travel experience stories.

Career Connection

Social Media Managers

Businesses are increasingly aware of the need for a person to manage all of the social media feeds that can have a huge effect on their business strategies. A social media manager coordinates all of the social media networking and marketing for an organization. Typically, the social media manager is someone who enjoys spending a lot of time online, has excellent writing skills, and enjoys communicating and connecting with all types of people. Jobs in social media management or strategy typically ask for individuals with degrees or diplomas in communications, public relations, or marketing.

EXPLORE FURTHER

Find a business in social media

As you have seen in this topic, businesses use social media in a variety of ways. In this activity you will look for a business that you are familiar with on social media websites to find out how they are using the medium to promote products or services or build loyalty.

1. Choose a business that you are familiar with not profiled in this topic and find its presence in a social media venue such as Facebook, Twitter, LinkedIn, or some other network.

2. Examine the way in which the business is using social media to promote or otherwise engage its customers or find new customers. Do you think the strategy is successful? Would you engage with the business on its social media site? Why or why not?

3. Create a document or presentation that describes the results of your research in this activity and answers the questions posed in Step 2. Include a screen capture or URL of the page you reviewed.

4. Save the document or presentation as **C6-SocialMedia-BusinessStrategy-Your Name**.

5. Submit the document or presentation to your instructor in the manner she or he has requested.

Concepts Review

Topic	Key Concepts	Key Terms
Social Networking	A social networking website provides tools for people to connect and interact with one another. A social network provides a means to publish a personal profile and establish a list of people with whom you want to share activities and exchange updates. Facebook is the most popular social networking site used by people who want to connect with friends and family. Google+ uses circles to group people you want to connect with by categories such as Family, Friends, Acquaintances, and Following. LinkedIn is a social network used to connect with business contacts. Popular social networking websites provide free apps for downloading to a smartphone so that people can stay connected from their mobile devices.	Social media Social networking website Facebook Google+ LinkedIn
Social Bookmarking	Social bookmarking websites let you save and share links to content on the Web such as articles, pictures, videos, blogs, music, or other web pages. A saved link is called a bookmark. Bookmarks are created by tagging a website with one or more keywords called tags. Bookmarklets are icons installed on your Favorites or Bookmarks bar that are used to link a page to a social bookmarking website. Pinterest is used to pin images that you want to save and share to a board at your Pinterest account. StumbleUpon is a social bookmarking website that shows you pages that might be of interest to you based on categories that you like. Delicious is a social bookmarking site for saving and sharing links and one that can import links you have saved to Favorites in your browser. Social bookmarking websites have connectors to Facebook and Twitter.	Social bookmarking Bookmarks Tagging Tag Bookmarklets Pinterest StumbleUpon Delicious
Sharing Media	Media sharing websites let registered users upload photos, videos, music, or presentations and share the content with others. YouTube is owned by Google and is the most popular video sharing website in the world. Viral videos are videos that spread quickly via forwarded links, shared links, or word-of-mouth. Flickr is a popular photo sharing website that provides tools for users to upload, organize, and share photos. Last.fm is a music streaming and recommendation service based in the United Kingdom. Last.fm uses a software app called Scrobbler that tracks the music you play so that recommendations can be tailored to your interests. Instagram is a popular photo sharing app for use with a smartphone.	Media sharing YouTube Viral videos Flickr Last.fm Instagram

continued....

Blogging	Blogs are online journals created at blog hosting websites, with the most recent post at the top of the page.	Blogs
	Bloggers create blog posts that are composed of text, photos, videos, or links.	Blogosphere
		Blogging
	Wordpress is a blog website that uses the open source WordPress blogging software.	Blog posts
		Blogger
	A blog is generally typed inside a word processor-style window.	WordPress
		Google's Blogger
	Blogger, owned by Google, is a popular blogging tool that uses templates and a user-friendly interface.	Microblogging
		Microblog
	Microblogging websites such as Twitter and Tumblr are used to create short posts or share links or photos.	Microbloggers
		Twitter
	Twitter is the most popular microblog with posts limited to 140 characters or less.	Tweet
		Hashtag symbol (#)
	The hashtag symbol (#) in a tweet precedes a keyword that the author wants to use to categorize the tweet.	
Wikis for User-Generated Content	A wiki website uses wiki software that allows users to add or edit content.	Wiki
		Wiki software
	Wikis that provide encyclopedic information have thousands of editors that edit content to ensure postings are well written and accurate.	Wikipedia
		Wikipedia Sandbox
	Wikipedia is the most used online encyclopedia.	wikiHow
	New contributors are encouraged to do a test edit in the Wikipedia Sandbox before editing a real article.	
	wikiHow is a wiki website with thousands of how-to instruction articles on a wide range of topics.	
Social Media Strategies for Business	Businesses use social media networks in a variety of ways to engage customers or find new customers.	
	Amazon.com's Facebook page includes space for customers to interact with the company and find customer service support.	
	Amtrak uses its Facebook page to publish deals and allow customers to upload photos and videos or post questions.	
	A coffee shop in Houston uses Twitter to tweet promotions and allows customers to send their takeout orders by tweets.	
	Southwest Airlines publishes a blog that uses a variety of multimedia in articles that promote brand loyalty and allows customers to share travel experiences.	
	Southwest Airlines also provides downloads at its blog for wallpaper, screen savers, and an app that alerts the customer when airfare specials are published.	

Multiple Choice

1. Google+ organizes your contacts into categories referred to as _____.
   a. Social groups
   b. Circles
   c. Friend shares
   d. Address books

2. This website is the most visited business-related social network.
   a. Facebook
   b. Google+
   c. My Space
   d. LinkedIn

3. This is the term that refers to a social network used to save and share links.
   a. Social bookmarking
   b. Social tagging
   c. Social sharing
   d. Social wikis

4. Pinterest is this type of social networking website.
   a. Social Bookmarking
   b. Social Pin Sharing
   c. Blogging
   d. Social Pinning

5. YouTube is referred to as this type of website.
   a. Social networking
   b. Social bookmarking
   c. Media sharing
   d. Blogging

6. This is the name of a popular app for smartphones that you use to share photos.
   a. Flickr
   b. Instagram
   c. Picasa
   d. Shutterfly

7. Which of the following is NOT a blog hosting website?
   a. Xanga
   b. Blog.com
   c. Blogger
   d. StumbleUpon

8. This blog hosting website is owned by Google.
   a. WordPress
   b. Blogger
   c. Twitter
   d. Tumblr

9. This is the software used at websites where the content is generated by users.
   a. Media sharing
   b. Social sharing
   c. Wiki software
   d. Bookmarking

10. This website posts articles with how-to instructions that are created by users.
    a. Wikipedia
    b. wikiHow
    c. Wikimedia Commons
    d. WikiDo

11. Coffee Groundz was profiled in this chapter as a business that uses this social network to accept takeout orders.
    a. Facebook
    b. LinkedIn
    c. Delicious
    d. Twitter

12. Southwest Airlines was profiled in this chapter for its use of this type of social media to promote brand loyalty.
    a. Social bookmarking
    b. Blogging
    c. Tweeting
    d. Wikis

Crossword Puzzle

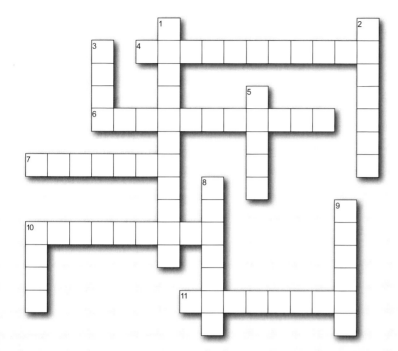

ACROSS

4 Social networking websites
6 Website that recommends pages
7 Most popular microblogging site
10 Open source blogging software
11 Most popular social network

DOWN

1 Button added to Favorites or Bookmarks bar
2 New contributors practice area in Wikipedia
3 Keywords used to create bookmarks
5 Type of media found at Last.fm
8 Precedes keywords in tweets
9 Popular photo sharing website
10 Website with user-generated content

Matching

Match the term with the statement or definition.

_____ 1. Social Networking
_____ 2. Google+
_____ 3. Delicious
_____ 4. Posts
_____ 5. Twitter
_____ 6. Pinterest
_____ 7. Flickr
_____ 8. Music sharing sites

a. Social bookmarking
b. Targets for copyright litigation
c. Photo sharing
d. Microblog
e. Connecting with friends
f. Blog entries
g. Virtual boards with pictures
h. Family, Friends, Acquaintances, Following

Project 1 Social Media at School, Work, or Volunteer Community

Individual
Deliverable: Presentation

How is social media used at your school, workplace, or volunteer organization? Does the school, business, or organization use Facebook, Twitter, LinkedIn, or blogs? If yes, how are these networks used to engage students, employees, customers, or other clients? Have you engaged with the school, workplace, or charity at these websites, and if so, how?

1. Create a presentation with your answers to the above questions summarizing your school, workplace, or volunteer social media activity only.
2. Save the presentation as **C6-Project1-SocialMedia-Your Name**.
3. Submit the presentation to your instructor in the manner she or he has requested.

Project 2 Establishing a Complete Profile at LinkedIn

Individual
Deliverable: Profile in PDF format

Having a complete profile on LinkedIn is a good idea since many businesses now use LinkedIn to look up prospective candidates. Starting now to build your professional presence before you graduate will give you a head start for your future job search.

1. Create a basic free account at LinkedIn if you do not already have one. If you already have a LinkedIn account, log in and go to your profile.
2. Edit your profile to enter a complete summary of your work experience and education by adding content similar to the information in your current resume. Make sure you have entered text for each of the LinkedIn headings *Summary*, *Experience*, *Education*, *Personal Information*, and *Skills & Expertise*. Be mindful of spelling, grammar, and writing style as this is your online resume.
3. Add a photo to your profile only if you have one that is of professional business quality. Consider asking a classmate to take a photo of you at school if you do not have a good quality picture suitable for a professional profile.
4. When you are finished polishing your profile, use the PDF button on the Profile page (located just above the Summary section) to export a copy of your profile in PDF format.
5. Choose the Save As option and name the PDF document **C6-Project2-MyLinkedInProfile-Your Name**.
6. Submit the PDF document to your instructor in the manner she or he has requested.

Project 3 Finding a Professional Blogger in Your Field of Study

Individual or Pairs
Deliverable: Document, Presentation, or Blog Entry

Blogging is an excellent forum for learning about new trends or issues in a field. Professional bloggers in many industries write regular posts about their fields. Specialized search engines that index blogs such as technorati.com can help you find a blog that is of interest to you.

1. Find a blog where the blogger writes about interesting topics or trends related to your field of study. Consider using technorati.com to locate a blog.
2. Read two to four blog posts and also read the comments posted as feedback.
3. Create a document, presentation, or blog entry with information about the blogger, the title of his or her blog, the two posts you read, the type of comments that were recorded, and your opinion on whether the blog is one that you will follow in the future. Provide the rationale for your decision to subscribe or not to subscribe to the blog. Include the URLs of the blog posts you read.

4. Save the document or presentation as **C6-Project3-ProfessionalBlogger-Your Name**.
5. Submit the document, presentation, or blog URL to your instructor in the manner she or he has requested.

Project 4 Social Media Policy for the Workplace

Pairs or Team
Deliverable: Document or Presentation

The popularity of social networking and blogging is blurring the lines between one's workplace and personal life. Organizations want to ensure that employees use web forums such as social networks and blogs to represent the organization in the best possible light and protect information that is considered confidential or intellectual property. How does a social media policy ensure employees do not post negative comments or photos, or misrepresent fellow colleagues or the organization in any way in social networks and blogs? How does the organization protect its intellectual property or confidential information from being disclosed by employees in blogs or on social networks?

1. Search the Web for examples of social media policies. Find and read at least two social media policy examples.
2. Within your team discuss each policy from both the employer's and the employee's point of view. What do you like and dislike about the policy for each side? Are there any parts of the policy you would rewrite? If yes, how would you rewrite the policy?
3. Create a document or presentation that links to the policies you reviewed and includes your assessment of the questions posed in Step 2.
4. Save the document or presentation as **C6-Project4-SocialMediaPolicies-Your Name**.
5. Submit the document or presentation to your instructor in the manner she or he has requested.

Project 5 Establishing a New Wiki on Green Computing

Pairs or Team
Deliverable: Document or Presentation

Assume that you want to establish a new wiki website with user-generated information about green computing. Are there existing wikis on green computing? If yes, how will you differentiate your wiki? What free wiki hosting sites are available that you can use to start a new wiki?

1. Search the Web for existing wikis on green computing and evaluate a wiki in terms of its organization and usefulness to someone interested in learning about green computing.
2. Plan the organization of pages at your wiki. Create a list of top-level headings or categories and subheadings that you might use for the structure of the new wiki.
3. Search the Web for free wiki hosting services. Choose one website and learn how to use the site to start a new wiki.
4. Create a document or presentation that summarizes your work in Steps 1 through 3. Include the URLs of all websites you used to help you complete this project.
5. Save the document or presentation as **C6-Project5-GreenComputingWiki-Your Name**.
6. Submit the presentation to your instructor in the manner she or he has requested.

Project 6 Greener Computing

Individual, Pairs, or Team
Deliverable: Blog Entry

Assume that you are an intern at a local business that sells pool care supplies. The company heavily promotes its pool maintenance products using print-based flyers with coupons that are distributed using direct mail campaigns. You want to convince the company to use social media tools to distribute coupon codes that people can use online or bring into the store instead of using the mass marketed print-based flyers.

1. Write and post a blog entry that will convince the management of the pool supplies store to consider using social networking tools to promote its products. Within your blog post include links to at least two companies that use social media for this purpose so that the manager can see a few models that support your suggestion.
2. Submit your blog URL to your instructor in the manner she or he has requested.

Optional

Read the blog entry for this project of at least two other classmates and post a comment to each. Submit the URLs of your classmates' blogs with Step 2.

Project 7 Ethics Discussion on Tagging Photos

Team
Deliverable: Document, Blog Entry, or Presentation

Assume that you and several workplace colleagues participated in a charity fundraiser that involved your team running a marathon. At the marathon event, a relative of one of your colleagues took several pictures of the team running at different points in the marathon. A few weeks later you found out that the relative uploaded the photos to his Facebook account and tagged your name in several pictures. You are upset because you never saw the photos, you were not in good running form near the end of the marathon, and you did not give your permission to have the pictures put on a social network where people you do not know will see them.

1. Within your team discuss the ethics involved in tagging someone in photos that are posted to a social network. Should you always get permission first before tagging someone in a photo? Is it OK to tag people in pictures they have not seen? Is it okay to tag people who are not in your network of friends or family? How should you share photos with your friends and family where someone else in the picture is a person they do not know? How should you handle this situation with your work colleague?
2. Prepare a summary of your team's discussion in a document, blog entry, or presentation.
3. Save the document or presentation as **C6-Project7-TagPhotoDiscussion-Your Name**.
4. Submit the document, presentation, or blog entry to your instructor in the manner she or he has requested.

Chapter 7

Computer Security and Privacy

After successfully completing this chapter, you will be able to:

Explain various types of network risks that occur when computers are connected to a network or the Internet

Describe techniques used to protect against network and Internet intrusions

Distinguish various types of malware and methods to prevent malware

Recognize privacy concerns when using the Internet and strategies for safeguarding personal information

Identify mobile device security risks and techniques for minimizing risk

Chances are you spend most of your time online browsing the Web, social networking, messaging, shopping, or doing research. A network intrusion can occur any time you are online, leaving you vulnerable to security and privacy breaches. According to Interpol, **cybercrime** (illegal acts involving a computer) is one of the fastest-growing crime areas, with organized crime groups increasingly controlling these illegal activities. Given the prevalence of cybercrime and other malicious computer threats, every person needs to understand and protect his or her computing equipment, data, and personal information from theft or misuse.

Computer security, also known as information security, includes all activities related to protecting hardware, software, and data from loss due to unauthorized access or use, theft, natural disaster, and human error. In this chapter you will learn about the various security and privacy concerns associated with using a computer connected to a network or the Internet. You will also examine computer security issues related to mobile devices.

Unauthorized Access and Unauthorized Use of Computer Resources

TOPIC 7.1

Connecting to a network at home, at work, or at school has many advantages that include sharing access to the Internet and its resources, storage, and software. However, these advantages do not come without risk. Network attacks at business and government organizations occur often. In this topic you will learn about the types of risks associated with using a network, which include unauthorized access and unauthorized use, and ways in which a network can be protected from these threats.

No network is immune from the threat of intrusion by cybercriminals.

Unauthorized access is often the result of network intrusions from hackers.

War driving is when someone drives around a neighborhood looking for unsecured wireless networks.

Unauthorized Access

Using a computer, network, or other resource without permission is referred to as **unauthorized access**. Unauthorized access happens when someone using programming or other technical skills gains entry without permission into a computer or other resource through the network. The term **hacker** refers to an individual who accesses a network without permission, and **hacking** describes activities involved in gaining unauthorized entry into a network's resources. Some hackers have good intentions; they attempt to pinpoint weaknesses in network security and may even be hired by an organization to hack into the organization's network. These types of hackers are called **white hats**. Hackers who gain unauthorized access with malicious intent to steal data or for other personal gain are called **black hats**.

Wireless networks are used often in homes and workplaces. These networks become a target for hackers because wireless networks are easier to infiltrate. An individual with a portable computing device who drives around trying to connect to someone else's unsecured wireless network is **war driving**. Connecting to someone else's wireless network without the network owner's intent or consent to provide access is called **piggybacking** or Wi-Fi piggybacking. This often occurs when a neighbor is within range of another neighbor's or businesses' unsecured wireless network.

Unauthorized Use

Using a computer, network, or other resource for purposes other than the intended uses is referred to as **unauthorized use**. Unauthorized use can occur when an employee uses the employer's computer for activities such as personal emails, personal printing, or personal online shopping without the employer's permission. Another unauthorized use could occur when a student uses a computer on a school campus to send inappropriate messages or participate in other unacceptable conduct.

Strategies to Prevent Unauthorized Access

At home and in the workplace, unauthorized access is prevented by making sure that each person is assigned a unique user name and password. Family members and employees are advised to choose a password that is not easy to guess and never to reveal it to anyone else or write it down in a visible location. At some workplaces, passwords are required to be changed every month, and the reuse of a password may be prohibited. When a device is not in use, the screen should be locked so that the password is required to log back into the computer. Every computer user should choose a **strong password**, which is a password that is difficult to hack by humans or password detection software programs. A strong password meets the following criteria:

- is a minimum of eight characters
- uses a combination of uppercase letters, lowercase letters, numbers, and symbols
- does not contain any dictionary words or words spelled backward
- does not contain consecutive or repeated numbers or letters
- has no personal information such as a birthdate

In the workplace, entry to rooms with computing equipment is often secured with physical locks. Entry to these rooms may also require additional authentication before the door is unlocked. For example, the use of **biometric devices** is becoming more common. Biometric devices authenticate a person's identity using physical characteristics such as a fingerprint, iris scan, or voice recognition.

All networked computers should have user accounts with strong passwords to gain access.

All networked computers should also have a **firewall**, which is hardware, software, or a combination of hardware and software that blocks unwanted access to your network. Operating systems such as Windows install with the firewall feature turned on by default (Figure 7.1). Incoming and outgoing network traffic is

Access to computing equipment may also be controlled using biometric devices such as iris or hand scans.

routed through firewalls that examine each message and block any communication that does not meet the firewall's security criteria. Some routers that are used to share network or Internet access have a built-in firewall, which adds an extra layer of protection. Many organizations with large networks install a piece of networking equipment that is a dedicated firewall.

All networked computers should have a firewall that blocks outside access to your computer.

In Windows, the firewall is turned on by default.

Figure 7.1 In Windows, the firewall is turned on by default. You can view the status or change the firewall settings in the Control Panel.

Securing a Wireless Network

www.onguardonline.gov/ media/video-0009-wireless-security

Go here to watch a video on steps to take to protect a home wireless network.

At home and at work, wireless routers and access points need to be secured from war drivers and piggybackers. The router or access point should require a security key to gain access. Some devices are sold with a preset password that should be changed to a strong password immediately upon installation. Wireless routers and access points should also be set to use the highest security and **encryption** standard available for the device. Encryption scrambles communications between devices so that the data is not readable. **Wi-Fi Protected Access (WPA)** and **WPA2** are the more recent security standards that authenticate users and employ sophisticated encryption techniques. Enable the WPA2 security standard if possible.

Organizations may also install **intrusion detection software** that analyzes network traffic for suspicious data and alerts network administrators to possible system threats.

A wireless access point should require a security key to connect and should use the highest level of security and encryption standard possible for the device.

Strategies to Prevent Unauthorized Use

An **acceptable use policy (AUP)** is a written policy that describes for employees, students, or other network users the permitted uses for computing equipment and networks. These policies will usually also spell out what is considered inappropriate use of the computers or networks. Some organizations allow employees to use a workplace computer for personal use while the employee is on breaks; however, other organizations prohibit personal use of any kind.

Some organizations use monitoring software that provides reports on activities at each computer. For example, some monitoring software will report on websites visited, web searches conducted, and may even record social networking activity. Email monitoring is also commonly practiced by employers.

Acceptable use policies spell out authorized and unauthorized activities on a network.

Video surveillance, although usually part of a broader safety and security strategy, is another method that can be used by organizations to monitor authorized access and authorized use of computers and networks.

 Blog Topic

Should employers monitor your smartphone?

Many employers provide mobile employees with company-paid smartphones for business use. Does the employer have the right to monitor your Internet and messaging use of the smartphone after business hours? Why or why not?

1. Write and post a blog entry that provides your response to the question.

2. Read at least two of your classmates' blogs and post one comment to each.

3. Submit your blog URL and the URLs of your classmates' blogs for which you provided a comment to your instructor in the manner she or he has requested.

EXPLORE   FURTHER

How can I create a strong password that is easy to remember?

Passwords that are eight or more characters that meet all of the criteria mentioned in this topic can be difficult to remember. How can one create a strong password that is also easy to remember?

1. Search for and read a minimum of two articles that describe techniques for creating a strong password that you can remember.

2. Create a presentation that could be used as a self-guided tutorial for a new network user who needs to create a strong password. Include the URLs of the articles that you read.

3. Save the presentation as **C7-Security-StrongPasswords-Your Name**.

4. Submit the presentation to your instructor in the manner she or he has requested.

TOPIC 7.2

Botnets and Denial of Service Attacks

Two types of attacks on a computer network that cause disruption to network service are botnets and denial of service attacks. These malicious activities cause widespread network slowdowns and sometimes block authorized activity from taking place. In this topic you will learn how a botnet spreads and how to prevent your computer from becoming compromised. You will also learn how a denial of service attack disrupts a network.

Botnets

A computer that is connected to the Internet and is controlled by a hacker or other cybercriminal without the owner's knowledge is called a **zombie** computer. A collection of zombie computers that work together to conduct an attack on another network is a **botnet**. Botnets are used by hackers or cybercriminals to send spam emails, spread viruses, or steal personal data. In some cases, the botnet may be used to conduct a denial of service attack.

A computer becomes a zombie by becoming infected with software (usually a virus) that is hidden from the user and that is controlled remotely by the hacker or cybercriminal. Generally, the infection happens from one of the following events:

- The individual clicks a link in an email or opens an email attachment that contains the malicious program code, which is then installed on the computer.
- The individual downloads a video, image, or program from a website without realizing the file is a cover for the malicious program code; this method is often used at media sharing or peer-to-peer sharing websites.
- The individual simply visits a website without realizing that the malicious code is being downloaded in the background.

Figure 7.2 illustrates a botnet spreading malicious code to a target computer. Once the target computer is infected, it joins the botnet. Table 7.1 lists signs that may indicate your computer has become a zombie. Keep in mind that some of the symptoms listed in Table 7.1 could indicate other issues such as lack of memory. If necessary, have your PC checked by a professional to determine the cause of any symptoms.

Did You Know ?

According to the Quarter 1 2012 McAfee Threats Report, between 4 and 5 million computers globally were infected by botnets, with Colombia, Japan, Poland, Spain, and the United States all seeing increases within the quarter.

To prevent your computer from becoming a zombie, make sure you have antivirus software automatically scheduled to scan and update, update the OS regularly, and have a firewall active at all times. If you think your computer is a zombie, immediately update your antivirus software and perform a full scan. In some cases, you may need to hire professional help to erase your hard disk drive and start from scratch by reinstalling legitimate programs and data.

hacker

"zombie" botnet network

Botnet makes contact with target computer and delivers malware application allowing stealth control by a hacker.

Figure 7.2 A zombie computer is a PC in which the owner is unaware that his or her computer is being used as part of a botnet to attack other computers.

Table 7.1	Signs That Your Computer May Be a Zombie
Your computer may be compromised if . . .	
Your Internet connectivity slows down consistently and dramatically	
Hard disk activity occurs when you are not running any programs (including automatic antivirus or software updates)	
Your computer or a device such as the keyboard or mouse becomes unresponsive	
Hard disk space is filling up unexpectedly	
A different default website appears when you open the browser window	
New desktop icons or toolbars appear that you did not install	
Undeliverable messages appear in your email inbox for people you did not email	

Denial of Service Attacks (DoS)

A **denial of service attack (DoS)** occurs when a network or web server is overwhelmed with network traffic in the form of a constant stream of bogus emails or other messages to the point that the server's response time becomes slow or shuts down completely. Legitimate users are denied access, usually receiving a message that the server is busy. Popular or well-known companies and government websites are often the target of DoS attacks conducted by botnets. Figure 7.3 displays how a DoS attack is orchestrated.

Hackers or other cybercriminals perform DoS attacks for a variety of reasons, some of which include to draw attention to a social or political cause, to embarrass a company or government, to gain notoriety, or to make demands on a company.

Organizations attempt to prevent DoS attacks by employing firewalls, intrusion detection software, and antivirus software tools.

Did You Know **?**

In August 2012, WikiLeaks (a website that publishes whistleblower documents) was the victim of a DoS attack that disrupted service for more than a week. Its server was swamped with 10 Gbps of phony network traffic from thousands of Internet addresses.

Figure 7.3 Denial of service attacks often target large corporate or government networks.

EXPLORE FURTHER

Best Practices for Preventing Botnets

In this topic you learned some strategies to avoid becoming a zombie computer that include regular updates to antivirus and OS software. Being diligent with email, downloading, sharing files, and web surfing will also help prevent botnets. What best practices should online users adopt?

1. Create a document or presentation with a list of Internet and Web use best practices that every computer user should adopt to help prevent the spread of botnets.
2. Save the document as **C7-Security-PreventBotnets-Your Name**.
3. Submit the document or presentation to your instructor in the manner she or he has requested.

TOPIC 7.3

Malware Infections

Any type of malicious software program that is designed to damage, disable, or steal data is called **malware**. Malware installs on your computer without your knowledge usually from email or online activities. Malware programs can delete files, damage files, steal personal data, track your activities, display pop-up windows or messages, or turn your computer into a zombie. In this topic you will learn about common malware that exists in the form of viruses, worms, Trojan horses, and rootkits as well as strategies to prevent malware from infecting your computer.

Viruses

A **virus** is a form of malware that, once installed on a host computer without the owner's knowledge, can replicate itself and spread to other media on the infected computer and to other computers on the network. A virus infects a computer through a variety of means, including:

- downloading and installing infected software
- opening an infected file attachment in an email message (Figure 7.4)
- visiting an infected website
- plugging in an infected USB or other peripheral device
- clicking links in messages (including instant messages) or at untrustworthy websites

A type of virus that is embedded in a document and infects the computer when the user opens the document and enables a macro is called a **macro virus**. Microsoft Office documents were once a favorite target for macro viruses because many people circulate documents via email attachments. Microsoft improved security in its Office programs so that macros are automatically disabled when a document is opened; however, one needs to be aware that enabling the macro may invoke the virus.

Check This Out

home.mcafee.com/virusinfo/

Go here for up-to-date virus information including recent threats, a virus threat meter, and a global virus map.

The receiver opens the attachment (with a virus) and is infected. The person then sends an email with the attachment to another person, and it infects that person's computer when it is opened.

email infected by virus

The receiver does not open the attachment, deletes the email, and is not infected.

email infected by virus

Figure 7.4 Opening an email attachment with a virus infects your computer and starts spreading the virus to others.

Worms

A self-replicating program that requires no action on the part of the user to copy itself to another computer on a network is called a **worm**. Your computer can become infected with a worm simply by being connected to an infected network (Figure 7.5). Worms typically exist to backlog network traffic or performance or may even shut down a network.

worm virus
introduced by a hacker

virus is spread throughout
unprotected network

Figure 7.5 **A worm automatically sends copies of itself to other computers on the network.**

Trojan Horses

A program that disguises itself as a useful program but then infects your computer with malware when you run the application is called a **Trojan horse**. This type of malware is named after the legend in which Greeks concealed themselves inside a hollow wooden horse to invade the city of Troy. Residents of Troy thought the horse was a victory trophy and brought the horse inside the gates of the city, thereby allowing their city to be overtaken. Similarly, Trojan horse malware often appears as a useful program such as antivirus software or an OS update to entice you to run the application that installs the malware. Trojans do not replicate themselves, but nevertheless the damage done by a Trojan can be disastrous as some are designed to send personal information back to a cybercriminal.

A Trojan horse is disguised as a useful program, tricking you into running the program that installs the malware.

Rootkits

A **rootkit** program hides on the infected computer and provides a **back door** (way to bypass computer security) for a hacker or other cybercriminal to remotely monitor or take over control of the PC. Using the remote access, the hacker or cybercriminal can run damaging programs or steal personal information. Unlike viruses and worms, the objective of a rootkit is not to spread to other computers but to control the target PC. Rootkits may end up on your computer by installing some other software in which the rootkit piggybacks or via a virus.

A hidden program called a rootkit can allow a hacker to monitor your activity or steal personal data.

Malware Protection

All computer users need to have an up-to-date **antivirus program** running on their computers at all times. Typically, these programs allow you to schedule automatic scans to run on a regular basis. Most programs are also set to scan all incoming emails automatically; however, you should check the settings in the program to ensure you have real-time protection turned on.

Most new computers are sold with an antivirus program already installed, and some OS's include malware protection. If you need an antivirus program or want to upgrade to a comprehensive suite of online threat protection, you can buy a program such as Norton 360 or McAfee All Access that includes protection for smartphones and tablets. You will also find antivirus software available free from companies such as Microsoft or AVG. Microsoft provides Windows Security Essentials free for computers using Windows 7 or earlier, and Windows Defender for computers using Windows 8. In Windows 8, Windows Defender (Figure 7.6) was enhanced to provide the same level of malware protection as Windows Security Essentials.

Norton 360 is a comprehensive package for protection from online threats including viruses, identity theft, and harmful websites.

Several other antivirus programs are available from reputable sources such as Sophos and Kaspersky; however, be wary of downloading free antivirus software from an ad or pop-up window that appears when you are on a website. Go directly to the website of a company that you know is trusted and download free software from there.

Regardless of the malware protection program you choose, make sure it is running automatically, scans regularly, and that a firewall is always active.

Check This Out
www.eset.com/us/online-scanner
Go here for a free on-demand scan of your computer that requires only your browser to work.

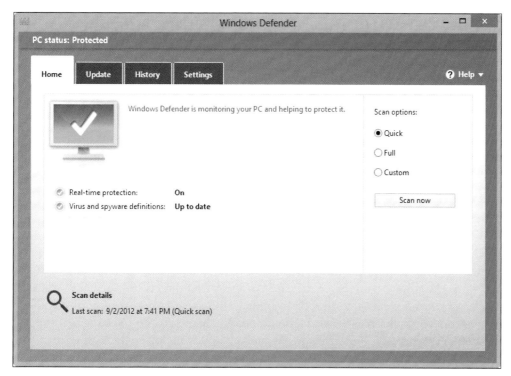

Figure 7.6 Windows Defender is included with Windows 8 and runs automatically to provide protection against malware and other unwanted software.

Do Regular Backups

Making regular backups of your data will provide the best protection of all. Create a routine to back up data regularly. Should malware strike your system, you will have another copy of important information safely stored somewhere else.

EXPLORE FURTHER

What is a logic bomb?

Another type of malware that can cause damage to your computer is a **logic bomb virus**. What are the characteristics of this type of malware? What is the most common type of activity that activates the virus? Are there uses for a logic bomb that are not malicious?

1. Search for information on logic bombs and read at least two articles to find answers to the above questions.

2. Create a document or presentation that summarizes in your own words what you learned about logic bombs. Include the URLs of the websites you used.

3. Save the document or presentation as **C7-Security-LogicBombs-Your Name**.

4. Submit the document or presentation to your instructor in the manner she or he has requested.

TOPIC 7.4

Phishing, Pharming, and Clickjacking Threats

A growing area of cybercrime involves online fraud or scams that are designed to trick unsuspecting users into revealing personal information so the criminal can steal money from the individual or engage in **identity theft**. Identity theft occurs when an individual's personal information is obtained by a criminal who then uses the information to buy products or services under the victim's name or otherwise pose as the victim for financial gain. In this topic you will learn about three scams that are designed to trick someone into revealing personal information.

Phishing

Phishing (pronounced *fishing*) is the term that describes activities that appear to be initiated by a legitimate organization (such as one's bank) in an attempt to obtain personal information that can be used in fraud, theft, or identity theft. A popular email phishing technique involves an individual receiving a message that appears to be from a bank or credit card company and directs him or her to click a link (Figure 7.7). The link goes to a bogus website that appears to be valid and may even include the real bank's logo and color scheme. At the phishing website, the user is prompted to enter his or her personal information such as a user name, password, bank account number, or credit card number. If the individual complies, he or she will have given critical personal information to a criminal who will use the information to transfer money from the individual's bank accounts or to charge purchases to a credit card.

Phishing is also growing on social networking sites such as Facebook and Twitter. With the high volume of activity at social networks, criminals are targeting these networks for new scams. One scam used a link to a video in a Facebook message that, when clicked, directed the person to a page that looked like the Facebook login page but was not genuine. Users typed in their email address and password thinking they were logging into Facebook but instead were providing the information to a cybercriminal.

Check This Out

www.antiphishing.org/report_phishing.html

Go here to submit a report about a phishing message you have received.

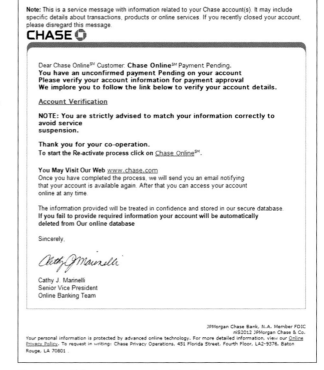

Figure 7.7 This message received by Chase customers was a phishing attempt to trick users into clicking the links and revealing account information.

Pharming

A **pharming** scam is similar to phishing except that the individual is tricked into typing in personal information at a phony website that appears to be the real website requested by the individual. For example, an individual enters a web address for his or her bank in the browser and is directed instead to a pharming website. The web page at the pharming website looks legitimate, so the individual proceeds to enter personal information.

Phishing and pharming scams employ **spoofing** techniques where a sender's email address is altered to a phony address that appears legitimate to the email recipient, or an IP address is altered to appear to be a trusted source.

Pharming scams redirect you to a phony website where you are prompted to enter personal information.

Clickjacking

Clickjacking occurs when a button, graphic, or link on a web page appears to be real but, when clicked, causes malicious software to run. The malicious software code is hidden on the web page so that an individual has no idea he or she is not clicking a real link. Clicking the bogus button, graphic, or link typically directs the person to another website where personal information is requested. Some clickjacks are used to download a virus onto a computer.

In January 2012, Facebook and the Washington State Office of the Attorney General filed a lawsuit against a company suspected of using clickjacking techniques. In one scheme, bogus Like buttons redirected users to advertising pages where the scammers received money for each wayward clicker.

Clickjacking scams use buttons, graphics, or links to redirect users from legitimate websites or run malicious software.

Phishing and clickjacking scams are often initiated in email. Delete messages you receive that ask you to click a link to update information. Never click links in unsolicited email messages. Before typing personal information, examine the URL and other text on the page. Phony websites usually have spelling or grammar errors, or the URL for a false website will have a slightly different domain name or character substitution in the name such as the number 1 instead of the letter i.

EXPLORE FURTHER

What is social engineering?

Security experts know that the weakest link in computer security is humans. Unfortunately, cybercriminals also know this and employ **social engineering** tactics to gain unauthorized access to a network or trick individuals into revealing personal information. What is social engineering?

1. Search for articles on social engineering. Find and read at least two articles that describe social engineering tactics including tactics used at social networking websites.
2. Create a document or presentation that summarizes in your own words what you learned about social engineering. Include the URLs of the websites you used.
3. Save the document or presentation as **C7-Security-SocialEngineering-Your Name**.
4. Submit the document or presentation to your instructor in the manner she or he has requested.

TOPIC 7.5

Information Privacy

With so much information collected and stored online, individuals and companies are increasingly concerned with information privacy. **Information privacy** is the right of individuals or organizations to control the information that is collected about them. Consider all of the websites at which you have set up accounts and the personal information you provided at each site. Consider also that some websites track the pages you visit and store information about you. Software may be installed on your computer that is tracking everything you do. In this topic you will learn about privacy concerns related to online activities.

Cookies

A web server may send a small text file to be stored on your computer's hard disk that contains data about you such as your user name and the pages you visited. This text file is called a **cookie** and is used to identify you when you return to the website. In many cases, the use of cookies is welcomed to prefill a login or customize your viewing preferences at an e-commerce site. However, cookies might also be used for unwanted purposes such as tracking your activities or gathering information about you without your permission.

All Internet browsers provide the ability for you to control how cookies are handled. Figure 7.8 shows the Privacy tab where you can choose how to manage cookies in the Internet Options dialog box of Internet Explorer 10. The default setting is *Medium*, which blocks first- and third-party cookies that might be used to contact you without your consent or that have no compact privacy policy.

Dragging the slider up to the top changes the privacy setting to block all cookies and all the way down accepts all cookies. In between, options set the privacy setting to Low, Medium, Medium High, or High.

As you move the slider bar up or down, the description for each level of privacy displays here.

Figure 7.8 Internet browser software such as IE10 provides tools to help you manage cookies.

Spyware

Software programs that exist on your computer without your knowledge and track your activities are referred to as **spyware**. Some spyware may be on a workplace computer so that the employer can monitor your online activities. Other spyware may be used by websites to target ads to your preferences. Antivirus programs typically include spyware detection and removal.

Software programs responsible for pop-up ads that appear on your desktop or while viewing web pages are the result of software referred to as **adware**. These unwelcome ads often piggyback spyware onto your computer.

Spyware tracks your online activities.

Keystroke Loggers   A version of spyware called **keystroke logger**, or **keylogger**, may be activated as part of a rootkit or Trojan horse that records every keystroke you type and sends it back to a cybercriminal. Keystroke loggers may be used to obtain your bank account number and password or other personal information that leads to identity theft. Some keystroke logger software is promoted on the Internet to businesses as a computer security tool and to parents who want to monitor their children's online activity.

Spam

Spam is electronic junk mail—unsolicited emails sent to a large group of people at the same time. Spam messages entice readers to buy something or are phishing messages. Spam messaging has infiltrated social networks and text messages. According to Symantec, more than 60 percent of email is spam. **Twitter bots** are software programmed to follow people based on popular keywords. When a user clicks a link in the comment that appears as a response to a tweet, they receive spam or malware. Beware of followers with strange handles.

Obtaining a store loyalty card or registering for free accounts often requires you provide your email address. These databases of names and email addresses are sold for marketing purposes, which is how you end up with spam. Many people use a free web-based email account such as Windows Live Hotmail or Gmail for online activities only. This prevents spam from invading a regular email inbox. Sign up for a new account when spam at the free account becomes onerous.

Data Privacy in the Cloud

When storing pictures, documents, or other data at a cloud provider's website such as Flickr or Dropbox, find out the privacy and security policies that affect your data. Typically, you control the data privacy by restricting who can see a file. However, unanticipated issues could arise such as an employee of the cloud provider being able to view the contents of your files. To be safe, never post files at a cloud provider that contain sensitive information,

Did You Know

In October 2011, a keystroke logger virus was found in the U.S. military's network that recorded pilots' keystrokes as they flew drone missions over Afghanistan and other war zones.

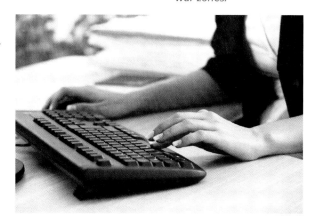

Spyware called keystroke loggers record every keystroke you type.

Spam is estimated to account for more than 60 percent of all email traffic!

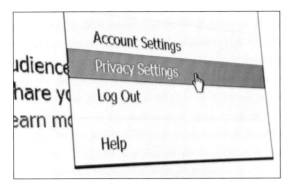

Change privacy settings at social networks such as Facebook and other cloud providers to control information about you that is available for anyone to view.

Check This Out

www.epic.org

Go here for up-to-date information on privacy issues.

such as your birthdate and social security number that could make you vulnerable to identity theft.

At social networks such as Facebook and Twitter, make sure you review and change privacy settings so that only the information you want public is viewable by anyone. When posting information at social networks, also consider that those friends who see the information could inadvertently share something personal about you with someone else. Cybercriminals are trolling social networks for personal data they can mine for financial gain.

Ways to Protect Personal Information

When shopping online or conducting other business that requires a financial transaction, make sure the URL at the website begins with *https* and that you see a small closed padlock next to the address bar or in the Status bar of the browser window. These signs indicate a secure website using a protocol that protects data sent to the site with **Transport Layer Security (TLS)**. TLS encrypts transmitted data so that the data is unreadable if intercepted.

Table 7.2 provides strategies you can use to protect personal information while pursuing online activities. Ultimately, the responsibility rests with you to keep sensitive information private and to be diligent at websites where you provide personal data. Check privacy policies and do not reveal information that you do not feel is necessary for the purpose of the visit.

Table 7.2   Strategies to Protect Personal Information
Ways to Minimize Tracking of Your Personal Information
Fill in only the fields marked with asterisks at websites that ask you for personal information when registering for an account; these are the minimum fields required to obtain an account.
Make sure the privacy setting for cookies in the browser you use is set to block cookies for sites that do not have a privacy policy or have not received your consent. You may want to consider blocking all cookies.
At websites that require a birthdate, such as Facebook, make sure you hide the date in your profile.
Have different user names and passwords for online shopping, social networks, and banking.
Do not allow apps or websites to tag your location. Geo-location apps on your smartphone sound cool, but consider that a third party could be tracking your every movement.
Use a free web-based email account for online shopping and social networks and keep your regular email address for other purposes.
If your ISP does not use a spam filter on your email account, find and install anti-spam software on your own.
Delete spam messages right away without opening them.
Unsubscribe to mailing lists that you think are selling your email address for marketing purposes.
Regularly clear the history in your browser.
Make sure the antivirus program you use includes anti-spyware and that the program is set to automatically update and scan your computer regularly.
Make sure a firewall is active at all times you are online.
Shred documents with personal information before discarding them.

Blog Topic

Should employers monitor employee activities?

Video cameras, email monitoring, website monitoring, and keystroke loggers are some of the ways in which employers can keep tabs on what their employees are up to at the workplace. Generally, employees should not have an expectation of privacy when using employer-owned computing equipment. Still, isn't all this monitoring of your activities an invasion of your privacy? What about using the employer's computer on your lunch hours and breaks? Shouldn't that be considered your personal time?

1. Write and post a blog entry that provides your opinion about the questions.

2. Read at least two of your classmates' blogs and post one comment to each.

3. Submit your blog URL and the URLs of your classmates' blogs for which you provided a comment to your instructor in the manner she or he has requested.

EXPLORE FURTHER

Learning about Privacy Notices

Websites that collect personal information also have a privacy notice that spells out how the organization will use the personal data you provide. Have you ever read a privacy notice? What should a typical privacy notice include?

1. Go to the website of an e-tailer that you have used in the past, and find and read the Privacy Policy or Privacy Notice link. If you have not made an online purchase, visit the website of a well-known e-tailer such as Amazon.

2. Create a document or presentation with a summary of how personal information will be used, stored, and safeguarded by the e-tailer. Include the URL to the policy you used.

3. Save the document or presentation as **C6-Security-PrivacyPolicy-Your Name**.

4. Submit the document or presentation to your instructor in the manner she or he has requested.

TOPIC 7.6

Mobile Device Security

Portable devices such as notebooks, ultrabooks, tablets, and smartphones have unchained people from their homes and offices; however, the portable nature of these devices makes them vulnerable to security risks. In this topic, you will examine the various security risks for mobile workers and methods used to protect hardware and data.

Mobile Malware

According to McAfee Security, **mobile malware** (viruses designed for mobile devices) increased 1,200 percent in the first quarter of 2012. Some of the increase is attributed to improved detection methods; however, a massive increase in viruses for mobile devices is still evident. Additionally, McAfee reported finding the first Android Trojan horse virus in 2012. Most mobile malware targets Android devices because of the open source nature of the mobile OS; however, no mobile OS is without risk. Make sure all mobile devices, including tablets and smartphones, have mobile security software to prevent malware infections.

Mobile malware is on the rise! Make sure your smartphone or tablet has mobile security software to stop the spread of viruses and spyware.

Lost or Stolen Mobile Devices

Securing a mobile device with locks, biometrics, or remote tools is a necessity to protect against the loss of a smartphone, tablet, or notebook computer due to theft or absentmindedness. Recent reports have shown an increase in the theft of mobile devices. While the hardware is easily replaced, the personal information and data stored on these devices is a major risk for individuals and employers. The following tools assist with securing mobile devices and data:

- Physical locks with cables that attach a notebook to a table or desk in a public place are a deterrent to thieves looking for an easy target.
- Many devices now come equipped with fingerprint readers that restrict access to the authenticated user only.
- Technology for remote wiping, locking, and tracking of a lost or stolen mobile device allows the owner to wipe the device clean of data and track the device's location.
- A strong password or passcode for access to the data should be enabled on all devices; should the device be stolen or lost, the password/passcode may provide enough time to employ remote wiping utilities.
- Regular backups of data stored on mobile devices should be mandatory.

Mobile devices can be secured with fingerprint readers, passcodes, and physical cable locks to restrict access.

Bluetooth Risks

Bluetooth technology, which wirelessly connects and exchanges data between two devices in close proximity, is subject to risk from intrusion from others within range. Bluetooth range is approximately 30 feet. When using Bluetooth in a public space with many people nearby, a risk exists that someone else can connect to your device and send you a virus or access personal data. Turn Bluetooth on only when needed and turn it off as soon as you are finished with it to prevent others from accessing your device. Consider installing a Bluetooth firewall app that will secure your device from unwanted intrusions.

Mobile devices carry risks unique to their portable nature. Employers may require employees with mobile devices to abide by a mobile computing policy that requires employees to take responsible measures to secure notebooks, tablets, or smartphones while away from the office, make frequent backups to a secure site, and password-protect all sensitive company documents stored on the device.

Turn off Bluetooth when using a mobile device in a crowded place.

Be Aware of Shoulder Surfers!

If you are viewing sensitive information on a mobile device, protect your screen from shoulder surfers. Privacy screens for notebooks, tablets, and smartphones prevent shoulder surfers from seeing personal or confidential information.

Career Connection

Computer Security Experts

Symantec CEO Enrique Salem told a New York Technology Summit group in June 2012 that the United States does not have enough security professionals. Computer security is a top priority for many organizations to combat the increase in network attacks and cybercrime. Security professionals are among the highest paid IT workers. A bachelor's degree in computer science or computer security is generally required for a computer security career. Certifications attract higher salaries with the Certified Information Security Manager (CISM) and Certified Information Systems Security Professional (CISSP) the most widely recognized security certifications.

EXPLORE   FURTHER

Using Public Wi-Fi Wisely

Many public places now provide free access to Wi-Fi networks. These networks are unsecured to make them as convenient to use as possible. What precautions should you take when using a public Wi-Fi network to connect your notebook, tablet, or smartphone?

1. Search for articles on public Wi-Fi hotspot security. Find and read at least two articles with tips for using these networks safely. Choose five tips you think are the most important.
2. Create a presentation with one slide for each tip where you describe how to use public Wi-Fi safely and securely. Include a sixth slide with the URLs of the articles you used.
3. Save the presentation as **C7-Security-PublicWi-Fi-Your Name**.
4. Submit the presentation to your instructor in the manner she or he has requested.

Concepts Review

Topic	Key Concepts	Key Terms
Unauthorized Access and Unauthorized Use of Computer Resources	Unauthorized access occurs when someone, usually a hacker, gains entry without permission to a computer through a network (referred to as hacking).	Cybercrime
	White hats are hackers that gain entry into a network to pinpoint weaknesses in the network security.	Computer security
		Unauthorized access
	Black hats are hackers that gain entry into a network with malicious intent.	Hacker
		Hacking
	Wireless networks are often the target of war drivers or piggybackers because unsecured wireless networks are easy to infiltrate.	White hats
		Black hats
		War driving
	Unauthorized use is performing activities on a computer other than the intended uses.	Piggybacking
		Unauthorized use
	A strong password is difficult to hack by humans or password detection software programs.	Strong password
		Biometric devices
	Physical entry to rooms with computing equipment at workplaces is secured by locks and biometric devices.	Firewall
		Wi-Fi Protected Access (WPA)
	A firewall is hardware, software, or a combination of hardware and software that blocks unauthorized access.	WPA2
		Encryption
	Wireless routers and access points should be protected with security keys and the highest possible encryption standards.	Intrusion detection software
		Acceptable use policy (AUP)
	Organizations may use intrusion detection software to thwart network attacks.	
	An acceptable use policy spells out appropriate and inappropriate use of computing equipment in the workplace.	
Botnets and Denial of Service Attacks	A zombie is a computer controlled by someone else without the owner's knowledge.	Zombie
		Botnet
	A collection of zombie computers that attack a network is called a botnet.	Denial of service attack (DoS)
	A computer becomes a zombie by being infected with software that is hidden from the user and is controlled remotely by the hacker or cybercriminal.	
	To prevent a computer from becoming a zombie, scan regularly with up-to-date antivirus software, update the OS regularly, and make sure a firewall is always active.	
	A denial of service attack (DoS) occurs when a botnet attacks a network by sending a constant stream of messages that slow down or completely shut down a server.	
	Corporate and government networks are often the target for DoS attacks.	
	Organizations use firewalls, intrusion detection software, and antivirus tools to prevent DoS attacks.	

continued....

Malware Infections	Malware refers to any type of malicious software.	Malware
	A virus is a form of malware that replicates itself, spreading to other media on the infected computer and to other computers.	Virus
	A macro virus is a virus that is embedded in a macro in a Microsoft Office document; when the user enables the macro, the virus infects the computer.	Macro virus
		Worm
	A worm is a self-replicating program that infects other computers on a network without user action.	Trojan horse
	A Trojan horse is a program that appears to the user to be a useful program but which in fact is malware.	Rootkit
		Back door
	Rootkit programs are hidden from the owner and are used by a hacker or cybercriminal to control a computer remotely.	Antivirus program
	Antivirus programs detect and remove malware.	Logic bomb virus
Phishing, Pharming, and Clickjacking Threats	Identity theft occurs when personal information is obtained by a criminal who uses the information for financial gain.	Identity theft
	Phishing messages include links to websites that appear legitimate but are intended to steal personal information.	Phishing
		Pharming
	Phishing is increasing on social networks.	Spoofing
	Pharming is where a phony website appears after the user types a web address into the address bar of a browser.	Clickjacking
		Social engineering
	Spoofing techniques alter a sender's email or web address to appear legitimate.	
	Clickjacking occurs when a user clicks a phony button, image, or link and is redirected to another website or a virus downloads.	
	Phishing and clickjacking scams are often initiated in email messages.	
Information Privacy	Information privacy refers to the rights of individuals to control information that is collected about them.	Information privacy
	A cookie is a small text file placed on your hard drive by a web server with information about your user name and the pages you visited.	Cookie
		Spyware
	Spyware tracks your activities without your knowledge.	Adware
	Adware displays pop-up ads on your desktop or at web pages.	Keystroke logger
	Adware will sometimes piggyback spyware onto your computer.	Keylogger
	Keystroke loggers, or keyloggers, record every keystroke you type and send the data to a cybercriminal.	Spam
	Spam is unsolicited email sent to large groups of people.	Twitter bots
	Find out the privacy and security policies in effect at cloud providing websites where you store pictures and documents.	Transport Layer Security (TLS)
	Review and change privacy settings at social networks like Facebook and Twitter.	
	Make sure *https* is the beginning of an address at any website at which you enter personal information for a financial transaction and that a closed padlock icon displays.	
	Transport Layer Security (TLS) encrypts data transmitted to a secure website.	

continued....

Topic	Key Concepts	Key Terms
Mobile Device Security	Mobile malware are viruses designed for mobile devices.	Mobile malware
	All mobile devices including tablets and smartphones should have mobile security software installed.	
	Android devices are attacked more frequently due to their open source mobile operating system.	
	Mobile devices should be secured with locks, biometrics, or remote wiping and tracking tools in case of loss or theft.	
	Using Bluetooth in a public space leaves you vulnerable; someone else with a Bluetooth device can access your smartphone, tablet, or notebook and send you a virus or steal personal data.	
	Employers may require mobile workers to abide by a mobile computing policy that requires them to take responsible measures to secure their devices.	
	Regular backups of data on mobile devices may be required as part of a mobile computing policy.	

Multiple Choice

1. A type of hacker that breaks into a computer network to pinpoint network weaknesses is known as a _____.
   a. Piggybacker
   b. Black hat
   c. White hat
   d. War logger

2. Hardware or software that blocks unwanted access to a network is a(n) _____.
   a. War driver
   b. Firewall
   c. Encrypter
   d. White hat

3. This term refers to a computer that is controlled by a hacker without the owner's knowledge.
   a. Botnet
   b. DoS
   c. Bot
   d. Zombie

4. This type of attack overwhelms a network server with the intent of slowing or shutting down the server.
   a. Denial of service
   b. Bot attack
   c. Piggybacking
   d. War driving

5. This type of virus is often embedded in a Microsoft Office document.
   a. Rootkit virus
   b. Worm virus
   c. Trojan horse virus
   d. Macro virus

6. This type of virus is hidden from the owner and allows the computer to be controlled remotely.
   a. Rootkit virus
   b. Worm virus
   c. Macro virus
   d. Logic bomb virus

7. This term describes activities that appear to be from legitimate organizations but that have malicious intent.
   a. Rootkit virus
   b. Logic bomb virus
   c. Phishing
   d. War driving

8. A phony button, graphic, or link on a website is used for _____.
   a. Phishing
   b. Pharming
   c. Spoofing
   d. Clickjacking

9. This is a small text file placed on your hard drive after visiting a website.
   a. Spyware
   b. Cookie
   c. Adware
   d. Spam

10. This type of spyware records everything you type.
    a. Adware
    b. Spam
    c. Cookie
    d. Keylogger

11. Bluetooth range is approximately _____ feet.
    a. 10
    b. 20
    c. 30
    d. 40

12. Viruses designed for a notebook, tablet, or smartphone are referred to by this term.
    a. Mobile malware
    b. Mobile mania
    c. Mobile risk
    d. Mobile software

Crossword Puzzle

ACROSS

7 Program disguised as useful software
8 Desktop pop-up ad
9 Software that tracks your activities
11 Scrambles data to make it unreadable
12 Bogus buttons at websites

DOWN

1 Devices frequently targeted for mobile malware
2 Malicious software
3 Wireless technology for short ranges
4 Often used to conduct DoS attack
5 Device authenticates physical characteristic
6 Junk mail
10 Links to phony websites in emails

Matching

Match the term with the statement or definition.

_____ 1. Mobile malware
_____ 2. WPA2
_____ 3. Denial of service
_____ 4. Worm
_____ 5. Botnet
_____ 6. Pharming
_____ 7. War driving
_____ 8. Https

a. Collection of zombies
b. Self-replicating virus
c. Spoofing a web address
d. Android Trojan horse
e. Transport Layer Security (TLS)
f. Breaking into a wireless network
g. Server is busy messages
h. Wireless security standard

Project 1 Computer Security Risks for Small Businesses

Individual or Pairs
Deliverable: Presentation

Assume you are helping an aunt who is working on opening a new café in your area. The café will feature daily lunch specials in addition to dessert treats, cold drinks, and fair trade coffee beverages. Free Wi-Fi access will be available to customers in the café. At a secure website, customers will be able to order and pay for lunch as well as receive daily coupons and specials at a Facebook page. Your aunt is also considering using Twitter to promote daily specials. To properly plan for her computing needs, your aunt has asked for your help in assessing the computer security risks that she may encounter.

1. Create a presentation that will summarize all of the risks and strategies for mitigating risks that have been explored in this chapter. The information presented should be a summary only of high-level points for your aunt to consider as she plans her business needs.
2. Save the presentation as **C7-Project1-SummaryOfSecurityRisks-Your Name**.
3. Submit the presentation to your instructor in the manner she or he has requested.

Project 2 Acceptable Use and Computer Security Policies

Individual or Pairs
Deliverable: Document or Presentation

Assume the aunt you have been helping launch a new café is now ready to hire staff and wants to have a solid Acceptable Use Policy and Computer Security Policy in place before employee training begins. She has asked you to develop a list of points that should be included in the two policies that include appropriate and inappropriate use of computer and network resources and responsibilities related to ensuring that the computing resources are not compromised with malware.

1. Create a document or presentation that provides your aunt with a list of points that should be included in the Acceptable Use Policy and a second list of points that should be included in the Computer Security Policy. *Hint: Use your school's AUP as a guideline.*
2. Save the document or presentation as **C7-Project2-AUPandSecurityPolicy-Your Name**.
3. Submit the document or presentation to your instructor in the manner she or he has requested.

Project 3 How Does AntiVirus Software Detect and Remove Viruses?

Individual or Pairs
Deliverable: Document or Presentation

The importance of regularly updating antivirus programs has been stressed throughout this chapter. How do antivirus programs work to detect a new virus on your computer? Why is updating the software so important? When a virus is found, how does the software remove the virus from your computer?

1. Search for information on how antivirus programs work to find answers to the above questions.
2. Create a document or presentation with a summary in your own words that describes the detection and removal techniques used by antivirus programs. Include the URLs of the websites you used.
3. Save the document or presentation as **C7-Project3-AntiVirusPrograms-Your Name**.
4. Submit the document or presentation to your instructor in the manner she or he has requested.

Project 4 College Students the Target of Identity Thieves

Pairs or Team

Deliverable: Information Flyer for New Students

According to the U.S. Department of Justice, individuals 18 to 24 years old are more likely to experience identity theft than others. College-age students represent one-quarter of identity theft victims. Why are college students the frequent targets of identity thieves? What can a college student do to minimize his or her risk of identity theft?

1. Search for information related to identity theft aimed at college-age students to find answers to the above questions.
2. Create a flyer that your school could insert in a new student's orientation package that warns students of the risk of identity theft and provides information on how to prevent it.
3. Save the flyer as **C7-Project4-StudentIdentityTheft-Your Name**.
4. Submit the flyer and the URLs for the websites you used to your instructor in the manner she or he has requested.

Project 5 Public Key and Symmetric Key Encryption

Pairs or Team

Deliverable: Document or Presentation with Diagrams

Encryption, a part of cryptography, is a method used to protect data as it is transmitted across a network. Encrypted data is scrambled so that a hacker will not be able to read intercepted messages. In this chapter, encryption was recommended to secure data transmitted on a wireless network and when conducting online financial transactions. Computer encryption systems are generally based on public key or symmetric key categories. How do these two encryption models differ?

1. Search for information on public key and symmetric key encryption. Read at least two articles that describe each encryption model process.
2. Next, search for images that diagram public key and symmetric key encryption models. Choose a diagram for each model that you think best illustrates each encryption model.
3. Create a document or presentation that summarizes in your own words how each encryption model works and include the diagram that you selected to illustrate the process. Be sure to cite the diagram in your document or presentation and include the URLs of the websites that you used.
4. Save the document or presentation as **C7-Project5-Encryption-Your Name**.
5. Submit the document or presentation to your instructor in the manner she or he has requested.

Project 6 Greener Computing

Individual, Pairs, or Team

Deliverable: Blog Entry

Cloud computing has been advocated as a way to practice green computing. By using SaaS tools at a cloud provider, a business or individual has no need for high-end computing devices to act as servers or PCs. Lower-powered hardware is a viable option that reduces an individual's or company's carbon footprint. Another advantage is the benefit of online collaboration reducing the need for travel by team members. However, adopting SaaS does not come without security and privacy risks. What are the risks and how can risks be mitigated?

1. Search for information on cloud computing security and privacy risks and methods to minimize risk. Read at least two articles that provide information to answer the above question.

2. Write and post a blog entry that describes in your own words cloud computing security and privacy risks and strategies for minimizing the risks.

3. Submit your blog URL to your instructor in the manner she or he has requested.

Optional

Read the blog entry for this project of at least two other classmates and post a comment to each. Submit the URLs of your classmates' blogs with Step 3.

Project 7 Ethics Discussion on Revealing Company Secrets

Team

Deliverable: Document, Blog Entry, or Presentation

You work in a company that is developing web-based software that homeowners can use to remotely adjust heating, lighting, and security systems in their homes. The software program is easier to use than others on the market and will be priced competitively. You have recently learned that a member of the team has been talking about the new software with her friends on Facebook. Another person in the company who is on the colleague's friends list has told you that she is revealing information about the program features and pricing. You have mentioned to her that she should not be discussing the project on a social network. She replied that it's OK because it's only her friends that see the postings.

1. Within your team discuss the ethics involved in revealing company secrets on a social network. Is it okay to discuss a project since only people in a friends list see the postings? Why or why not? Are there security and privacy issues the colleague is not considering when she responded that it was OK? How should you handle this situation? Is there any action the individual who told you about the matter should have taken? How can a company prevent an individual from revealing company secrets on a social network?

2. Prepare a summary of your team's discussion in a document, blog entry, or presentation.

3. Save the document or presentation as **C7-Project7-CompanySecretsDiscussion-Your Name**.

4. Submit the document, presentation, or blog entry to your instructor in the manner she or he has requested.

Appendix A

Buying a New Computing Device

B uying a new notebook, tablet, or smartphone requires an understanding of some of the technical jargon that fills a computer ad. An experienced electronics sales associate will help you choose the right device; however, some people like to shop online or know in advance the features that are important to consider. In this appendix you will learn tips for shopping for a device that meets your needs in a step-by-step buying process model.

Buying a New PC, Tablet, or Smartphone

Are you in the market for a new computer or are you looking to add a second device to supplement a computer you already own? Many people own more than one computing device. Perhaps you have a desktop PC and want a notebook or tablet to use for school. You may have an older cell phone and want a newer smartphone that you can use to access the Internet or view documents while you're on the go. The following pages will guide you through a decision-making process that will help you make an informed purchase. Spending a little time planning your requirements will save time and money and help you avoid making an impulse purchase that you may regret.

A section with tips for making a smartphone purchase is included at the end of the appendix. The following steps are geared toward deciding how to buy a personal computer or tablet.

Step 1 Determine Your Maximum Budget

Before you start browsing computer ads, know how much money you can afford to spend. Computers are sold in a wide range of prices from a few hundred dollars to a few thousand dollars to suit a variety of budgets. Setting the maximum price will help narrow the search when you are ready to shop.

Start by setting the maximum budget.

Step 2 Decide on a Desktop, Notebook, Ultrabook, Netbook, or Tablet

Desktop PCs are declining in usage, but nevertheless, some people prefer the stationary system unit that sits on or under a desk with an attached monitor, keyboard, and mouse. If you normally work in one place and have the physical space to accommodate the larger PC, a desktop is a good value. The desktop PCs of today last longer than earlier desktops and are easier to upgrade than most mobile devices. All-in-one PCs pack all of the system unit components behind the monitor, which requires less desktop. Desktop PCs also generally include a large screen.

Decide between a desktop PC, notebook, Ultrabook, netbook, or tablet.

If you are looking for a portable computer for school or work, or one that you can move around your house, then a notebook, Ultrabook, or netbook is a good choice. Which option you choose will depend on how you plan to use it. A notebook computer provides everything that a traditional desktop PC provides in a portable case that you can carry around. An Ultrabook is lighter and slimmer than a notebook but sacrifices an optical drive to achieve the slim, lightweight design. Consider if you want to watch DVD or Blu-ray movies on your computer; if you do, you'll need a notebook. If your computing needs are primarily just surfing the Web and sending and receiving email, a netbook with its smaller screen size may be for you. A netbook will limit your choice of applications and does not include a DVD or Blu-ray drive, so if you have the money to afford a notebook, you may be better off with a more powerful unit.

Tablets are smaller and lighter than notebooks. If screen size is important to you, a notebook or Ultrabook will be your preference. Typically, people buy a tablet as a secondary device to a desktop or notebook PC. However, newer tablets, convertible tablet PCs (screens rotate 180 degrees to fold over a keyboard), and tablets that are supplied with a docking station that includes a full-size keyboard are available. If you want to use touch-enabled screens or a stylus to handwrite notes, a tablet is the way to go.

Step 3 Decide on the Software Applications and Operating System

Computers come with an operating system and some software applications preinstalled so you may be tempted to skip over this step. However, watch for systems that preinstall limited trial editions of software applications. These applications usually expire within a short time frame such as 90 days or at some point within the first year after purchase. Following expiration, you have to pay a software license fee to continue using the software. This will affect your budget, so you need to find out in advance if you will need to set aside money to pay for software applications separately.

Choosing the software applications you need will determine the hardware and operating systems requirements.

Check your school's computer store to see if you can buy software applications at academic pricing. Some academic licenses have to be purchased, through your school to qualify for student discounts; however, increasingly, retailers are able to offer the same pricing upon proof of student registration.

It pays to shop around for the best price on the software application you want to install. Some software publishers offer coupons for web-based purchases and some retailers can offer attractive pricing when you package the software with your hardware. Look for a software suite that will bundle together multiple applications in one product. These are always a better value than buying individual applications.

Deciding on the software applications you want to use will help you choose the appropriate hardware and OS. All software applications will specify the system requirements that are needed to run the software. You will notice that software companies will specify minimum and recommended system requirements. Go for the recommended requirements in a new purchase since the minimum requirements usually mean performance is slower than the recommended requirements. Pay particular attention to the specified operating system that is needed to run the application, the amount of RAM, the processor speed, and the disk storage used by the application(s).

Apple PCs and mobile devices are generally more expensive than Windows-compatible computers.

Mac versus PC Software applications are typically available in a Mac or a Windows-compatible PC edition. With the popularity of cloud-based software solutions, the computer platform is becoming less of an issue than it was for early computers. Deciding between Mac and PC is becoming more a personal choice and a budget issue. Apple PCs are more expensive than Windows-compatible PCs. Apple's iPad and iPhone are also more expensive than Windows-compatible or Android tablets and smartphones.

Apple fans are fiercely loyal to the brand and will argue that the extra money for Apple is well worth the investment. Ultimately, if you are not partial to either platform or OS family of products, you should try both environments at your school or at a store to determine if you become a Mac or a PC owner.

Step 4 Compare Hardware Components to Match Software Needs

Table A.1 provides an overview of specifications you should check in a typical ad for a Windows-compatible notebook computer. If necessary, review Chapter 3 for more information on any of the hardware components that are listed.

If you can afford to spend more, buy more than you need to meet the recommended requirements. This will ensure you have a computer that will meet your needs into the future. In a nutshell, go for the computer with the fastest processor, most RAM, and largest internal hard disk drive. These systems will typically be packaged with other components that will be adequate for an average computer user who needs a device to use Office applications and the Internet. If you cannot afford to spend more now, look for a computer ad that says the RAM is expandable. This will be a better choice than one that cannot be upgraded or that can have only a limited amount added later.

Look for the Energy Star logo or something in the ad that says the device is Energy Star qualified. This means the computer will use less energy than one that is not rated.

Examine the width, height, and weight specifications to get an idea of the physical characteristics. Pay particular attention to weight and screen size if you will be carrying the notebook around at school in a backpack.

Table A.1	Hardware Components Typically Advertised for a Notebook PC
Processor	Intel Core, Atom, AMD, or ARM processors are commonly found in notebooks and tablets. Notebooks and tablets are sold with multiple-core CPUs, usually dual- or quad-core at the time of writing. Look for the amount and type (L1, L2, or L3) of cache memory with the CPU and the highest processor speed (1.5 GHz and higher).
RAM	RAM works with the CPU to give you high-speed performance. The more RAM you have, the better your system will perform. Look for a minimum of 4 GB of RAM on a notebook and 1 to 2 GB on a tablet. Check if RAM is expandable in modules that can be added to the device at a later time. A system with a higher level of expandable RAM will last longer.
Screen	A desktop PC will have a larger screen than a notebook or tablet, typically 19 inches or higher. A notebook or Ultrabook will have a screen size in the range of 15 inches or higher. Netbook and tablet screens are the smallest in the range of 9 to 12 inches. Recall that screen size is measured diagonally from corner to corner.
Video Card	In most cases, the video card supplied with a notebook is adequate; however, if you are going to use your computer for gaming or high-end graphics design, pay attention to the graphics card, video memory, and the GPU. Look for higher specifications for these items to achieve faster graphics processing capabilities.
Hard Disk Space	The larger amount of hard disk storage space you can get the better; however, keep in mind that you can always buy external hard disk drives to store all of those digital photos, videos, and music files. Higher end notebooks at the time of writing are supplied with 1 TB HDDs, while lower end notebooks may only have 500 GB.
Optical Disc Drives	Notebooks include a DVD or Blu-ray Disc drive. If watching movies on your computer is important, remember that Ultrabooks and Netbooks do not have optical drives (although you can purchase one as a peripheral).
Digital Media Reader	Transferring data from a digital camera or smartphone is easier if the notebook has a digital media card reader. Most notebooks are equipped with a reader or include a slot for one.
Networking Capabilities	Notebooks and tablets are equipped with wireless networking capabilities. Some also come with Bluetooth-enabled connectivity. An Ethernet port will provide you with the added capability of plugging in to a wired network using a twisted-pair cable (sometimes called an RJ-45 connector). At school, some classrooms, lounges, or libraries may be equipped with network plug-ins that will give you faster Internet access than the wireless network.
Battery Life	Check the battery life to see how long the computer will operate before requiring power from an outlet. Battery life is important if you will be using the notebook away from power outlets for most of the day or evening.
Ports	Check the number and type of ports that are available on the notebook. The more USB ports the better, although you can buy an inexpensive USB hub if you need to expand the port availability. An HDMI port will allow you to plug in the notebook to a high-definition television screen for watching movies. A video port is also typically included to allow you to plug in an external monitor. Look for a FireWire port if you plan to transfer digital video from a peripheral device to the PC.
Integrated Web Cam	Most notebooks are equipped with a web cam. If you plan to do video calling, this feature will be important to you.

Choose the options you want to purchase in addition to the computer.

Step 5 Choose Options

If you will be using the notebook in place of a desktop PC, you may want to consider buying an external monitor, keyboard, and mouse. These peripherals will allow you to design an ergonomically correct workspace at home to avoid the repetitive strain and eye strain that occur from prolonged use of notebooks. Wireless keyboards and mice allow you to adjust your workspace to more comfortable positions. If you like listening to music or watching movies, you may want to invest in external speakers or high-quality, noise-canceling headphones. A headset with a microphone is desirable if you plan to use voice technology in many applications.

If you need to print at home, consider whether you want a laser or inkjet printer. Compare the cost of toner versus ink and the number of pages you can print before replacing supplies to help you decide on the type of printer. Some computers are bundled with a printer. Make sure the printer included in such a package is one that you want, and if it isn't, negotiate a discount on a better quality printer rather than accepting the packaged device. Consider an all-in-one printer that includes scanning and copying capabilities. All-in-one printers are a good value and will use less desk space than having multiple devices.

Think about how you will carry the device, and buy a well-padded case or backpack. Consider buying a case with wheels if you will be carrying the notebook along with your textbooks at school. For tablets, consider buying a sleeve or case that you can use to protect the screen's surface.

Many mobile devices are subject to theft or loss. Consider biometric options such as a fingerprint reader or tracking software and hardware that will allow you to remotely monitor or wipe the device should it be stolen or lost.

Step 6 Decide Whether to Buy an Extended Warranty

Computers come with a limited parts and labor warranty that is typically good for one year. Consider if you want to buy the extended warranty plans that are offered when you buy a new computer. These warranties are priced depending on the notebook's value, and some retailers' warranties will fix mishaps not covered by the manufacturer. Decide if you want to spend the money on these plans. Some people believe extended warranties are a waste of money, while others prefer the peace of mind knowing they are covered for anything that might happen.

If you have a credit card that includes a buyer protection plan, check the policy first to see if the credit card insurance will cover you for any accidental damage or loss. Sometimes these policies supply enough coverage that you do not need the extra protection from a retailer's extended warranty.

Most computer equipment carries a one-year parts and labor warranty.

Step 7 Shop Around, Ask About Service, and Check Reviews

Spend some time on the Web before deciding what to purchase by comparing two or three notebooks in the same price range that you can afford. Compare the pricing at in-store electronics retailers and online etailers. Be mindful of shipping costs that you may incur if you buy from a web-based store. Consider creating a spreadsheet to compare a few options side by side.

Make sure to visit your school's computer store. Schools often offer attractive deals from hardware manufacturers that have discounts negotiated for the large school audience. School staff will also be able to help you choose a computer for programs with specialized hardware or software requirements.

If you are comfortable negotiating at an electronics store, find a retailer that you may be able to convince to upgrade some options for you in a package price. For example, it won't hurt to ask the sales associate if he or she will throw in a wireless keyboard or mouse or a set of speakers with a new notebook PC.

Make sure to inquire about service options. If the computer you buy requires repairs, ask where the warranty work is performed. Some stores will do warranty repairs or out-of-warranty repairs onsite, while others have to ship the PC back to the manufacturer. If the retailer ships the computer elsewhere, ask how long a typical repair will take. In some cases, you could be without your PC for more than week if the store ships the repair offsite. Ask who pays for the shipping to and from the repair center. Finally, some stores do not offer any assistance with repairs—avoid these locations if you are not technically savvy or are adverse to risk.

Some people prefer to pay a little more for a computer that they can have serviced at the store of purchase in case of malfunction. You will have to decide how important the repair facility is to you before making a purchase. Be sure to ask all of these questions to help you make the choice with which you are most comfortable.

Search the Web for reviews of the product you are considering and the retailer from which you want to purchase it. While reviews are not always helpful (many are negative and the positive ones may not be authentic), they do provide insight into the questions you should ask and the issues for which you want to be on the alert.

Compare prices at in-store and online retailers, investigate service options, and read reviews on the Web.

Considerations for Buying a Smartphone

Before choosing a smartphone, choose the provider with which you want to subscribe and the data plan that will meet your needs. Often, the wireless provider will provide a base model smartphone free of charge or upgraded models at a low price if you sign up for a specified contract period. If you are willing to commit to a long-term plan, you may be satisfied with the smartphone that comes free with the plan. Watch for limits, caps, and time-of-use charges that may apply. For example, a plan may advertise unlimited use, but the unlimited use may apply in certain hours only. Note that some tablets may also need a data plan from a wireless carrier.

Once you have chosen a data plan, compare the smartphones the carrier is offering. Visit a store where you can try out a few smartphone models in advance. You will want to note the screen size and the type of input. Some smartphones have smaller screens than others. You will want to try out messaging and browsing on different size screens to find the one with which you are comfortable. Input can be touch-based with an onscreen keyboard or a keyboard with trackpad input. Keyboards may slide out or be built in below the screen. Try a few tasks with a touch screen to make sure you are comfortable with touch input. Some people prefer keyboards over touch; however, touch-enabled screens are definitely the mode of input for future devices.

Compare the battery life of various smartphone models. Battery technology is improving and newer batteries last longer, but often battery life does not live up to the advertised specifications. Talk time is the standard by which to base comparisons. Look for reviews on the Web that have tested models and provide actual talk time statistics. You may want to inquire about purchasing a second battery if you will often be away from charging stations and think you will use the phone more robustly than the advertised specifications.

People often want to take pictures with their smartphones, use them to play music, and communicate using messaging applications. These apps need storage space on a memory card. Check the size of the memory card that comes with the smartphone and consider if you will need to buy a larger

When acquiring a smartphone, start with a data plan and then try out various smartphones to choose the one that suits you. Consider the screen size, input method, battery life, and memory card options.

memory card. Check the compatibility of the memory card with your notebook or other computing devices so that you can easily exchange media files among them.

Ask if a car charger adapter comes with the smartphone or if you have to buy the car charger separately. This could be a negotiating item if you think you will use a car charger often.

Replacing an Older Device?

Try selling your older device using online classified ads or donate the equipment to a charity. If you cannot sell, give away, or trade in older electronics, remember to look into disposal options for e-waste that will properly recycle the device. Go to www.epa.gov/epawaste/conserve/materials/ecycling for more information on recycling electronics.

Appendix B

Wireless Networking

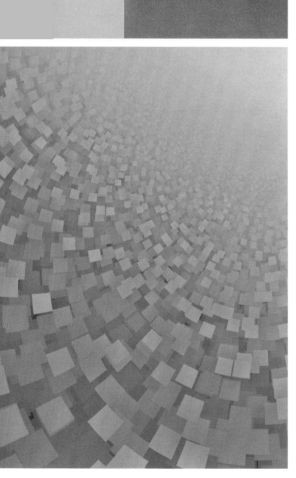

Most people prefer a wireless network so that a network cable does not have to be installed from room to room through floors or ceilings in their homes. With a wireless network, you can move freely around the house and outside to your yard with your computing device without losing a network connection. With a wireless network, you can connect PCs, tablets, smartphones, and gaming consoles. Internet-enabled televisions allow you to connect your television to a wireless network so you can browse Internet content such as YouTube or watch movies from a service such as Netflix on your TV. In this appendix you will learn the basic steps for setting up a wireless network and connecting devices to the network.

Setting Up a Wireless Network at Home

Most home networks are a Wireless Fidelity (Wi-Fi) network. Wi-Fi uses a combination wireless router/wireless access point and radio signals to transmit data. Wi-Fi networks have a limited range and a connection speed that vary depending on the equipment. Most routers used today are referred to as Wireless N (802.11n) routers and have the ability to support speeds up to 300 Mbps. A new technology called Wireless AC (802.11ac) is coming into the marketplace at the time of writing. Expect to see this technology become popular as it is estimated that Wireless AC is capable of delivering speeds of more than 6.0 Gbps. While this speed sounds lightning fast, bear in mind that the equipment can only deliver the Internet speed for which you have subscribed (see Step 1). You also need to have devices that are compatible with the wireless router to take advantage of newer technology.

A modem provides Internet access. A wireless router allows you to share that access among multiple devices.

Even with a wireless network, some homes will have a desktop PC that is connected by a network cable to the wireless router. In the steps that follow, the process to set up a wireless network is described. Different routers provide slightly different software interfaces; however, the general steps will be the same.

Step 1 Subscribe to High-Speed Internet Service with an ISP

As you learned in Topic 2.2 in Chapter 2, to connect to the Internet you need an account with an Internet Service Provider (ISP). Contact your telephone or cable provider for high-speed Internet access. Each provider will offer different pricing levels for Internet access that vary according to the speed you want, with faster speeds costing more per month than slower speeds.

A telephone company will provide you with a DSL modem and a cable company will provide you with a cable modem. Newer modems provided by ISPs are a combination wireless router and modem in one piece of equipment called a *modem router*. Some installations may require two pieces of equipment: a DSL or cable modem plus an additional wireless router. To proceed to Step 2 you need the ISP service activated, as well as a DSL or cable modem router or modem plus wireless router. If necessary, you can buy a wireless router at an electronics store if your ISP does not provide one. Brand names for wireless routers that are popular are Linksys, D-Link, and Cisco.

Your ISP will also provide instruction documentation when you subscribe for service and may give you a USB or DVD that automates the setup process. If the documentation from your ISP contains instructions that vary from the steps below, complete the steps according to the ISP's instructions.

A modem router or cable modem provide high-speed Internet access.

Step 2 Connect the Networking Hardware Equipment

Connect one end of a coaxial cable
(cable modem) or twisted-pair
cable (DSL modem) to the
modem and the other end
to the cable or telephone
line coming into your house.
Plug the power adapter into
the modem and into a power
outlet. You should see lights
illuminate on the front of the
modem, indicating power and
connectivity are live.

Next, connect the modem to the wireless router
if you need a standalone router (your ISP did not
provide you with a modem router device). To do
this, plug one end of a network cable into the back
of the modem and the other end into the back of
the wireless router. Plug the power adapter into
the wireless router and into a power outlet. You
should also see lights illuminate on the front of the
standalone router.

Connect a cable or DSL modem to a wireless router using a
network cable.

If you have a desktop PC in the same room as your
networking equipment, you can connect the PC to the integrated modem router
or standalone router by plugging one end of a network cable into the PC's network
port and the other end into the back of the modem router or standalone router.
This allows the PC to use a wired connection to the router, while the remaining
devices in your home will use a wireless connection.

Once the networking equipment is connected and has power, you can move on
to Step 3, where you will configure the router.

Step 3 Configure the Wireless Router

Integrated modem routers or standalone routers all come with an installation CD,
DVD, or USB flash drive that walks you through the steps to set up the router. One
computer used to configure the wireless router will need to be plugged into the
wireless router while you configure it. After this step, you can unplug the PC from
the router and connect wirelessly afterward.

If you have a desktop PC already connected to the router, proceed to insert the
installation medium into the desktop PC and begin the configuration process. If you
do not have a PC connected to the router, attach a network cable from an open
port on the back of the wireless router to the network port on your notebook,
insert the installation medium, and begin the configuration process (Figure B.1).

To configure the wireless router, follow the instructions that appear in the setup
program. The software interface is user-friendly and prompts assist you at each
step. Generally, you need to do three tasks: assign the router a name (called the
SSID) and security key, change the router's administrative password, and choose the
security standard you want to use.

If you did not receive an installation medium with a preprogrammed setup
process, look for instructions that came with the equipment that provide a URL or

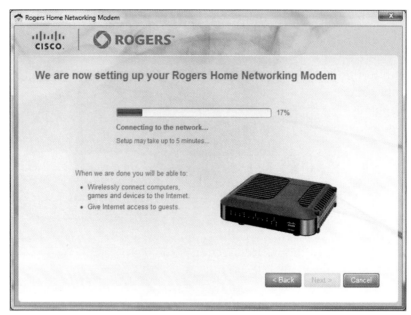

Figure B.1 Insert the CD, DVD, or USB flash drive into a PC to start the router's setup program.

IP address to configure the router. Open a browser window and type the URL or IP address to start the software interface.

Wireless routers come with a default user name and password that is usually *admin* (for both user name and password) or *admin* and *password*. Log on to the router device and proceed to change the settings as needed.

When giving the router a new name, try not to use obvious names that will identify you with the router. For example, do not use your name or your address. This way when someone is within range of your router, they will not associate the network name with you and try to break into your Internet access (such as a neighbor trying to piggyback your connection). A good idea is to prevent the router from broadcasting the router's SSID. Free public Wi-Fi networks such as those at airports, coffee shops, and libraries use a recognizable name because they provide unsecured network access to everyone who is within range. Also assign a security key that your neighbors or anyone who knows you would not be able to guess.

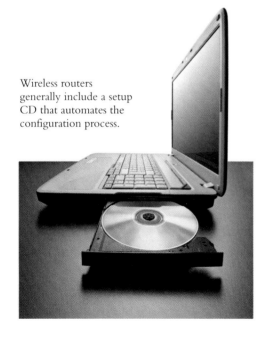

Wireless routers generally include a setup CD that automates the configuration process.

Change the default administrator password to a strong password known only to you. The administrative password will be needed if you ever want to change the router settings in the future. If necessary, write down the user name and password for administering the router and store it in a secure location.

Activate the router's security standard using Wi-Fi Protected Access WPA2 if possible. Some older devices may not support WPA2 and you may need to use WPA instead. Avoid using the less secure WEP standard. WPA2 secures your wireless network with encryption. People will not be able to connect to the wireless router unless they know the security key, and data transmitted across the wireless network will be encrypted.

When you have finished configuring the wireless router, unplug the notebook PC used to configure the wireless router and proceed to connect each wireless device to the router as per Step 4. You can leave a desktop PC plugged into the router if the desktop PC does not have a wireless network adapter or you do not want to use it wirelessly.

Step 4 Connect Individual Devices to the Wireless Router

Notebooks, tablets, and smartphones come equipped with a built-in wireless interface card, called a network adapter. Generally, the wireless network adapter turns on by default when the device is powered on. For smartphones and some tablets you may need to turn on Wi-Fi.

If a PC or other computing device does not have a built-in wireless interface card, you can purchase a network adapter for wireless networking. For a desktop PC, buy a USB wireless network adapter; for a notebook PC, buy a wireless network card adapter. A tip for ensuring a smooth setup process is to buy a wireless network adapter made by the same manufacturer as your wireless router.

Generally, the installation medium you used to set up your wireless router can be used in each other device that you want to connect to the network. If necessary, you can manually connect to the router by following the steps shown in Figure B.2 for Windows 7 and Figure B.3 for Windows 8.

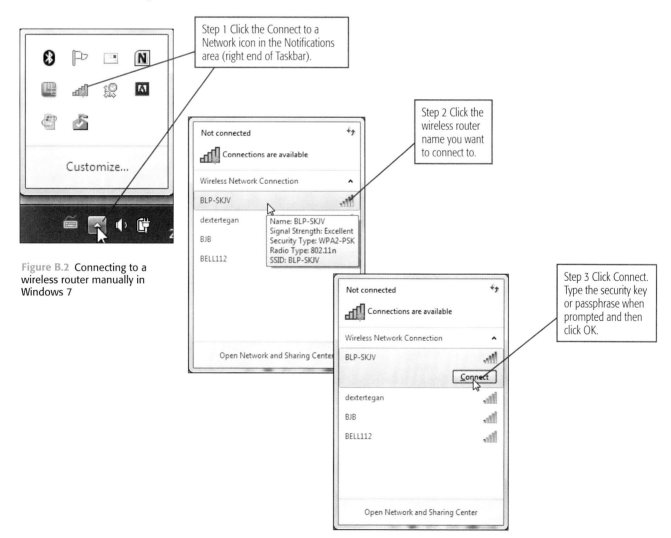

Figure B.2 **Connecting to a wireless router manually in Windows 7**

Step 1 Swipe in from the right edge of the Start screen or point at the top right or bottom right screen edge to display charms, tap or click the Settings charm, and then tap or click the Networks icon.

Step 2 Tap or click the wireless router name you want to connect to.

Step 3 Tap or click the Connect automatically check box and then tap or click Connect. Type the security key or passphrase when prompted and then tap or click OK.

Figure B.3 Connecting to a wireless router manually in Windows 8

Connect a computing device, television, or gaming console by following instructions provided by the device manufacturers. In most cases, you have options to use a push button on the router to automatically detect the wireless router or to manually connect by providing the device name and security key by using buttons on a remote control and on-screen menu.

Setting Up a Wireless Network on Apple Equipment

To set up a wireless network with Apple computers, you will need to purchase and configure a Wi-Fi base station (called Airport Express, Airport Extreme, or Time Capsule) that connects to your high-speed cable or DSL modem. Plug in the networking equipment by following steps similar to Step 2 above and then go to www.apple.com/findouthow/mac/#wirelesssetup to watch a video that shows you the steps to configure the wireless network on an Apple computer using the Airport Utility software.

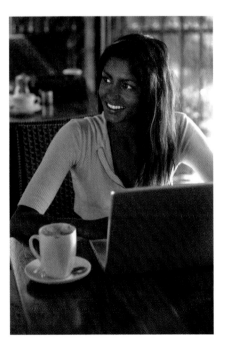

Connecting to a Public Wireless Hotspot

Follow the steps to manually connect to a public wireless hotspot as shown in Figure B.2 for a Windows 7 device and Figure B.3 for a Windows 8 device. The network name should be obvious in the list of available networks; however, if necessary you can ask a store clerk, hotel clerk, or airport staff member for the network name and password. Exercise caution when using a public Wi-Fi hotspot, and do not transmit personal or confidential data as these networks are not secured with encryption and are at risk of interception by hackers. Never perform financial transactions or log on to websites where you need to provide your user name and password.

Wireless networking has unchained people from fixed locations and allowed for freedom of movement without losing Internet access. With more home devices becoming Internet-enabled, such as smart appliances and televisions, wireless networking is becoming even more advantageous. Setting up a wireless home network is relatively straightforward. Always implement wireless network security to ensure your personal data is not subjected to unwanted access.

Glossary

A

acceptable use policy (AUP) a written policy that spells out for employees, students, or other network users the permitted uses for computing equipment and networks.

accounting software application business software used to record and report financial information related to assets, liabilities, equity, revenue, and expenses.

adware software programs responsible for pop-up ads that appear on your desktop or while viewing web pages.

Android the mobile operating system for many smartphones and tablets.

Android Open Source Project (AOSP) a program operated by Google through which the Android is maintained and developed.

animation software programs used to create images or objects that have movement or otherwise interact with users.

antivirus program a program that detects and removes malware.

application software (apps) programs used by individuals to carry out tasks or otherwise get things done.

audio recording and editing software programs that include tools for recording and editing music, sound clips, and podcasts.

B

back door a way to bypass computer security.

backup utility a program that allows you to back up selected files or an entire disk to a removable storage medium.

bar code reader a device that optically scans bar codes to identify products in warehouses or at checkout counters.

binary system the location for the digital data temporarily stored in RAM, processed by the CPU, and eventually saved to permanent storage when you save the document. In the binary system, only two possible values exist—0 and 1.

biometric device a tool that authenticates a person's identity using physical characteristics such as a fingerprint, iris scan, or voice recognition.

biometric scanner a device used to identify people by individual human characteristics such as a fingerprint, iris, or voice pattern.

BIOS (Basic Input Output System) programming code stored on a ROM chip that includes instructions used when starting a computer.

bit the smallest unit for digital data in the binary system.

black hats hackers who gain unauthorized access with malicious intent to steal data or for other personal gain.

BlackBerry OS the operating system designed for BlackBerry devices.

BlackBerry thumb the pain that develops in BlackBerry users in the thumb or wrist from excessive texting.

blog a journal posted on a website.

blog posts entries on a blog.

blogger an individual who writes blog content.

blogging writing and maintaining a blog.

blogosphere the collection of all of the blogs on the Web.

Bluetooth a technology that offers the ability to connect to another Bluetooth-enabled device such as your smartphone.

Bluetooth headset a device that can be paired to a smartphone to hear a conversation when making and receiving voice calls.

bookmark a link on a social bookmarking site.

bookmarklet a social bookmarking site icon that allows you to bookmark the page instantly by clicking the icon.

booting starting a computer.

botnet a collection of zombie computers that work together to conduct an attack on another network.

broadband any always-on connection capable of carrying a large amount of data at a fast speed.

byte each group of eight bits that represents one character.

C

cable Internet access Internet access provided by the same cable company with which you subscribe for television service.

cache memory a system that stores frequently used data.

carpal tunnel syndrome (CTS) a common computer-related RSI injury that occurs when the nerve that connects the forearm to the palm of the hand becomes inflamed. It is caused by excessive typing, mouse scrolling, mouse clicking, and thumb typing/movements on mobile devices.

ccTLDs two-character TLDs that are country codes such as us and ca.

central processing unit (CPU) a computer chip that carries out the instructions given by the software to perform the processing cycle.

Chrome Google's free Web browser that runs on Windows-compatible PCs.

Chrome OS Google's Linux-based cloud operating system that is available on specific hardware called Chromebooks.

clickjacking when a button, graphic, or link on a web page appears to be real, but when clicked causes malicious software to run.

client a computer that connects to a server.

clock speed the number of instruction cycles the CPU can process per second, typically measured in gigahertz (GHz).

cloud computing software and computing services accessed entirely on the Internet.

cloud storage a storage option in which you log in to a website and copy documents, photos, or other information to a web service.

cold boot turning on a computer that has been shut off.

command-line interface a system used to interact with an OS in which you type commands on the keyboard at a prompt to tell the OS what to do.

communications device any component used to facilitate the transmission of data such as a cable modem, DSL modem, or router.

computer an electronic device that has been programmed to process, store, and output data that has been accepted as input. It needs hardware and software to work.

computer security all activities related to protecting hardware, software, and data from loss as a result of unauthorized access or use, theft, natural disaster, and human error. Also known as information security.

computer vision syndrome (CVS) a temporary condition caused by prolonged computer use that involves eye strain; weak, blurred, itchy, burning, or dry eyes; double vision; difficulty with focus; sensitivity to light; headaches; and neck pain.

computing platform the combination of hardware architecture and software design that allows applications to run.

content aggregator an organization that searches the Web for new content, and collects and organizes the content in one place.

cookie a small text file stored on your computer's hard disk that contains data about you such as your user name and the pages you visited.

cybercrime illegal acts involving a computer.

D

data buses wires that allow data to travel between the components on the motherboard to the CPU and memory.

database management application software that organizes and keeps track of large amounts of data.

Delicious a social bookmarking website that allows you to save and share links to pages on the Web that have articles, pictures, videos, blogs, or some other content that you want to bookmark.

desktop computer a PC that includes a system unit and a separate monitor, keyboard, and mouse.

desktop publishing software an application that incorporates text, graphics, and colors to create high-quality documents for marketing, communication, or other commercial purposes.

dial-up Internet access in which you connect your PC to your telephone system via a modem built into your PC.

digital copier an output device that can be used as a traditional paper photocopier and also accept output from computers for printing.

Digital Subscriber Line (DSL) Internet access provided by your telephone company that connects using telephone lines.

Disk Cleanup a Windows utility that allows you to scan a particular storage device or drive to select various types of files to be deleted.

disk defragmenter a utility that rearranges fragmented files back together to improve file retrieval speed and efficiency.

document management system (DMS) a program that manages the creation, storage, retrieval, history, and eventual disposal of information stored in a central repository.

Domain Name System (DNS) a server that holds the directory that associates an Internet address with a Web address.

drive a storage device that is identified by a unique letter and label or assigned a name.

drivers small programs that contain the instructions the OS uses to communicate and route data to/from the device.

E

e-commerce (electronic commerce) buying or selling over the Internet.

e-tailers (electronic retailers) businesses that sell online to consumers.

e-waste (electronic waste) discarded or unwanted electrical items. Also known as e-trash.

educational software programs designed for children and adults to learn about subjects such as math, spelling, grammar, geography, and history.

802.11 protocol the standard developed to facilitate wireless communication among several hardware providers.

email (electronic mail) the sending and receiving of digital messages, sometimes with documents or photos attached.

email address used to connect to your email account at the ISP server.

email client a program such as Microsoft's Outlook or Apple's Mail that sends and receives messages.

embedded computer a processor programmed to perform a particular task that is incorporated into a household appliance and consumer electronic.

Embedded Linux applications that run smart appliances, in-flight entertainment systems, personal navigation systems, and a variety of other consumer and commercial electronics.

embedded operating system a specialized operating system designed for the limited use of a specific device.

encryption the act of scrambling communications between devices so that the data is not readable.

enterprise resource planning (ERP) a software solution designed for large-scale organizations.

entertainment software programs for playing interactive games and videos.

ergonomics strategies involving the design of equipment and a person's work space to promote safe and comfortable operation.

Ethernet port a device that facilitates connection to the Internet. Also known as a network interface card (NIC).

expansion card a device that plugs into an expansion slot on the motherboard to provide or improve functionality.

external wireless adapter a device that has a built-in radio transmitter and receiver that allow you to connect to a wireless modem or wireless router.

F

Facebook one of the most popular social networking sites used by people who want to connect with friends and family.

Fiber-to-the-Premises (FTTP) Internet access that involves the ISP running a fiber-optic cable directly to your home or business. Also known as Fiber-to-the-Home (FTTH) or Fiber-Optic Service (FiOS).

file the collection of bytes that comprise the saved document.

File Explorer a file management system in Windows 8 in which you can move, copy, delete, and rename files.

File History the location where you back up or restore files.

file name the unique name assigned to a document when you save.

Firefox the Mozilla Foundation's free Web browser.

firewall hardware, software, or a combination of hardware and software that blocks unwanted access to your network.

fixed wireless Internet access Internet access that involves installing an antenna outside your home to send and receive radio signals.

flash memory chip-based technology where data is stored electronically on a chip instead of magnetically like a traditional HDD.

flash memory card a small card that contains one or more flash memory chips.

Flickr one of the most popular dedicated photo-sharing websites.

folder a placeholder name for where you want to store related files.

4G (fourth generation) a network for mobile devices that provides Internet access through cell towers. The average speed for 4G devices is often advertised as 10 times faster than 3G.

fragmentation occurs when file clusters needed for a document are not stored adjacent to each other.

Freeware software that can be downloaded and installed at no cost and without restrictions.

G

generic top-level domains (gTLDs) TLDs with three or more characters such as com, gov, and edu.

gigabyte approximately 1 billion bytes.

gigahertz (GHz) 1 billion instruction cycles per second.

Google's Blogger a popular choice for creating a blog.

Google+ a Google social networking site.

graphical user interface (GUI) a system that presents visual images such as tiles, icons, or buttons that you tap or click to tell the OS what you want to do.

graphics software programs for creating, editing, and manipulating drawings, pictures, photos, clip art, and scanned images.

green computing the use of computers and other electronic devices in an environmentally responsible manner.

H

hacker an individual who accesses a network without permission.

hacking activities involved in gaining unauthorized entry into a network's resources.

hard copy a printed copy of computer output.

hard disk the storage medium upon which the operating system and application software programs are stored as well as data files. Also known as a hard drive or hard disk drive (HDD).

hashtag symbol (#) precedes a keyword or topics in a tweet to categorize messages.

Help and Support a program that allows you to search for solutions to a computer issue in extensive online resources.

hobby software applications programs that support leisure activities such as creating a family tree, scrapbooking, planning trips, and creating custom greeting cards.

home page the first page of a website that displays when the Web address is requested.

hotspot an area where a Wi-Fi network is within range.

HTML (Hypertext Markup Language) markup language used to create web pages.

hyperlinks addresses that when clicked or tapped on a touchscreen take you to a related Web page.

I

ICANN (Internet Corporation for Assigned Names and Numbers) a nonprofit organization that keeps track of the Internet addresses and names all around the world.

iCloud Apple's cloud operating system that provides access to email, contacts, calendar, documents, and more.

identity theft when an individual's personal information is obtained by a criminal who then uses the information to buy products or services under the victim's name or otherwise pose as the victim for financial gain.

information the result of software programs providing instructions for a computer to process and organize the data into a meaningful and useful way.

information privacy the right of individuals or organizations to control the information that is collected about them.

Information Processing Cycle four operations—input, processing, output, and storage—involved in transforming data into information.

information technology (IT) the use of computers, software, networks, and other communication systems and processes to store, retrieve, send, process, and protect information.

inkjet printer an output device that forms text and images on the page by spraying drops of ink from one or more ink cartridges that move back and forth across the page.

input device any device used to enter raw data or communicate instructions to the computer.

Instagram a popular, free app for sharing photos from your iPhone, iPad, iPod Touch, or Android phone.

instant messaging exchanging text messages in real time.

instruction cycle an action in which the CPU retrieves, decodes, executes, and stores an instruction.

interactive whiteboard a device that displays the computer's output on a large whiteboard, on which special pens can be used to annotate and draw.

Internet (Net) a global network that links together other networks such as government departments, businesses, nonprofit organizations, educational and research institutions, and individuals.

Internet Explorer (IE) the web browser included with Microsoft Windows.

Internet Protocol (IP) address a unique address assigned to a computing device when it is connected to the Internet so that the device can communicate with other computers. An IP address is a series of four numbers from 0 to 255 separated by periods.

Internet Service Provider (ISP) a company that provides access to the Internet's infrastructure for a fee.

intrusion detection software programs that analyze network traffic for suspicious data and alert network administrators to possible system threats.

iOS Apple's mobile operating system used for its iPhone, iPod Touch, and iPad.

K

kernel the core of the OS that manages memory, devices, and programs, and assigns resources.

keyboard a device used to type and input data into a computer.

keystroke logger spyware that is activated as part of a rootkit or Trojan horse that records every keystroke you type and sends it back to a cybercriminal. Also known as a keylogger.

kilobyte (KB) approximately 1,000 bytes.

L

laptop computer a PC that has a monitor that when swiveled up reveals a keyboard with the remaining components housed below. Also known as a notebook.

laser printer an output device in which a laser beam electrostatically charges a drum with the text and images sent for printing. A dry powder called toner sticks to the drum and is transferred to the paper.

Last.fm an example of a music-sharing website.

legal software programs that help you prepare legal documents such as wills, contracts, leases, loan agreements, and living trusts.

Level 1 (L1) cache cache memory that is built on the CPU chip and operates the fastest of all memory.

Level 2 (L2) cache cache memory stored on the CPU chip or built on the motherboard that feeds the L1 cache.

Level 3 (L3) cache cache memory that is usually built on the motherboard and feeds the L2 cache.

Light-Emitting Diode (LED) a flat-panel technology that consumes less energy and costs more than LCD.

LinkedIn a professional network through which you connect with your business contacts.

Linux an operating system created by Linus Torvalds and based on UNIX; it can be used as a standalone OS or as a server OS.

Liquid Crystal Displays (LCD) flat-panel, widescreen technology widely used for new desktop PC monitors.

LTE network the fastest network for mobile devices.

M

Mac OS a proprietary operating system created by Apple.

magnetic strip reader a device that can read data from the magnetic strip on the backs of cards such as debit cards, credit cards, or cards used to open doors or parking gates.

mainframe a large, powerful, and expensive computer used by the government and large organizations such as banks, insurance companies, and other corporations to connect hundreds or thousands of users simultaneously.

malware any type of malicious software program that is designed to damage, disable, or steal data.

media sharing websites that allow you to share, view, and download photos, videos, music, and presentations.

megabits per second (Mbps) the speed for broadband connectivity in which data transfers at the rate of 1 million bits per second.

megabyte approximately 1 million bytes.

metasearch search engines search engines that send your search phrase to other search engines and then compile the results in one list.

microblog a blog that restricts posts to a smaller amount of text than a traditional blog.

microblogger individuals who create posts that are typically about what they are doing, where they are, what they are thinking about in the moment, or links to interesting content they have seen on the Web.

microphone a device used in conjunction with software to create a digital audio file from voice input or other sounds.

microprocessor a silicon chip. Also known as a central processing unit.

midrange server used in small and medium organizations that need to connect hundreds of client computers at the same time.

mobile applications a different edition of software that is designed specifically for mobile use.

mobile broadband sticks portable modems that plug into a USB port on your mobile device and connect via a cellular network.

mobile computer a PC that can be moved from place to place.

mobile device a handheld computing device smaller than a notebook.

mobile malware a virus designed for mobile devices.

mobile operating system an operating system designed specifically for a mobile device.

mobile web browser a browser designed to quickly display web pages optimized for the smaller screens on devices such as tablets and smartphones.

monitor an output device that houses the screen on a desktop PC.

motherboard the main circuit board in the computer.

mouse a device used to point, select, and manipulate objects on the screen.

multi-core processor independent units on the same chip that can process data simultaneously, which significantly increases speed and performance.

multimedia software programs that use text and images with video, audio, and animations to create engaging and interactive applications that market products or services, educate, or entertain users.

N

netbook a smaller version of a notebook designed for people who primarily need access only to web-based applications such as email and the Internet.

netiquette short for *Internet etiquette*; rules for acceptable social interactions over the Internet.

network two or more computers or other devices (such as a printer) that are linked together to share resources and communicate with each other.

network adapter any device used to connect a computer to a network. Also known as a network card.

network interface card (NIC) facilitates connection to the Internet. Also known as an Ethernet port.

note-taking software programs used to store, organize, search, and share notes.

O

Open Handset Alliance a consortium of several mobile technology companies of which Google is a member.

open source program a program in which the source code is available to the public and can be freely modified or customized.

open source software programs that generally are available for free and downloaded from a website.

operating system (OS) a system that provides the user interface that allows you to work with the computer, manages all of the hardware resources, and provides the platform for managing files and application programs.

optical disc a CD, DVD, or Blu-ray disc.

Optimize Drives a utility used to analyze a drive for the percentage of fragmentation.

Organic Light-Emitting Diode (OLED) a newer flat-panel technology that does not require backlighting like an LCD.

output device anything used to view the information processed and organized by the computer.

P

packaged software a bundle of traditional software suites.

parallel processing a procedure that involves having multiple microprocessor chips or a multi-core processor to execute multiple instructions simultaneously.

peripheral hardware used for input, output, connectivity, or storage that you plug in or connect to your computer wirelessly.

personal computer (PC) a computer in which the input, processing, storage, and output are self-contained.

personal finance software programs that allow you to download activity from your banking account directly into the software.

personal information management (PIM) software programs that help you organize messages, schedule, contacts, and tasks.

petaflop a measurement used in scientific calculations that represents a quadrillion floating point operations per second.

pharming a scam in which an individual is tricked into typing in personal information at a phony website that appears to be the real website requested by the individual.

phishing activities that appear to be initiated by a legitimate organization in an attempt to obtain personal information that can be used in fraud, theft, or identity theft.

photo editing software programs used to edit and add special effects and text to photos.

photo printer an output device that connects directly to a digital camera to print high-quality photos on photo paper using inkjet technology.

piggybacking connecting to someone else's wireless network without the network owner's consent.

Pinterest a virtual pinboard on which people pin pictures of things they have seen on the Internet that they like and want to share using the Pin It button.

pixels the picture elements that make up the image shown on the display screen. A pixel is square with red, green, and blue color values that represent each color needed to form the image.

plasma a flat-panel technology that provides truer color representation and costs more than an LCD.

plotter an output device that moves one or more pens across the surface of the paper to produce a drawing.

Plug and Play a platform in which the OS searches a newly plugged-in device for the driver, loads it automatically, and displays a message when the device is ready to use.

plug-in a software program that allows the browser to display enhanced content that it cannot display on its own. Also known as add-on or player.

port a connector located at the back of a desktop PC or at the sides, back, and sometimes the front of a notebook or other mobile device that is used to plug in external devices.

Portable Media Player a device on which to play music, watch videos, view photos, play games, and/or read electronic books.

presentation application software used to create slides for an electronic slideshow that may be projected on a screen.

processing a cycle carried out by the central processing unit.

productivity software a group of programs that includes word processing, spreadsheets, presentations, and database management.

project management software programs that allow you to enter all of the tasks needed to get a project done, establish time frames, assign resources, and allocate budget money to each task.

protocol a set of rules that defines how data is exchanged between two devices.

Q

QR (Quick Response) code a type of bar code that looks like a matrix of black square dots.

R

Radio Frequency Identification (RFID) reader a device that scans an embedded RFID tag to identify an object.

random access memory (RAM) temporary storage for instructions and data that is emptied when power to the computer is lost.

raw data characters that are typed or otherwise entered into a computer.

read-only memory (ROM) memory built on the motherboard that is used for storing computer instructions that do not change.

Really Simple Syndication (RSS) a specification used by content aggregators to distribute updates to subscribers.

reference software programs that use multimedia tools to provide rich content information in encyclopedias, dictionaries, translation guides, atlases, and other reference resources.

repetitive strain injury (RSI) an injury or disorder of the joints, nerves, muscles, ligaments, or tendons.

resolution the number of pixels that make up the image shown on the display screen, which affects the quality of output.

restore utility a program that allows you to copy files from a backup to a disk drive in their original state.

rootkit a program that hides on an infected computer and provides a back door for a hacker or other cybercriminal to remotely monitor or take control of the PC.

S

Safari Apple's browser for mobile devices.

satellite Internet access Internet access available to those who live in a rural area where cable or DSL is not available.

scanner a device that uses optical technology to analyze text and/or images and convert them into data that can be used by a computer.

search engine a company that searches Web pages and indexes the pages by keyword or subject.

server a computer with hardware and software that allows it to link together other computers to provide services and share resources.

server room a controlled room where high-performance computers are stacked in racks and stored to avoid heat, humidity and dust.

Shareware software that is available to download for a free trial period.

Short Message Service (SMS) a service that facilitates texting.

smartphone a cell phone with a built-in camera that offers apps, web browsing, and messaging capabilities.

social bookmarking a category of social networking that provides tools with which you can organize, store, and share content with others.

social media any online tool in which users generate content and interact with others.

social networking website a website that provides tools for people to connect and interact with groups of people.

Software License Agreement (SLA) a license agreement that you are required to accept when you install software. Also known as End User License Agreement (EULA).

software suite a bundled group of productivity software applications. Also known as productivity suite.

software-as-a-service (SaaS) the delivery of software applications using the Internet.

solid-state drive (SSD) a newer type of hard disk drive technology that uses flash memory.

spam electronic junk mail.

spiders programs that read Web pages and other information to generate index entries. Also known as crawlers.

spoofing techniques in which a sender's email address is altered to a phony address that appears legitimate to the email recipient, or an IP address is altered to appear to be a trusted source.

spreadsheet application software in which you work primarily with numbers that you organize, calculate, and chart.

spyware software programs that exist on your computer without your knowledge and track your activities.

storage device the piece of hardware with the means to write new data to and read existing data from storage media.

storage media any device where data and information are saved for later use.

strong password a password that is difficult to hack by humans or password detection software programs.

StumbleUpon a social bookmarking website on which you can browse recommended web pages and save the pages you like to your profile.

stylus a digital pen.

subscription software programs purchased from cloud computing providers who generally charge a monthly fee per user for access to the provider's software and storage services.

supercomputer the fastest, most expensive, most powerful computer, capable of performing trillions of calculations per second.

System Restore a program that will undo a recent change while leaving all documents intact.

system software programs, including the operating system, that are designed to work with the present hardware as well as a set of utility programs that are used to maintain the computer and its devices.

system unit a horizontal or vertical case in which the computer's processing, memory, and main storage device are housed.

T

tablet PC a lightweight notebook with a smaller screen that you interact with using a touch screen or stylus.

tag a keyword you assign to content to describe or categorize a photo, article, or item from a Web page.

tagging creating bookmarks on a website.

tax preparation software programs that guide you through the completion of the complex forms required to file your income taxes.

technological convergence the place where innovation merges several technologies into a single device.

tendonitis a common computer-related RSI injury that occurs when a tendon in the wrist becomes inflamed. It is caused by excessive typing, mouse scrolling, mouse clicking, and thumb typing/movements on mobile devices.

terabyte approximately 1 trillion bytes.

text messages short text exchanges using mobile devices.

texting sending text messages to another mobile device.

thermal printer an output device that heats coated paper as the paper passes over the print head; usually used for receipts.

thin client a computer connected to a network that does not store any data or software on the local PC.

3G (third generation) a network for mobile devices that provides Internet access through cell towers. Average speed for a 3G connection is around 1 Mbps.

top-level domain (TLD) the part of the domain name that identifies the type of organization associated with the domain name.

touch-enabled display a technology that accepts input from finger gestures and is found on many of today's mobile devices. Also known as touchscreens.

touchpad a rectangular surface with buttons, located below the keyboard on a notebook, that is used in place of a mouse to move the pointer on the screen and manipulate objects. The touchpad senses finger movement and taps similar to a mouse.

Transport Layer Security (TLS) a program that encrypts transmitted data so the data is unreadable if intercepted.

Trojan horse a program that disguises itself as a useful program that infects your computer with malware when you run the application.

tweet a post on Twitter.

Twitter the most popular microblog, with posts limited to 140 characters or less.

Twitter bots software programmed to follow people based on popular keywords.

U

ubiquitous computing an idea that computing technology is everywhere within our environment and used all of the time.

Ultra-Mobile PC (UMPC) a small handheld computer that supports touch or digital pen input, or includes a compact keyboard.

ultrabook a type of notebook that is thinner and lighter, but just as powerful as a traditional notebook.

unauthorized access using a computer, network, or other resource without permission.

unauthorized use using a computer, network, or other resource for purposes other than the intended use.

universal serial bus (USB) port the most common type of port that is used to connect an external device such as a keyboard, mouse, printer, smartphone, or external storage media to a computer.

UNIX an operating system designed for servers that originally was designed to be multi-user and multitasking.

USB flash drive a portable storage device that contains flash memory inside the case.

USB wireless adapter the most common type of external wireless adapter. Also known as a USB dongle.

user interface (UI) the means with which you interact with the computer.

V

video card a device used to process the data needed to display the text and images on your monitor, projector, or television.

video display an electronic device that visually presents information from a computer.

video display projector (VDP) a device used when a computer's output needs to be projected on a large screen.

video editing software programs that provide tools to create video clips.

viral videos video clips that spread quickly via forwarded or shared links or word-of-mouth.

virtual memory the hard disk space allocated to store RAM contents.

virus a form of malware that can replicate itself and spread to other media on the infected computer and to other computers on the network.

Voice over Internet Protocol (VoIP) the ability to call someone using the Internet and engage in a voice conversation.

voice recognition technology used to recognize voice commands as input for hands-free operation at work, with your car's navigation and communications system, or with your mobile device. Also known as speech recognition technology.

W

war driving the act of driving around trying to connect to someone else's unsecured wireless network.

warm boot restarting a computer without turning off the power.

wearable computer a computing device that can be worn on the body and functions while the individual is walking or otherwise moving around.

Web 2.0 websites that encourage and facilitate collaboration and sharing and allow users to add or edit content.

Web 3.0 the next generation of the Web that is under development in which meaningful connections between data and web pages will exist, allowing you to find more complex information more easily and more quickly. Also known as Semantic Web.

Web address a text-based address to navigate to a website. Also known as uniform resource locator (URL).

web authoring software a program designed to create content to be provided over the Internet.

web conferencing a program that allows a group of individuals to connect online to engage in a meeting.

web page a document that contains text and multimedia content such as images, video, sound, and animation.

web server a special server where all the web pages and resources that make a website work are stored.

web-based operating system an operating system that operates like a virtual desktop where settings, documents, pictures, contacts, and other files are stored in the cloud.

webcam a video camera built into a video display screen or plugged in as a peripheral and used to provide images to the computer.

website a collection of related web pages for one organization or individual.

white hats hackers who pinpoint weaknesses in network security and may even be hired by an organization to hack into the organization's network.

Wi-Fi adapter a device that communicates with a wireless access point or wireless router using radio frequencies to transfer data.

Wi-Fi Protected Access (WPA or WPA2) security standards that authenticate users and employ sophisticated encryption techniques.

wiki a website that allows anyone to create and edit content.

wiki software programs that allow anyone to create and edit content on the website.

wikiHow a website that contains more than 140,000 how-to instruction articles.

Wikipedia Sandbox a Wikipedia entry that contains instructions on how to edit content.

Wikipedia the most-used online encyclopedia on which content can be created by anyone.

Windows Action Center used to view messages about issues encountered on your computer and provides buttons and links to tools that can be used to resolve the issues.

Windows an operating system created by Microsoft Corporation that is the most popular OS because a wide variety of hardware is designed to run it.

Windows Backup where you back up or restore files.

Windows Embedded a family of operating systems based on the familiar Windows

Windows Explorer a file management system in Windows 7 in which you can move, copy, delete, and rename files.

Windows Phone Microsoft's mobile operating system used on Windows smartphones.

wireless ExpressCard an adapter that plugs into a narrow slot on a notebook or other mobile device.

Wireless Fidelity (Wi-Fi) a network in which wireless access points and radio signals are used to transmit data.

wireless interface card allows you to connect to a network using wireless technology.

word processing application software used to create documents containing mostly text.

WordPress a blog-hosting website that uses the WordPress open source blogging software.

World Wide Web the global collection of electronic documents circulated on the Internet in the form of web pages. Also known as Web or WWW.

worm a self-replicating program that requires no user action to copy itself to another computer on a network.

Y

YouTube the most popular video sharing website; owned by Google.

Z

zombie a computer that is connected to the Internet and is controlled by a hacker or other cybercriminal without the owner's knowledge.

Index